How to Develop Excellent Skills in Your Children
to Face the Challenges of the Future

The Secrets
of Successful Parenting

Volume 1: Being - Gabellini Model

ALBINA GABELLINI

DANIELE GIANNINI

LORELLA PUCCI

RAOUL PUCCI

LAURA MAZZA

This is a work of nonfiction.

Ordering Information:

Prime Seven Media
518 Landmann St.
Tomah City, WI 54660

Printed in the United States of America

Dedication

To Allegra, the joy of a lifetime.

Don't give up. You might do it an hour before the miracle.
(Arabic proverb)

Table of Contents

BE AWARE OF THE DANGERS

PAY ATTENTION TO OUR CHILDREN'S FUTURE
2.5 million young people unemployed

In Italy, there are 2.5 million unemployed individuals between the ages of 15 and 29 who are neither studying nor working.

They are classified as NEETs (Not in Education, Employment, or Training).

This shocking data comes from an OECD report.
75% of NEETs live with their families.

Young NEETs in Italy make up 27% of the labor force and cost the state 1.4% of its GDP. Italy holds the negative record for NEETs in Europe (Milano, Sole 24 Ore Italia) (Centro Studi Impresa Lavoro).

Across Europe, the total number of unemployed people, 33 million, is expected to rise. This is an alarming trend, especially given that employment policies are typically medium- to long-term solutions!

(You can find solutions from Strategy 1 to Strategy 9: Enhancing character and attitude).

Attention to the Future Economy

By 2030, Italy will have fallen to 15th place among the world's developed economies (The Bureau). The United States, which we currently look to as a model, will lose its leading position, falling behind China. What will happen to Europe, with countries developing (or lagging) at very different rates?

Today in Italy, one million families have no income, another million rely on a single income (from the mother), and 200,000 single women are completely without income. Innovation is minimal, and productive companies are leaving. The infrastructure is crumbling. Public services, though good, have yet to be modernized.

In this impoverished economy, what will we, along with our children, do? (Find solutions in Proposals 1, 2, 3, 4.)

Attention to the Future of Politics

The average age of politicians and leaders in Italy remains very high. There is no rapid generational turnover. In 10 years, who will we elect? Who will be honest and efficient in governing wisely? Who will be willing to take on the responsibility of representing us? How can we hold our leaders accountable if we don't understand public budgets or the legislative process? We are not educating our children in the management of the *ResPublica*, the state. (In France, they have a dedicated school for this, the ÉNA.) How will we defend our interests in Europe without competent successors? How will we protect our reputation in the eyes of the world?

(Find solutions in Proposal 4: A school for public administration.)

Attention to Research and Development

Italy has hundreds of thousands of brilliant minds (our researchers are among the best in the world) who have emigrated in search of new opportunities, many of whom never returned. Some have become world-renowned figures—take Dr. Sabina Berretta, for example: while in Italy she wasn't even considered worthy of a janitor's position, at Harvard she now serves as the Director of the Brain Bank!

Each year, 100,000 young Italians leave the country, while we fail to attract a significant number of foreign talents. Our budgets for Research and Development are simply not competitive. In 10 years, the number of emigrated intellectuals will reach one million.

With this approach, we are systematically depleting our human capital. Will the country have the intelligence needed to create technology rather than buying it from abroad, thereby avoiding becoming digital subjects?

(Find solutions in Proposal 3: Digital Natives.)

Attention to Future Pensions

The year zero for pensions is 2030, when pension payments will be at risk (La Stampa.it). If the retirement income, the result of many years of work, becomes uncertain, how will we be able to support ourselves, our families, our children, and our grandchildren? What will we live on from 2030 onward, just 13 years from now?

Today, out of 16 million pensions granted for various reasons, around 63% are paid out at less than 750 euros per month. We are already on the poverty line. What still saves us is the careful savings culture of the older generation (we were once among the top savers in the world). The new generation, however, has little opportunity to save, barely managing to cover mortgage payments.

Whatpathshouldwetake?Whatmeasuresshouldweprepareinadvance? (Find solutions in Proposal 1: The Entrepreneurial Family.)

Answers to the Questions: Some Solutions

"If you think education is expensive, wait and see how much ignorance will cost you." (J.M. Capozzi)

You will find some answers along the way. You can participate too. If you wish to collaborate, write to info@gsm-online.it. Your proposals will be published in the next version.

A) For Job Guidance and Reducing Social Discomfort

For jobs: Create new realities—the digital family with adolescents. Educate a multidimensional personality: there is a new pedagogy to develop the Being in our children. Foster their adaptability to the future and their resilience to face challenges. Listen to our proposals. (Solutions can be found in Strategy 1 through Strategy 9, Entrepreneurs 4.0.)

The family of 2030 will be a network of online entrepreneurs—grandchildren, grandparents, and parents working together. This reduces the risk of relying solely on pensions. Meanwhile, we need to retain some of the 150,000 graduates leaving Italy each year. Let's explore how. (Find solutions in Proposal 1: The Entrepreneurial Family.)

C) For Economic Development: Expanding Businesses—Italy's Beauty and the Expertise of Millions of Artisans and Professionals

Italy is the most beautiful country in the world, a vast wealth waiting to be tapped. If we updated the state's balance sheet by including cultural assets, our children would be the richest in the world—they would inherit assets, not debts.

If we create hubs of attraction around our centers of excellence, foreign companies would be keen to join, benefiting from economies of scale and returning to Italy. (Find solutions in Proposal 2: The Beauty of Italy.)

D) For Competent Internal and Foreign Policy: A School for Efficiency in Public Administration and International Relations

Establish a school to train the next generation of politicians (our children and grandchildren) to represent Italy with excellence and defend national interests on every front. We need a team of elected officials—honest, capable of fixing our accounts—who will become a model for the world.

In times of massive socio-economic changes, there are two ways to profit: seizing new opportunities or cutting costs. This would lead to reduced taxes, attracting new investors and businesses to Italy.

E) For Research: Recovering Our Intellectual Heritage

There are three paths:

1. Attract fresh talent from abroad by implementing educational policies that draw young students from other countries. This would become a business in itself—defending and promoting the reputation of excellence that Italy deserves. This will provide new resources to partly fund institutions (particularly inviting students from emerging countries, as they are the future leaders). (Find solutions in Proposal: Digital Natives.)

2. Reinvest in Research and Development at a national level, recalling our best minds from abroad by providing the necessary resources.

3. Encourage young creative minds, starting in adolescence, in schools and labs, and fund promising young talent. In 20 years, we could have a world-class team and cutting-edge technology for our own use and for export to other countries.

F) To Replace Pensions: Adopt a New Mindset—Open Your Heart and Mind, Look Beyond, and Share

We need to create a new type of family relationship—a digital family consisting of two or even three generations, working together to create their own alternative family income source beyond traditional employment. Small and medium-sized online businesses can leverage the experience of grandparents, the skills of parents, and the digital proficiency of children.

With additional income, we can continue to save, a typical Italian habit (we are among the top in the world in this regard), and ensure a secure future. When parents retire or grandparents pass away, the family will still have its accumulated capital, which it managed independently. To prevent becoming a social burden, it will be enough to maintain mandatory savings without intermediaries. (Find solutions from Strategy 1 to Strategy 9.)

Two pillars are fundamental in all proposals:

- Training our children and ourselves to be strong people capable of overcoming challenges
- Creating the economic-financial-technological conditions to operate effectively

Education is the link that connects everything. Our success will be measured by how well we harmonize these elements, a responsibility we all share.

"If you think jobs will increase, wait and see how much your naivety will cost you."

This book is dedicated to you, the parent, who cares about the future of your children.

"If you think job creation is the state's responsibility, wait and see how much your indifference will cost you."

The world is changing too quickly—it has become a global market, with expanded points of reference. Often, we don't even know where we stand or who we are dealing with. Today, you are recognized for the work you do, and a person's dignity is perceived through their role. In the rush, no one investigates a person's true inner qualities. Tomorrow, if jobs no longer exist, how will you be identified?

You will agree that we need a new orientation on roles and how to create an effective response to defend the dignity of our children that satisfies their personality (Strategic Pedagogy).

Some Key Points Need to Be Addressed:

- **Information:** It is the greatest asset of a role or profession that young people must possess. With the right guidance, they can find solutions to develop excellence, talent, overcome obstacles, and become experts. There will always be a market for such individuals.
- **Adjustment to New Social Equations:** It is likely that purchasing power will erode, necessitating a change in lifestyle. Roles can be defined without flaunting wealth. Two elements intersect here: future socioeconomic situations and the children who will need to manage them. We can mitigate the former and empower the latter.
- **Awareness:** We need to open our eyes. We desire a generation of winning children! Sociology, tasked with monitoring population behavior, has fallen behind. It does not strongly demand public attention, just as governments struggle to address this phenomenon affecting all families.
- **Control of Dangers and Risks:** Due to automation and robotics, in ten years, jobs will continue to diminish, leading to a rise in NEET (Not in Education, Employment, or Training) individuals, potentially including your children. We must develop an adequate labor policy today to counteract this trend.

Alessandro Rosina, a professor of Demography at the Catholic University of Milan, asserts that: "Increasingly, graduates are falling into this inert universe of NEETs, unable to leave their homes even years after defending their theses." The wait for opportunities that the market does not offer has stripped away motivation and enthusiasm.

Do you agree that this situation is critical, important, and urgent? The NEET phenomenon reflects the inefficiency of "our" politics, created by us (families and the State together), which fails to provide a concrete response. No one is innocent.

Is there a solution? Yes, we can reverse this trend if each of us contributes by playing our part starting now. Let's explore how. Stand with us!

PREFACE
BOOK OBJECTIVE
FUNDAMENTAL CONCEPTS
IMPLEMENTATION OF THE GABELLINI MODEL

BOOK OBJECTIVE

The Parent Coach Oriented Series comprises three volumes addressing an individual's core dimensions: Being (personality), Possessing (instrumental capabilities), and Executing (actionable strategies).

This series is predicated on Cognitive Coaching methodology, designed to train and orient parents in transforming their children into adaptable, resilient individuals capable of thriving in diverse future environments.

By utilizing the Gabellini Model, parents will acquire advanced coaching competencies that are equally applicable in professional business contexts.

The genesis of this series emerged from a consistent, critical inquiry posed by professionals—managers, entrepreneurs, coaches, and trainers—following coaching sessions:

"What systemic implications will speculative economic fluctuations have on our children's future, and what potential consequences should we anticipate?"

Contemporary economic landscapes present significant challenges. Consider representative scenarios: Dr. P.P., who experienced substantial asset loss through corporate bankruptcies, or Engineer D.C., whose strategic investments in market research ultimately failed. Such narratives underscore the volatility of current economic structures, where prosperous families can experience rapid financial destabilization.

Current economic systems are substantially compromised by financial manipulation. Empirical evidence from global markets—particularly evident in the United States—demonstrates how large productive enterprises struggle with restrictive credit access and complex power dynamics.

As reported by Il Sole 24 Ore, "The 4 trillion-dollar mechanism that inflated Wall Street's valuation systematically prioritizes stock market performance over substantive corporate investments." Similar patterns emerge in Italian banking, where small and medium enterprises encounter significant obstacles in securing essential credit facilities for business revitalization.

Prevalent parental perspectives frequently misconstrue financial education as developmentally inappropriate for younger demographics. This conventional wisdom—that monetary management should be exclusively adult-managed—requires comprehensive reevaluation. Contemporary socioeconomic landscapes offer unprecedented opportunities for youth to generate personal economic value through innovative engagement strategies.

Our fundamental objective is to provide a strategic framework that prepares families to navigate complex, evolving economic challenges. By fostering an integrated family ecosystem characterized by intergenerational alignment and mutual empowerment, we aim to cultivate resilient, emotionally intelligent individuals capable of autonomous decision-making.

The proposed pedagogical approach offers a comprehensive developmental roadmap spanning from early childhood through emerging adulthood (ages 25-29), with a focus on cultivating excellence as a fundamental problem-solving mechanism.

Our core message to contemporary parents is unequivocal:

Recognize the accelerating pace of global transformation. Traditional employment guarantees have been eroded, necessitating proactive, strategic educational interventions. While institutional education provides informational frameworks, genuine personal transformation remains a parental responsibility.

The emerging professional landscape demands dynamic, adaptable coaching methodologies. Parents possess a unique "Proximity Factor"—intimate familial understanding that enables more nuanced, effective coaching interventions.

Professionals can strategically position themselves as "Parenting Coaches," meeting the growing market demand for sophisticated, personalized developmental strategies that transcend traditional educational models.

A STRATEGIC PEDAGOGICAL APPROACH WILL SYSTEMATICALLY MITIGATE PARENTAL PSYCHOLOGICAL CONSTRAINTS.

BASIC CONCEPTS

Human beings can be fully understood through three core concepts, and human existence can be described within three dimensions or areas. This series, which examines and proposes a new pedagogy for children, is deliberately divided into these three parts:

1. **Being: Strategic Pedagogy.** A framework to create unique personalities and exceptional talents while avoiding NEET (Not in Education, Employment, or Training) situations.

2. **Having: Operational Pedagogy.** Strategies to plan for health and wealth during adolescence and navigate new family dynamics and resources.

3. **Doing: Frontier Pedagogy.** Approaches to implement and experiment with new protocols both within the family and society, fostering super-capitals, super-companies, and champion-level skills.

We are online and available for any inquiries at **info@gsm-online.it** or on the **Facebook Group "Genitori Orientati."**

To better understand the paths we will explore, it is helpful to clarify some fundamental concepts.

PSYCHO-PEDAGOGICAL LEXICON

Pedagogy is the science of educating human beings. Rooted in anthropology, like sociology, psychology, and neuropsychology, it harnesses synergies between diverse disciplines for both knowledge and practice. As Socrates said, *"Know thyself."* This timeless maxim remains the cornerstone of education—understanding your child is the starting point of any meaningful upbringing.

Types of Pedagogy

- **Strategic Pedagogy** focuses on long-term education, guiding children to maturity. Its vision is grounded in values like peace, justice, fraternity, and freedom, with the mission to use knowledge as a means of improving the world. It emphasizes planning, programs, strategies, and tools while evaluating markets and costs. This pedagogy constitutes the largest part of this book, as it addresses medium- and long-term futures, aiming to enrich individual personalities. Public and private schools should ideally fulfill this role, at least regarding instruction.

- In Italy, we take pride in having the world's leading public early childhood education system, located in Reggio Emilia. Founded by the late Loris Malaguzzi, this pedagogical approach is globally recognized as the best applied to early childhood.
- While Italy's public school system generally exceeds European standards, the private sector tends to prioritize specialization over general education. Unfortunately, public investments and teaching resources are dwindling.

- **Operational Pedagogy** addresses teaching techniques and best practices that foster positive behaviors. It focuses on implementing advice in daily interactions with teachers and finding immediate, urgent solutions.

  - Italian teachers boast world-class training, thanks to general education programs. Complementing this, Italian mothers (and grandmothers) traditionally enrich education through empathy, care, mirror neurons, and food as a social tool—an epigenetic and ancestral practice often applied intuitively without theoretical knowledge.

- **Frontier Pedagogy**—our area of focus—studies, invents, and tests new or adapted technologies and protocols, leveraging advancements across disciplines. It thrives on live experiences and cutting-edge research and is highly sought after by affluent families.

  - In the U.S., universities directly fund these groundbreaking studies, producing exclusive results accessible only to a select few. This is particularly evident in the shift from traditional education to participatory coaching and training.

Education is the essence of pedagogy. Derived from the Latin *"e-ducere,"* meaning "to draw out," it extends to cultivating "attributes" for society where our children will thrive. Parenting involves an unspoken contract, safeguarded by civil codes, where parents harmonize their children's personalities within a demanding, highly organized society that harshly penalizes mistakes and imposes social proof, often neglecting opportunities for recovery.

Instruction refers to the volume of information schools are mandated to provide, even without religious content. In Italy, schools deliver a substantial amount of general, non-specialized knowledge.

Ethics encompasses the rules of "social living," respecting values, principles, belief systems rooted in religion and philosophy, and the rights of humans, animals, plants, and all environments within Nature.

Teaching Methods are pedagogical strategies aimed at developing effective, specialized tools. These strategies emerge from the fusion of philosophy, psychology, and technology—disciplines that interpret life's ultimate goals and delve into the psyche.

PARENT AND CHILD ROLES

Parent

Who is a parent? Someone who biologically generates a child, exercises parental duties, maintains a family where children are born, or plans and desires to have a child? The roles and responsibilities vary depending on where the emphasis is placed.

- **How do you see yourself?** Are you a guide, an educator, a role model, a friend to your children, or both father and mother as a single parent?
- Do you feel responsible emotionally, financially, or socially?

These are profound questions, shaping different approaches to relationships with children. Whatever your parental identity, your child's future undoubtedly remains your top priority. Have you clarified your role? Do you reflect on it?

Child

Legally, a child is a human recognized as born to a couple, a single mother, or a father who acknowledges/adopts them. This concept ties to minority status and the obligation of care and support until maturity (or economic independence). On an emotional level, one remains a child for life.

"Education is not preparation for life; education is life itself." Let us embark on this journey together to redefine and elevate our children's futures.

APPLYING THE GABELLINI MODEL

Many people know everything, except for themselves. (Proverb)

What are the current pedagogical models? There are several. Montessori, Steiner, Yale University's schools, the Reggio Emilia approach early childhood (considered the best in the world), and many others. Not all of them are innovative; some prefer to remain in their comfort zone. They often conflict with each other. We have developed a new model.

From childhood, it's essential to introduce (or recover) additional disciplines alongside the subjects already being taught (languages, sports, math, history, geography, science, etc.). Many of the derived insights are not content that children need to study but rather methods and behavioral models to apply.

The model addresses various needs.
When digging deep into our personality, we may risk encountering a stranger. (Michelangelo)

First, we must understand who our children are, where they are going, and how they think. For this purpose, we have built a model based on specific schematizations. Like any synthesis, it has its limits, but it is highly effective in quickly providing clarity.

Every challenge in life—love, work, earning, playing, studying—has its typical level to respect. Each role—parent, instructor, coach, provider, modeler, psychologist, consultant, educator, relative—must be aware of its utility, which in this case is to raise a healthy and happy family.

The model tackles the challenge/role/skill themes to find personalized solutions to implement immediately. The framework is divided into seven parts:

PARTS OF THE MODEL

Section	Purpose	Outcome: Knowledge for Action
1. Definitions	Sharing concepts	What am I talking about?
2. Skills/Attitudes	Understanding our "know-how"	What do I need to improve?
3. Maximum Points	Ideals to strive for	What do I want to achieve? Excellence.
4. Minimum Points	Situations to avoid	What do I want to leave behind?
5. Resilience	Recovery ability	The defense mechanism to regain energy.
6. Questionnaires	Tools to gather data	The information I need for coaching.
7. Success Cases	Stories of achievements	Motivating and reassuring examples.

The questionnaire organizes questions to collect personal data for creating coaching plans, improvement strategies, and tactics. It also includes significant examples of people who have succeeded.

The reasoning model is a framework that brings order to our self-knowledge. When we face a difficulty, we'll know where to place it and can quickly identify effective solutions. It is, of course, only a synthesis, valuable for saving time and gaining clarity. Practicality is of great value, even though life is far richer and more nuanced.

GABELLINI MODEL - AREAS/LEVELS FRAMEWORK

1. **BEING**: Who we are, identity, role, personality, mission
    - **Level 1: Spiritual Themes**
    - **Level 2: Rational and Cognitive Themes**
    - **Level 3: Emotional Themes**

2. **HAVING**: What we have, skills, know-how, body, and assets
    - **Level 4: Physiological Themes**
    - **Level 5: Economic-Financial Themes**
    - **Level 6: Logistical-Organizational Themes (Time Management)**

3. **DOING**: How we behave with family/society/environment
    - **Level 7: Relational-Family-Affective Themes**
    - **Level 8: Eco-Environmental Themes**
    - **Level 9: Behavioral Themes**
    - **Level 10: Social Themes (with external validation)**

HOW TO FRAME THE THEMES?

For example, if you want to study a thought, you'll refer to Level 2. If it's an emotion, Level 3. If it's healthy, Level 4. For family love, Level 7.

HOW TO EVALUATE THEM?

If 100% represents the total, the sum of your attention or energy can be distributed across the 10 levels, each representing 10%. The areas have a weight of 40% for the spiritual, and 30% for each of the other two dimensions. These are just guidelines. What matters is observing the tendency—where more energy and attention are directed.

The knowledge of the levels is enriched by introducing new study subjects, both in content and techniques. The Reggio Emilia approach, for example, uses ateliers and the "hundred languages of children."

We continue researching, integrating advancements in neuroscience into practical applications. Our American colleagues often call us "modelers," smilingly acknowledging our role.

The Gabellini 10-level framework is a fast, comprehensive approach designed to answer one key question:
"Before acting or reacting, have I considered everything I need?"

The framework is graphically represented by a circle, the "Wheel of Life," where the segments represent our situations, themes, and topics in life and work. It is a well-known circle, which we had initially designed to include various aspects relevant to coaching, aiming for happiness, wealth, and health. Today, after over twenty years, we see it everywhere, with a touch of pride.

The circle also applies to companies, with two types of tests:

a) **Personal:** Measures individual progress from zero (center) to 100% (circumference).
b) **Corporate:** Assesses a company's position relative to its objectives and the socio-economic realities of 1994-1996.

You can request them for free by writing to info@gsm-online.it.

We strongly believe that the 10-level model should be taught to everyone as a mental framework because we've realized that human beings are complex. The 10 aspects of life constantly compete for our

attention and energy. With this model, we can determine where to direct those limited resources.

All aspects are important, but after acknowledging them, we need to assign them balanced precedence and priorities minute by minute. Often, we forget this, creating unnecessary difficulties for ourselves. We are incredibly skilled at doing so!

For example: if we focus too much on studying (Level 2, Cognitive), we may isolate ourselves and lose friends (Level 7, Relational) because we're not sharing moments of fun. On the other hand, if we spend every night in clubs, Level 2 (Knowledge) will suffer. Our friends won't take exams on our behalf! If we dedicate all our time to making money, we may lose friends because we can't give them our attention.

It's also been discovered that if a specific level is neglected for an extended period, it will eventually trigger a crisis on its own (first through unconscious messages, then conscious ones), and the individual will suffer the consequences.

We'll provide many other examples along the way.

EXAMPLE 1: ANNA'S STORY, 16 YEARS OLD, LEFT BY HER BOYFRIEND

Anna begins overeating. She gains weight. She isolates herself. Her behavior is clearly unhealthy. She was betrayed and then abandoned by her boyfriend.

Let's analyze the levels.

It's an offense to her identity, **Level 1, Spiritual**. What happens to the other levels? The boyfriend's abandonment causes a crisis in **Level 7, Relational**, creating a lack of love that conflicts with **Level 3, Emotional**. This results in profound suffering. **Level 3, Emotional** is directly connected to **Level 1, Spiritual**, leading to a loss of self-esteem.

To help Anna, we need to monitor all 10 levels and act quickly. Compulsive eating is a behavioral issue at **Level 9, Behavioral**, which harms **Level 4, Physical Health**. This creates a cycle of lost self-esteem and declining health.

1. BEING: ANNA HAS LOST HER IDENTITY	Damages
Level 1 - Spiritual Themes	Damage to self-esteem
Level 2 - Rational, Cognitive Themes	Damage to cognitive clarity
Level 3 - Emotional Themes	Damage and suffering
2. HAVING: ANNA IS LOSING HER HEALTH	
Level 4 - Physiological Themes	Health threatened
Level 5 - Economic, Financial Themes	Damage, no more work
Level 6 - Logistical, Organizational, Time Management Themes	
3. DOING: ANNA HAS LOST LOVE AND TRUST IN OTHERS	
Level 7 - Relational, Family, Affectionate Themes	Damage, loneliness
Level 8 - Eco-Environmental Themes	
Level 9 - Behavioral Themes	Damage, errors in eating habits
Level 10 - Social Themes with Validation from Others	Damage, conflicts

WHAT TO DO? WHAT ARE THE PRIORITIES?

Level 1: If her perception changes from negative to positive, her morale will improve.

Level 3: She will suffer less and feel motivated to stop overeating.

Level 9: Improved behavior will restore **Level 4**, her physical health.

Level 4: With better health, her energy will increase, enabling her to pursue new relationships (**Level 7**).

Level 7: She starts socializing and exploring new opportunities, eventually resuming work.

Level 10: She begins engaging with people, creating new opportunities.

Level 5: This level benefits as well. With more resources, she can improve her appearance.

Level 6: She finds money to better manage her image, enhancing **Level 1** and **Level 3**.

This creates a virtuous loop that should be followed immediately for her to bounce back.

Today, Anna has forgiven her ex-boyfriend and found a new one who's better suited for her.

By following the model, Anna didn't overlook any aspect, speeding up her recovery with great responsibility.

EXAMPLE 2: GIOVANNA'S STORY, 18 YEARS OLD, AT HER FIRST JOB

She had an argument with her boss. She refuses to reflect on it and wants to quit her job.

We help her think through it using this model. We ask her 10 questions:

What's happening at Levels 1, 2, 3, 4, 5, 6, 7, 8, 9, and 10?

Here are her answers:

- **"I wouldn't have money to live or take care of myself."** Levels **5** and **4**, financial and health.
- **"I'd have to depend on my family, who doesn't have money. Without money, I'd feel restricted and suffer."** Level **3**, emotional.

1. BEING: Giovanna feels her role is threatened	DAMAGES
Level 1 - Spiritual Themes	Damage to self-esteem
Level 2 - Rational, Cognitive Themes	Damage due to limited knowledge
Level 3 - Emotional Themes	Damage: Suffering, Impulsiveness, Anger
2. HAVING: Giovanna is losing peace and her job	
Level 4 - Physiological Themes	Nervousness
Level 5 - Economic, Financial Themes	Damage: No job, no money
Level 6 - Logistical, Organizational, Time Management Themes	Poor communication
3. DOING: Giovanna had lost trust in others	
Level 7 - Relational, Family, Affectionate Themes	Damage: Rebellion without dialogue
Level 8 - Eco-Environmental Themes	
Level 9 - Behavioral Themes	Damage: Escapism, irrational decisions
Level 10 - Social Themes with Validation from Others	Damage: Conflict she refused to resolve

After analyzing her personal framework, she agreed to accept the advice: find clarity with her boss, navigate through the painful episode, and improve Level 6, logistics, by learning the right way to communicate.

What advantages and benefits did she gain?

Now she is happy. Staying at that company turned out to be the right choice.

- **Level 1:** Increased courage and strength.
- **Level 10:** Affirmation of her value in front of her boss and colleagues.

- **Level 6:** Improved communication skills.
- **Level 7:** Greater effectiveness in relationships, and so on.

With the help of the model, self-awareness becomes immediate, allowing for the avoidance of many mistakes.

First Part:
The World Around Us

- **The Unknown That Awaits Us**
- **Acceleration – Universal Rule**
- **How to Interpret Signals**

The Unknown That Awaits Us

The fascination with the unknown dominates everything.
(Homer)

We live on Earth within a vast Universe, in an environment populated by living beings, interconnected in a morphogenetic world. ***(Sheldrake)*** Life is consciousness; everything is interconnected. An action by one person reverberates on all others across geographical boundaries. How we live depends on all of us. Each person contributes something important and receives back from others in return (synchronicity). The responsibility toward the world is great, and we must uphold the mission to improve.

Talents, excellence, artists, scientists, researchers, and experts have a duty to lead by example. Educating people about responsibility toward the world is the virtuous path. ***(Level 8 – Environment)*** The effect grows with sharing and acceptance from others, social proof, like word-of-mouth.

In this universe, young people will face two unknowns: a journey inward and a journey outward. For the former, they can use the Gabellini Model discussed earlier, while for the latter, they can use Big Data Analysis and signals from newspapers, the web, as we will explore further.

Acceleration as a Universal Rule

Over the past 70 years, humanity has produced a quarter of all output from the past 2,000 years! Our society is no longer static but operates in a dynamic regime: not at high speed, but in acceleration. At this pace, our brains are not accustomed to such rapid change.

What does this mean? That our children will be required to make great efforts to adapt. In both local and global markets, nothing remains stable – everything is in motion, and that very movement will continue to undergo change.

Change of change = acceleration. Acceleration generates stress.

To prevent this, they must increase efficiency and improve data management, as those who possess dynamic, accelerated, and up-to-date information will have the advantage.

We need to train our youth to adopt an accelerated, yet stress-free, mental habit—one that looks ahead with an emerging mindset. We must retrain our brains to adapt to this pace, using techniques such as Transcendental Meditation.

Meditating, slowing down, in order to regain greater precision, an essential skill for excellence. Refer to the attached "Transcendental Meditation" document. Specifically, the Maharishi Foundation promotes and develops the "Stress-Free School" program, based on Transcendental Meditation techniques, already implemented in many schools worldwide with thousands of young people. Beyond rising stress levels, youth can address anxiety, learning difficulties, poor academic performance, addictions, youth violence, bullying, and even school dropout.

Acceleration is now an ongoing social dynamic. We cannot avoid it, but we can learn to confront it with new and effective tools, like Transcendental Meditation.

How to Interpret Signals

Being able to see and interpret the signals of events that may impact on our children's lives protects them from potential dangers.

These signals include:

1. **Political signals** that generate social and economic trends.
2. **Spiritual signals** of vision and values that shape attitudes.
3. **Technological signals** that impact work, roles, and daily life. (Refer to the appendix for further details.)

There are various techniques for interpreting these signals:

1. **Open your mind: look beyond politics and techniques to neutralize surprises.**
2. **Identify the signals: classify them by order of importance and timing.**
3. **Evaluate the risks: assessing them in advance will serve as a strategic advantage.**

Part Two:
The New Pedagogy

School Subjects to Consider

The Coaching Model for Children

BEING AND ITS EXPRESSIONS

> "To be yourself in a world that is constantly trying to make
> you something else is the greatest accomplishment."
> — Ralph Waldo Emerson

> "Being yourself in a world that is constantly trying to make
> you something else is the greatest accomplishment."

What a beautiful statement! Children are individuals, distinct from us.

SCHOOL SUBJECTS TO CONSIDER

> "Be like the sea, which, breaking against the rocks,
> always finds the strength to try again."
> — Jim Morrison

It is worth noting that perseverance in studying is often more powerful than knowledge itself. Practical information and strategies make life easier. As Isaac Newton once said, "If I have seen further, it is by being patient more than by any other talent."

In Gabellini's Pedagogy, the focus of study is personal development. The field of scientific knowledge has expanded enormously since the 1600s, making patience an essential virtue. Today, this is needed to cultivate strong character and skill in using digital tools. As parents, we often serve as poor examples.

Below is a list of 12 subjects (not exhaustive) that aim to create new paradigms. These disciplines should be introduced from early childhood. Many will integrate non-content-transfer methods already effective in Italy. While traditional subjects remain comprehensive, these 12 are supplemental, leveraging the latest scientific discoveries in fields such as the mind, the brain, sensory pathways, and quantum medicine.

LIST OF DISCIPLINES WITH CORRESPONDING GOALS (ORGANIZED BY 10 LEVELS)

LEVELS	DISCIPLINES	OBJECTIVES
level 1	Epigenetics and Use of Family Documents	Defense of Identity
level 2	Lateral Thinking, Speed Reading, Quantum Thinking	Creativity, Logic
level 3	Cognitive Psychology, NLP, Hypnosis	Personal Improvement
level 3	Transcendental Meditation/Stress Management/Yoga	Against Hyperactivity
level 4	Physiology, Anatomy of Senses, 18 Biofeedback Techniques	Excellent Performance
level 5	Savings, Finance, Business Management	Wealth
level 6	Technology, Databases, Social Media	Source of Self-Income
level 7	Relational Communication	Peace, No Conflicts
level 8	Domestic Economy, Hygiene, Environment, Recovery	Health and Autonomy for Singles
level 8	Artistic Education	Italian Territory and Heritage
level 9	Coaching, Choices, Behaviors	Transformation
level 10	Sociology, Empathy, Politics, and Rights	Persuasion and Acceptance

Let's examine a few of them

(Note: The following section includes some theoretical concepts necessary to understand the importance of these subjects. If you prefer to move directly to practical applications, feel free to skip this part and revisit it later at your convenience.)

Epigenetics

It is the "branch of molecular biology that studies genetic mutations and the transmission of hereditary traits not directly attributable to the DNA sequence." DNA chromosomes inform cells and behave differently depending on the environmental accelerators they encounter. Unlike genetic processes, epigenetics is not mechanistic but rather an interaction between potentialities and an environment conducive to their manifestation. Stimuli can vary: chemical, physiological, hormonal, energetic, dietary, electrical, magnetic, auditory, or pollution-related.

The "epigenome" is active during the prenatal period and approximately the first two years of a child's life, playing a crucial role in the development of synapses and knowledge. An epigenetics teacher would work on two parallel fronts:

1. **Protecting the child's physical health**
    They would educate the child on proper dietary and environmental hygiene, including suitable diets, exercises, and ways to mitigate potential pollutants. The teacher would also guide parents on how to regulate the environment, select appropriate physical and energetic measures, and promote their child's well-being.

2. **Safeguarding psychological health**
    Behavioral epigenetics (Meane and Szyf) has discovered that ancestral fears and anxieties experienced during childhood may be inherited, influencing behavior in seemingly irrational ways (through enzymatic methylation). Research indicates

these inherited traits can resurface in adulthood during periods of stress, trauma, substance abuse, or painful experiences, reactivating emotional wounds linked to parental neglect, abuse, alcoholism, or violence in prior generations.

Epigenetics has shown that the genome is no longer a fixed DNA code; the epigenome can alter it. An epigenetic coach can break the chain of inherited errors. Proper care, tactile affection, hugs, and kisses can perform wonders (e.g., through tapping exercises). For further reading, consider Roberto Giacobbo's book *"Le carezze cambiano il DNA"* (**Hugs Can Change DNA**), which explains how such interactions reshape neuronal connections in the hippocampus.

Children subjected to abuse or psychological and physical violence, especially during early childhood, often grow into adults with stress and disrupted memories. Their hippocampi show excessive methylation, leading to emotional blocks, heightened fear, and despair. Conversely, sensory input like touch, love, and affection fosters brain development, emotional intelligence, calmness, and learning abilities.

A critical point:

Children subjected to physical punishment during their formative years risk damaging their tactile pathways and reducing sensory abilities, including those related to sexuality.

Current biotechnological research aims to eliminate methyl groups that contribute to anxiety, stress, depression, and emotional deficiencies. An epigenetic pill could cleanse the hippocampus, calm the mind, enhance memory, and accelerate learning—a promising hope for the future.

A new profession:

An epigenetic coach for children. Learn alongside your children and specialize in this field, which promises a bright future.

Meditation, Transcendental Meditation, Yoga, Stress-Relief Techniques

There is an extensive body of literature on meditation techniques. Transcendental Meditation (TM), introduced globally by Maharishi Mahesh Yogi, is a simple, natural practice accessible to all, and its effectiveness is confirmed by over 700 scientific studies. It is regarded as one of the most effective techniques.

It's remarkable to observe children practicing TM with precision. The primary benefits are calmness, even when practiced for just a few minutes in the morning and evening. The second benefit is improved concentration, and the third is enhanced learning.

New Professions

Consider becoming a Transcendental Meditation instructor—a valuable profession for helping to prevent the rise of future NEETs (Not in Education, Employment, or Training). Learn alongside your children and specialize in this field, which has a promising future. Additionally, coaches in yoga and mindfulness for children offer effective solutions.

We recommend reading the attached document, which delves deeper into the work of the Maharishi Foundation and the "School Without Stress" program, designed for students and implemented worldwide.

Financial Literacy for Personal and State Economics

Who decided that children and teenagers should be excluded from discussing "vile money"? In today's ever-shifting world of spending, investments, risks, the stock market, capital, savings, profits, and earnings, it's essential to educate them. They need to understand the difference between economic phenomena and financial ones, between the initial cost of a product and its final cost, because this understanding can profoundly impact their lives—and perhaps even the lives of some adults. We have assisted numerous young entrepreneurs in trying to correct these financial errors.

For those who wish to participate in government activities or public administration as adults, it's crucial to study and understand how real calculations are made in state accounting.

EXAMPLE: ANDREA'S STORY – A DESPERATE ENTREPRENEUR AT 45

Andrea, a new entrepreneur, excitedly secures a potential client. Him and his wife invest their time and energy into securing the order, offering a very low price in hopes of generating some revenue. They agree to be paid in 120 days. However, they neglected to consider guarantees, credit lines, or the client's reliability. By the due date, they are unable to collect the payment, leaving them indebted to suppliers and eroding their working capital, borrowed from their parents. A huge disappointment— potential NEET status looms.

Producing, delivering, invoicing, and selling a product is an economic phenomenon. Collecting payment, however, is a financial phenomenon that is essential—without it, businesses fail. Better to refuse an order (economic) than to go into debt and have a zero balance (financial).

This is just one example but a significant one.

FINANCIAL EDUCATION FOR SAVING

Another common financial education error passed down by parents is regarding product prices. When we purchase an item, like an appliance, we say it costs 500 euros and that we paid that amount. No! True financial savvy involves calculating the total cost of products over time and space. The useful life of a washing machine is approximately 7 years, with maintenance costing about 50 euros per year. If a breakdown occurs, the repair cost doubles. Additionally, where will it be located? How much space does it require? How much does that space cost? In the end, after accounting for all these factors, the true cost of the washing machine may be around 1,000 euros. At the end of its life, how much does disposal cost? Educating your children on this type of calculation will help them buy only what's necessary, avoiding the superfluous—essential financial education.

SELF-REFLECTION

Try calculating how much you spend on superfluous items in your home. How much on toys that are discarded? Remember, there's an inverse relationship between the price of something and the time you dedicate to your children. Often, we spend on unnecessary things as a form of guilt for being absent. It's better to pay more attention to them and educate them on managing their savings for the future. Instead of consuming excessive, unnecessary items suggested by trends, buy educational tools that aid in their growth.

NEW PROFESSION: PRIVATE AND PUBLIC FINANCIAL COACH FOR ADOLESCENCE

The teacher of this subject, which is not accounting, will have a wide range of choices. These will depend on the family's type and the child's characteristics.

Regarding the management of state, regional, provincial, and municipal finances, how will our children understand the right or wrong actions? We're currently being governed without understanding finance and its consequences. We are relinquishing our future and the freedom of our children to outsiders. Due to absenteeism, our votes are no longer truly democratic, as they no longer represent the majority of the population.

New Profession: A financial coach for private and public adolescence. Learn with your children and specialize in this field, which has a bright future.

Profitable Use of Technology

Admit it or not, acknowledging the inevitability of technology has become redundant. Training children carefully to use digital tools is not only a necessity but also a mission that can serve as a potential tool for redemption, especially for NEETs. By guiding them into professions related to technology, in collaboration with parents, grandparents, and friends, we begin to break down their isolation—the primary cause of NEET status.

New Profession: Computer Coach, Particularly in Coding for Children

Learn with your children and specialize in this field, which has a promising future.

Cognitive Psychology

Various techniques such as NLP (Neuro-Linguistic Programming), hypnosis, transactional analysis, biofeedback, and others will be explored briefly in the examination of the 10 models across the three volumes. For detailed insights, you may request them at info@gsm-online.it.

New Profession: Cognitive Coach for Children, Adolescents, and Youth

Learn with your children and specialize in this field, which offers vast opportunities both professionally and in business.

Interpersonal Communication

People need to learn from a young age how to:

- Communicate their thoughts, emotions, and states to others.
- Understand others' thoughts, emotions, and states just as effectively.

No one teaches us this scientifically. However, it's crucial to become authoritative adults. Many NEETs suffered from a lack of communication and, to avoid further pain, withdrew into their own worlds. Many adults who attended our courses lacked communication skills and struggled to speak in public. If you wish to improve, join ToastMasters. You'll learn public speaking in both Italian and English at a minimal investment. There are numerous ToastMasters clubs throughout Italy, and we attend the Como chapter.

For further exploration of Public Speaking and Leadership, consider contacting ToastMasters. Many successful entrepreneurs and politicians in the U.S. are former ToastMasters members.

LET'S REMEMBER

---

1) Epigenetics
Disciplines like epigenetics help us better understand ourselves. A skilled epigenetic teacher supports students with care, affection, a proper diet, hygiene, and kind words, helping modify their DNA by clearing away any negative inherited genes from ancestors.

---

2) Communication
Effective communication is essential for building healthy relationships. Through cognitive psychology, children will learn various techniques to understand themselves and others from an early age, helping prevent the growth of NEETs.

---

3) Transcendental Meditation
Transcendental Meditation is a natural technique that should be initiated as early as possible to promote calmness, mindfulness, conflict reduction, and the prevention of hyperactivity and inattention commonly linked to NEET behaviors.

THE COACHING MODEL FOR CHILDREN

The **Gabellini Model** (a part of the Method) is a "Reasoning Model," a tool designed to organize and frame the topics we want to address in a specific order. It is also the coaching process that monitors behavior, highlighting benefits and measuring successes.

Imagine guiding travelers from one city to another in a vehicle. The coach is the one who steers, overseeing every move and change. The coach's **dashboard** is represented by the Model they must follow. In doing so, following codified rules, we gain time, clarity, serenity, and arrive at our destination safely and more aware.

As a metaphor, we can think of the Model as an **effective shortcut** to navigating intersections and traveling successfully. In a non-figurative sense, the Model will guide in managing every important aspect of life and quickly realizing our dreams. It can also be applied to children.

We can calculate the benefits and measure them through the **three main areas**:

The Gabellini Model and Powerful Questions

1 BEING	Where is the child and where does he or she want to go?	Who do you want to be?
Level 1	Spiritual, purpose, mission, goal	What role or job?
Level 2	Rational, cognitive, what thoughts, calculations, memory	What do you think about…?
Level 3	Emotional, what feelings, sensory pathways, alertness	How do you feel?
2 HAVING	With what means and tools, and in what time frame	What do you own?
Level 4	Physiological, how is health and body functioning	How is your body?
Level 5	Economic-financial, how much money to invest or from whom?	How much wealth, money?
Level 6	Logistical-organizational, competencies or assistance from others	How to proceed?
3 DOING	With whom and for whom to gain experience and how to act	How, with whom to act?
Level 7	Relational-family-affective collaboration, love	How much support?
Level 8	Environmental respect, how to respect the environment	Do you respect nature?
Level 9	Behavioral, what virtuous actions to take	Correct actions?
Level 10	Social, feedback from others, how to live in the community, and public management of state resources.	Am I accepted?

Then we will add level 11

Level 11 Luck, attraction in the material realm

In a few years, this level—how to manage coincidences, synchronicities in the morphogenetic field—will also be available. Today, we are teaching these techniques experimentally, working in cross-over (seeking possible convergences) across three related sciences:

1. a) quantum medicine
2. b) quantum physics
3. c) epigenetics

We examine phenomena, attitudes, behaviors, and character, adopting the perspectives of these three approaches (like wearing three different pairs of glasses) as they have now become scientific disciplines.

We repeat: the Gabellini Model is designed for both children and parents to seek efficiency. Try it and train together. For those already successful, look for the Advanced Model. (See attachments)

Advantages of the Model (framework)
Follow the Model in your mind, use it as a reasoning method, and you can achieve the following benefits:

- Control important aspects of business or life
- Monitor behaviors from 10 different perspectives
- Rapidly judge conflicting situations
- Quickly identify critical points
- Increase the number of correct actions

Benefits of the Model

This model is suitable for everyone, especially those who feel lost, unclear, struggling, or suffering.

SITUATION IN SUFFERING	RESULTS
Level 1: Those who have lost their sense of purpose and self-esteem.	Finds out who they are
Level 2: Those who live in confusion of concepts and uncertainty.	Clarify their ideas
Level 3: Those who suffer unjustly.	Moves toward serenity
Level 4: Those with chronic pain or health issues.	Improves health
Level 5: Those who lack financial well-being.	Identify the right resources
Level 6: Those who procrastinate.	Learning how to act in time
Level 7: Those who have lost love, friends, or connections.	Rebuilds connections
Level 8: Those who have harmed the environment.	Revalues nature
Level 9: Those who struggle without success.	Finding winning strategies
Level 10: Those who face rejection or setbacks from others.	Communicates effectively
Level 11: Those who witness Fortune slipping away.	Recognizes the right moment

This mental framework, used to assess things, will make a quality difference: a chaotic "before" and a structured, goal-oriented "after."

It's useful for everyone, parents, and efficiency! Teach it to your child!

And for those already successful? Seek the Advanced Model! (See attachments)

LET'S REMEBER

Coaching works when the Attention of children is activated, serving as an Energy Accelerator. In children, attention management occurs through specific phases, depending on age:

- **From 0 to 3, maximum 5 years:** Attention is Sensory. The child dedicates it to one object at a time, which they copy and imitate, but they cannot yet judge it; they capture it perfectly, often better than adults.
- **From 5 to 7 years:** Attention becomes more Emotional. Children observe an object through a filter, assessing whether they like it, if it sparks curiosity or other feelings, and then accept and study it.
- **From 8 to 10 years:** Judgment from experience begins, and attention becomes Cognitive. The child follows rules, processes, analyses, and synthesizes. They direct energy perfectly to define things they want to explore with curiosity.
- **From 11 to 14 years:** Attention becomes Functional and multi-directional, with a strong desire to challenge, rebel, and create alternative approaches.
- **From 14 to 16 years:** Attention is Hormonal. It should be already directed by the brain/ mind with intentional focus. However, during puberty, hormones and emotions moderate attention, making it either low or intermittent.
- **Above 16/18 years:** Once development is complete, attention becomes Focusable, similar to adults. Controlled by will, unless there is sensory or sexual imbalance disrupting it.

We must respect these phases because children simply cannot understand our commands; they don't yet have the cognitive tools. When we ask them to act as small children, it's best to show them our requests with patience, perhaps through drawings and figures, rather than explaining with words. Patient repetition is always beneficial.

Adults achieve results by providing attention, hence Focused Energy. Our little ones are not capable of "focusing," meaning intentionally directing a message. This is one reason why children we label as inattentive or clumsy make mistakes—they lack the ability and should not be scolded for it.

Thinking about results, children should learn to ask themselves the right questions regarding their attention objectives and measure the overall cost required, such as:

"Do you want to achieve this thing (name), at the cost of what (name)?"

"To increase that thing (name), how much do you need to reduce here (name)?"

"Having this thing (name or figure), how much does it cost in terms of time, energy, money?"

"Do you have enough resilience (adjective) to sacrifice to get what you want (name)?"

Explain what resilience is to them as soon as possible, as it's essential to overcome obstacles and difficulties. In this way, they'll learn a "Game of 10 Resilience and 10 Abilities" to operate, from their control panel, the various areas of focus (see the levels models you'll find later).

By activating a new pedagogy, such as coaching pathways, these are the areas of intervention:

Levels	Disciplines to Apply
1. Intuition	Psychology, Transcendental Meditation
2. Confidence	Mathematics, Sciences, Logic, Art
3. Serenity	Epigenetic/Genetic Psychology
4. Physical Resilience	Sports, Hygiene, Diet, Biofeedback
5. Productivity	Financial Education, Household Economics
6. Skills	Coaching for Each Category
7. Empathy	Public Speaking Psychology
8. Harmony	Ecological Education
9. Efficiency	Virtuous Behavior in Every Subject
10. Persuasion	Transactional Psychology, Communication

Example Four: The Story of Manuel, 38, Career Ambition

Is achieving a result always a true success? No! It can be a boomerang. Coaching doesn't always need to focus solely on results. It's not necessarily the highest aspiration in life!

At times, one can be a "loser" and still be happy. If success is achieved at the expense of other vital or priority areas, then it's not worth it, as the cost will be too high. Manuel's story illustrates this.

Manuel hopes to quickly climb the societal ladder. "For the love of my three children, whom I want to give the best," he dedicates himself entirely to this goal. How? By working from morning to night and reducing his presence in the family.

Manuel is in a rush to succeed. Meanwhile, his partner, with a very distracted husband, seeks attention elsewhere. The children grow up as strangers. He becomes wealthy, but alone—exactly the opposite of what he worked for! We've since worked to restore his relationship with his children and are now addressing the one with his wife. How many can relate to this story?

LET'S REMEMBER

The Gabellini method, as an approach, can be learned and memorized in a short period:

- Basic Program: 21 days, 10 minutes a day
- Accelerated Program: 10 days, 10 minutes twice a day

The recommended situation is the accelerated program.
Result: By committing, you'll learn to think 360 degrees in 10/20 days. The responsibility and joy of success will remain entirely yours.

The value of repetition and consistency

This book is designed with the needs of a busy parent in mind. Since you'll use it frequently, always carry a physical copy or a tablet version so you can make use of any free five minutes. Simply reading isn't enough—you must apply every part of it. If you consistently follow the program, you'll learn how to Focus and Choose effectively. Through repetition, you'll become better at asking the right Questions to meet your needs. You'll learn to think in goal-oriented, balanced ways, facing even complex challenges with direction and a clear sequence of priorities. Your attitude will change: your plans will be organized, and you'll eliminate bad habits, limiting beliefs, unfinished work anxieties, and the "pending." You'll feel the purpose of your actions, training yourself to succeed in new opportunities. We can all do this—it depends only on us!

Being and its Expressions

Being Yourself: The first rule in the command area.

Let's begin by highlighting the "first area" of personality that we'll train using our model.

Being means existing as individuals, as citizens within a society, with defined roles in both work and family.

Do parents truly strive to make their children different from themselves? Even schools or society? How can we defend ourselves— our children, small, insecure beings who trust everyone? Does becoming oneself really require effort?

We've been taught that if something is already itself, in its state of rest or motion, it doesn't need energy to become what it already is. It can't even absorb energy without becoming something else, changing state. It's a physical law, the first of dynamics. Where, then, is the mystery?

Let's define the battlefield.

The Being area represents our inner self and encompasses the three most important levels of our personality:

1. **Spiritual:** The Spirit in its truest sense, our soul, the deeper reason for our presence on this earth. Our creative power.
2. **Cognitive:** The Mind, all faculties that enable us to reason, its processes, the organization of thought, calculation, and memory.
3. **Emotional:** The Heart, all sensory pathways transformed into feelings, carrying their load of joy

Their corresponding breakdown would be:

Spiritual Level 1, broken down into 3 sub-levels:

a. Identity
b. Mission
c. Motivation

Cognitive Level 2, broken down into 3 sub-levels:

a. Thoughts
b. Calculation
c. Memory

Emotional Level 3, broken down into 3 sub-levels:

a. Sensations
b. Feelings
c. Conflict Alerts

The tree of being, as you see, is quite crowded. Its branches are numerous. Following this model, you will know immediately where to categorize a situation, giving you clear ideas to defend your sense of self.

At which level do others—parents, teachers, society—attempt to create beings different from themselves? Each of these concepts will clarify how you and your children operate as human beings. Perhaps you need further clarification.

It seems the greatest misunderstandings about us arise from the overlap between two images: the one we emit (our sense of self) and the one others perceive of us.

The next step is to understand which image others want us to become to conform to their distorted perception.

The lesson becomes: Clarify where you believe your child is strong, where their talent lies. Then, let them express, in their own way, who they want to be or become. Your role is to intercept those signals. We have all, consciously or unconsciously, tried to influence our children's choices for what we believed was their best interest. We all make these mistakes.

TECHNIQUES – THE MAPS OF BEEING

A) Drawing and building a tree:

1. Drawing a Tree:

- Start by drawing a tree, where each branch represents an action, event, a victory, a help, an example, a pain, or an offense.
- Each branch has its own path of actions, behaviors, and events that occur.
- A full tree will immediately show your successes.

B) Drawing a Circle:

1. The Big Circle Method:

- Draw a large circle and place the subject (yourself, your child) in the center.
- Starting from the center, add concentric circles.
- Inside the circle, draw your child's best traits, abilities, as arrows based on the questions.
- Draw a new circle from the center each time the ability achieves success.
- Remember, this is a map, and you can modify it as you please.

2. Creating Additional Layers:

- The thickness of the rings represents the ability that comes into play.
- Make an additional ring whenever the ability achieves success.

3. **Reflect on Environments and Advantages:**

- Reflect on the environment, advantages, and ensure energy is directed in the right way to build resilience.
- When the circle space runs out, create a new one with other goals or abilities.

4. **Memories and Reflections:**

- These are beautiful memories: your child will revisit them as they grow and understand how to improve further.
- Often, some circles are forgotten, giving insight into their life's direction, especially through their silence.

YOUR CHILD
Abilities
Attitudes
Tendencies
Interests
Attention to
family Requests

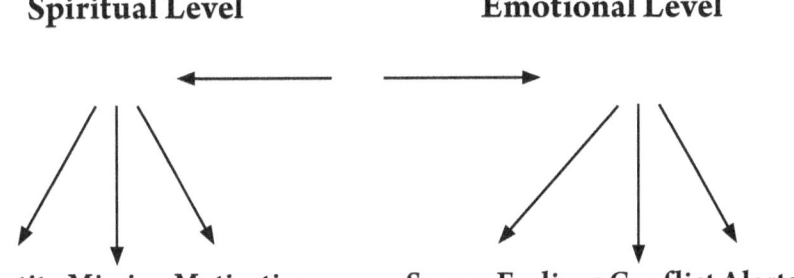

Spiritual Level   **Emotional Level**

Identity Mission Motivation   **Senses Feelings Conflict Alerts**

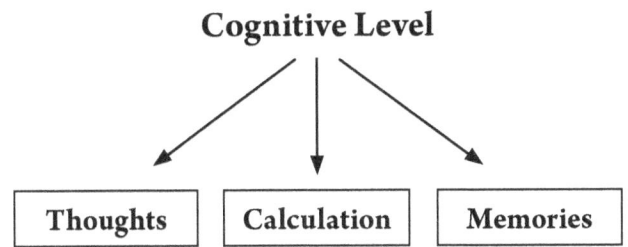

Cognitive Level

| **Thoughts** | **Calculation** | **Memories** |

Part Three:
The Spiritual Level

Strategy number 1 - Define identity
Strategy number 2 - Find the mission
Strategy number 3 - Always motivate your children

The spiritual level 1 Level 1 The Spirit

> *"Who works with his hands is a worker. Who works with*
> *his hands and his head is a craftsman. Who works with his*
> *hands, his head, and his heart is an artist." - St. Francis*

Note: In the first thirty pages, we outlined the concepts from a theoretical perspective. Now, we will familiarize ourselves with the models to define the personality of our children.

Let's remember that we have created a framework examining the main aspects of the expressions of being: definition and purpose, character attitudes, the ideal maximum, and the worst-case scenario, resilience, and advice.

Questionnaires for improvement.

Spiritual Level

Definitions	Goal	Attitudes - Skills - Abilities	Maximum	Minimum
	Goals	Competences	Excellences	
Identity	Finding ourselves	Will Determination	Enlightenment Reputation Confidence Self-esteem high	Alienation Depression
Mission	Messages to define the role	Role Personality Passion Clarity Sync	Vision High Values Principles References Positive Beliefs	Darkness False Myths Negative Beliefs
Motivation	Feel driven and push towards a direction	Enthusiasm Courage	Leadership Charisma	Despise Demotivate Negative Judgments

1 IDENTITY

LEVEL 1 SPIRITUAL

The true calling of everyone is one: to know oneself. (Hermann Hesse)

The expressions of the spirit are many, but we summarize the three most important: identity, mission, and motivation.

Definition	Goal	Attitudes, Skills, Capabilities, Competencies	Maximum - Strengths	Minimum - Weaknesses
Identity	Finding Ourselves Whole	Will - Determination	Enlightenment, Reputation, Authority, High Self-Esteem	Alienation, Depression

1 . Definition and purpose of identity

"O man! Journey from yourself to yourself."
(Galal al-Dın Rumı)

To recognize a person's identity is to affirm their right to existence. Society classifies us in two main ways:

a) by our roles (e.g., parent, child, spouse, leader, priest, doctor, etc.),
b) through identity cards and passports.

The role of parents is to provide an identity foundation for their children. Teachers, coaches, and other mentors are also entrusted with this responsibility. Adolescents often face painful experiences of depersonalization. Most NEETs emerge from the spiritual struggles of identity. Defeats, self-esteem losses, and repeated offenses create destructive beliefs. The first is: "Perhaps it's true that I'm nobody, that I'm worth nothing. I'm invisible, as if transparent. Maybe they're right."

The purpose of identity is to have a place in the world, with the ambition to be whole, recognizable, unique, respected, and with a good reputation. Today, this often includes visibility or fame.

LET'S REMEMBER

The first step to success is strengthening one's identity.

Immediate Action, Recovery

If you have suffered humiliation, shame, who better than you can become an expert in defending identity and self-worth? If this block and belief were instilled in you around the age of 4, it's difficult to remove, but necessary unless you want to live an anonymous life as a depersonalized person. If it has happened to your child, you can help them while simultaneously rebuilding your own self-image and restoring their integrity!

This limitation is overcome through the Anchoring Technique: repeating positive affirmations with self-conviction. It helps even when you think you're not capable in certain situations. Repeating affirmations like "I am capable, I am good, I can do it" or "I believe in my abilities, I am skilled in creating these outcomes… I want this to happen, and it will." for about 3 months. Consistent repetition works. In practice, you use induction and thought restructuring techniques from NLP. It works.

---

2. ATTITUDES AND SKILLS THAT DEFINE IDENTITY

Note:

To improve various dimensions of Being and learn how to achieve excellence—ultimate goals of education—different levels must be ascended. The "ladder of competence" consists of knowledge and operational skills. From the least operational to the most advanced, these are the steps:

a) **Attitudes** are innate dispositions of a person. Tendency, vocation, inclination, and talent are variations of this. Dreams and expectations can emerge, but they must be transformed.
b) **Skills** are the first steps in putting attitudes into practice. Expertise, dexterity, caution, and resourcefulness are variations.
c) **Capabilities** are the operational realization of skills. We've transformed the attitude and mastered it. We can demonstrate how it's done.
d) **Competencies** are mastery (both theoretical and practical) of how things are done. We can teach others how to do it and justify the reasons behind it.

There are those who are experts in information and those who are experts in results. Here, we focus on the latter—those who have gained experience firsthand, improving by overcoming trials, obstacles, and challenges.

To achieve excellence, which distinguishes us from others and leads to high performance, it's essential to find and navigate these steps in every dimension (Identity, Mission, Motivation).

Let's begin with those related to Identity.

IDENTITY Steps of "Knowing How"	Signals	Benefits
Attitude	Tendency to express oneself, frequently using "I"	Self-definition, recognition, and acknowledgment
Abilities	Emergence, multiple attempts to express one's character, and assert opinions	Gaining confidence and presence in the world, in roles, and at work
Capabilities	Diversification and assertion of one's personality, seeking advice, imitation	Self-esteem and respect from others, receiving praise
Competence	Awareness of one's value, pride, and defense of one's identity	Excellence and success as a person: social recognition of charisma, leadership, and authority

Note How to use the model: the signs are general indications, on this track you can create your own map, marking those that are most important for you and your child.

LET'S REMEMBER

Every identity is perfect. Attitudes naturally emerge if we don't suppress them. However, others judge us based on our actions and our role within the context we operate in. We must not confuse the actions we are capable of with our personality. Incorrect actions are not synonymous with a flawed personality, which remains excellent.

You might be a person who tends to be introverted, shy, and wouldn't naturally dive into the middle of a dance floor. In contrast, you'll likely be precise and reliable.

With these attitudes, you can become someone perceived as highly dependable. By developing this tendency, your ability might become helping others stay consistent, completing tasks, and being precise and punctual, just as you are.

If you enjoy this ability, you can turn it into a capacity—transferring your solutions (based on your lived and learned experiences) to increase others' self-esteem and awareness of their role's value.

Over time, with added study and personal growth through your struggles, you'll become the authoritative expert others seek when facing character-related obstacles.

You'll establish a reputation as a competent professional. You can succeed in fields where precision and the perfection of individual elements are crucial. Staying within this theme, you could become a time management consultant, a human resources leader, or an effective manager in Research and Development.

These professions align with your shy yet trustworthy and meticulous identity. You can become a champion in sports and much more.

Admired by your audience, you can sell your high-value-added services.

To strengthen this journey, you need willpower, determination, and self-confidence.

Example Five: Marco's Story, Age 6, and the Broken Cup

One of the most common communication mistakes regarding identity is as follows:

Marco is a restless child; he dropped a cup, which broke.

His mother scolds him: "You need to be more careful, you're always so inattentive."

Marco looks at her, eyes wide: "Stop calling me names! You're always saying that!"

For a small child who believes in their parents unconditionally, the message they receive is: "I am foolish, I am inattentive. My mom is right."

Repeated over time, this message reinforces itself, leading to a drastic drop in Marco's self-esteem regarding his attention and intelligence.

This devaluation will cost much more than a broken cup if it becomes a belief!

Marco may begin to fear cups, calculations, weight, space, and precision!

When we spoke with Marco to address his insecurity and fear, the conversation became:

"We see you broke a cup. You're a good boy. Next time, hold the cup this way!" with a gentle tone.

"If you keep holding the cup like this, you'll pay for it. What if I take the cost out of your allowance next time?"

We reached an agreement (be firm about conditions).

Not humiliated, but now responsible, Marco pays attention and hasn't broken another cup since.

In line with his shy tendencies, to help a timid child (from age 6 onward) develop confidence and precision, aside from your example, tasks of increasing difficulty that he enjoys and are short can be given.

He will become accustomed to trusting his abilities.

Recognition of results should be shared by the whole family.

In this way, his identity is reinforced through shared esteem.

For example, a reward ritual could be created during Sunday lunch.

And if he makes a mistake? Nothing serious. We start over.

The communication error with Marco, if repeated with a child of an independent character (after age 6), who is already emotionally strong, verbalizes, and abstracts, becomes a boomerang.

Instead of suffering from your criticism, the child won't lower their self-esteem but will stop believing you.

They may react in different ways:

- Lying
- Hiding
- Not listening
- Shrugging
- Shifting attention to other topics
- Interrupting dialogue with fake stomach aches

In short, they no longer consider your words important, lose trust in you, and rebel.

Has this happened to you? How many times have you unintentionally harmed their self-esteem?

Recovery begins if you reframe those experiences with them. Your communication and their trust will rise again.

3 MAXIMUM SITUATION of identity. Excellence (the benefits you get if... The pleasurable situation toward which you want to go)

"What lies behind us and what lies before us are tiny
matters compared to what lies within us."
(Ralph Waldo Emerson)

The maximum aspiration of identity is to realize ourselves, to be admired, applauded, and to become leaders.

Excellence aims for the highest possible level. A memorable identity, a champion, a gold medal, a Nobel prize.

Desirable results are enlightenment if we are in the field of truth and knowledge, authority if we speak of society, and fame if we aim to reach our audience.

Above all, the highest aspiration is to achieve a state of strong self-confidence as a unit, known as self-esteem, the vehicle that allows us to maintain good mental health and psychological well-being.

LEADERSHIP

Leadership is the result of long preparation, facilitated by a natural tendency. To transform it into excellent leadership, there are several stages:

Stages of coaching to transform a person with a tendency to lead others into an excellent leader, including mini strategies that cultivate ambitions, attitudes, actions:	
Steps	Mini Strategies That Cultivate Ambitions, Attitudes, and Actions
A Attitude	Love others, be extroverted, and care for important global issues.
B Skills	Build relationships with people through empathy, kindness, and active listening.
C Capabilities	Communicate, persuade, and use special techniques for public speaking and covert persuasion to assert your role.
D Competencies	Study key authors, models, and theories of personal development, and apply them.
E Excellence	Transform yourself into a master opinion leader with strong eloquence.
F Flow-Enhancing Techniques	Use psycho-physiological techniques to enter a mental state where you anticipate success, visualizing outcomes like engaging with audiences, receiving applause, and recognition. Build a network of supporters and followers, managing large groups with both fans and detractors (whom you'll need to get accustomed to).

There are at least 6 steps to identity excellence. The gifted person must be trained in the various steps as the muscles of a sports player are trained.

LET'S REMEMBER

Talent is a dimension of identity.

Identity is singular but can express itself through multiple talents.

Michelangelo, Leonardo, Bernini, Donatello—all possessed extraordinary talents: in painting, architecture, research, and science.

Our task is to bring out all our talents to their fullest potential. Since obstacles will inevitably arise, we must develop and refine them to achieve excellence. This requires consistent effort and sacrifices. Let us not be deceived—it demands relentless practice and perseverance.

4 MINIMAL IDENTITY SITUATION (the price you pay if you don't… The painful state you want to escape from)

This is the condition where we no longer know who we are and feel trapped. Such a void allows others to overpower us. People sense our weakness and take advantage.

This is a dangerous state that parents must be vigilant about. The most noticeable signs include neglect of personal hygiene, disinterest in school, sudden nail-biting, minimal or reduced communication, and forgetting important belongings. When children lose self-esteem, they may start to withdraw, isolate themselves for hours in front of the computer or TV. It's a pathway leading to NEET status.

Prolonged inaction and self-deprecation can lead to depression, eating disorders such as bulimia and anorexia, and in extreme cases, more severe conditions. If you suspect such risks and the situation persists, seek medical support as it could become a serious pathological state.

Example six: the story of Verde, 11 years old, a victim of bullying

Verde was subjected to severe bullying by four older students in middle school.

Teens who are bullied often come to believe they are worthless and comply with the rules of the dominant group, following blindly. Verde started stealing from the supermarket, like many others, hoping to ingratiate himself with the leader and escape the abuse.

But in his case, the bullying continued, even after he was caught by the police and referred to social services. A sad story of absent parents for all five of these children.

Today, Verde is doing well. He lives in a protected community, excels academically, and shows strong artistic talent. He has regained his identity, stands up to "the big guys," and helps "the girls."

In families where women are victims of domestic violence, they often lose self-esteem and enable the abusive partner to continue. The consequences are widely reported.

Low self-esteem is a social indicator of damage to identity. How can we entrust people with such mental handicaps with responsibilities? Would we place our children in the hands of someone so insecure?

A self-esteem test should be mandatory in schools and workplaces.

When people are humiliated, suffering until reaching a breaking point, they may lash out at themselves or others as a misguided response to mistreatment. They may become aggressive towards those they perceive as weaker. They replicate the negative model they were victims of. Let's avoid unpleasant surprises. Cultivating self-esteem is a lifelong task that starts from birth and continues into adulthood.

Managers and employees who fear their superiors, undervalue themselves, and perform poorly at work need their self-esteem boosted. A good coaching process can resolve these issues within 3-6 months, definitively. Our statistics show personal and group performance increasing by at least 20%.

5 RESILIENCE OF IDENTITY

The resilience of personal identity is the ability to withstand attacks on one's personality while maintaining good self-esteem.

It is the most crucial form of resilience.

In practice, various offenses to our appearance or intelligence that call into question our capacity for attraction and seduction make us feel "stupid, incapable."

We perceive two key signals: aesthetic and intellectual:

- If we perceive ourselves as less attractive, the reaction is twofold:
  - We stop caring, give up, thinking "it doesn't matter anymore."
  - Alternatively, we become obsessed with excessive care of our physical appearance.

- If we perceive ourselves as less intelligent, the reaction is threefold:
  - Our enthusiasm diminishes, we laugh less, and we have a "dour" expression.
  - We increase resentment, expressing it with a harsh, abrasive, and acidic tone.
  - We reduce our kindness, responding negatively to people who haven't even offended us (transfer).

Recovery

Recovery happens through Logos (effective words) and actions.

The recovery of identity resilience goes through two phases:

Logos: using powerful words towards the external offender, and/or internally towards ourselves.

Behaviors: through personal actions and/or with the support of others.

Logos with personal actions:

- Defend yourself externally against those who launched the offenses, responding calmly and restating their incorrect opinion. Sometimes offenders apologize and change their behavior.
- Internally, dialogue with ourselves, using mantras, if possible out loud. Messages that work best in the face of any cruelty are:

"I know what I'm worth."

"They think this way? I'll show them what I'm worth!"

"Thank you for this experience! I'll learn more." (The preferred one)

"My actions are not me, a mistake is a wrong action. I am whole, capable of correcting myself."

"You don't want me? You don't deserve me!" and react by doing better.

Repeat these phrases consistently. They are effective mantras.

Logos (effective words) with the support of others:

Share your experience in detail with friends, parents, or those close to you who listen, which will help reduce the emotional impact, making you more objective and ready to respond. (They can also intervene on your behalf, especially against bullying.)

To regain self-esteem, you can use two conscious techniques:

- Seducing better, communicating better (this is the greatest challenge).
- Temporarily buying the acceptance of the offender with a "gift" that conveys your willingness to win their favor.

Don't criticize this action; it's not weakness, but a tactic. First, regain confidence in yourself, and when stronger, rebalance the relationship.

(Even a dog uses these strategies; it lies down on its back when scolded. This submissive act doesn't make it weaker, but rather strengthens the bond with the owner and gains more!)

We are not dogs, but if we are offended regarding our identity by authoritative figures, we unconsciously tend to develop a reactive psychology that seeks others' love and seduction, like a dog.

If this becomes a learned behavior in early childhood, we tend to be overly servile, available, as if we are generous.

However, we confuse this "generosity of spirit" with our need to be accepted.

We feel a debt, a duty to give, and end up losing in every relationship.

By fixing resilience, we'll escape this tunnel. Learning to say no will make us feel lighter. At first, it will be more painful, but eventually, we'll feel free.

Are you part of this cycle? You're in good company. Reflect on your relationship with parents, teachers, or friends from different social backgrounds.

The vulnerability to words, excessive defensiveness, and susceptibility are indicators of low resilience. This decreases the necessary enthusiasm for any initiative, leading to low available energy. At a minimal level, without strong identity defenses, humiliation, offenses, violence, and abuse become acceptable. With low resilience, there is no response, increasing the risk of becoming a NEET, sinking into exhaustion, and suffering from depression.

An effective measure: if you find yourself in a difficult situation and feel low in identity resilience, sing your favorite song loudly. Music energizes the sense of self. Reclaim your self through your personal tastes. Some coaches use the formula of intense, deep prayer. Others focus on the image they had of themselves as children, surrounded by their parents. These anchors work, especially if the memories are positive, giving a brief burst of energy, like when rubbing and blowing on a dead battery.

Alarm-inducing phrases are:

"I am worth nothing. I have nothing. Nobody wants me. I can't do anything. I mess everything up. I am a disaster. I am a burden." Fortunately, these are rare in children but more frequent in old age.

Identity resilience fluctuates greatly during adolescence. Teens are searching for stability in their roles and sexual identity. Adolescents oscillate between robustness and fragility, identity resilience and vulnerability, struggling daily for social validation due to hormonal shifts. They fear appearing ridiculous. No one wants the role of the loser, though sometimes it may be beneficial. It's a time when you must increase attention toward your children.

Support your child. If you're angry about low school grades, avoid generalizations, insults, or lowering their resilience. If they're clearly at fault, perhaps due to superficiality, boost their identity resilience by giving them small, achievable challenges. Redirect attention to positive achievements. The difficulty level of the task doesn't matter as much as sincere confirmation that they did well. They deserve genuine praise. Over time, increase the challenge levels as they build confidence in their abilities.

If there's a long gap between failure and restructuring, the risk of raising NEETs increases. They become passive, give up, lose motivation, become shy, and moody.

Talk to them—perhaps encourage them to read stories of extraordinary individuals in their field, like Gianluca Genoni, the freediver who conquers deep-sea abyss through mental preparation, yoga, breathing techniques, and meditation. He dispels myths about diving limits. Share the stories of Enzo Maiorca, who passed recently, a record-breaking freediver, and Umberto Pellizzari, another champion.

High identity resilience attracts others and allows you to seduce those around you.

If you want to become a leader, cultivate this identity resilience. (For further details, you can read "Resilience, Coaching & Training" in Italian and attend courses.)

EXAMPLE SEVEN: THE STORY OF HOW IDENTITY RESILIENCE WORKS IN BUSINESS

In the economic field, low identity resilience of a brand drives it out of the market. Nobody likes to buy things they don't value or identify with. To regain this resilience, it's essential to gauge customer opinions, using experts in image who conduct market research to understand the causes weakening resilience and, consequently, sales.

Today, market research has become accessible and inexpensive. The 1960s, when market research was mainly available to large companies like IBM, Galbani, Ferrero, Beretta, and Coca-Cola, are long gone. Back then, we worked with professionals like Prof. Luzzatto Fegis and Dr. Ennio Salamon. Today, quantitative market research—using questionnaires requiring simple yes/no answers or checkmarks—can be deployed online, even on platforms like Survey Monkey, Facebook, or Google.

Market trends can also be extracted from data-driven tools like Noble Samurai, Google Trends, or Facebook insights.

The online identity campaign for social positioning should reinforce the brand, its message, and reputation, supported by authoritative testimonials. The advertising campaign will employ various strategies: samples, giveaways, contests, prizes, guerrilla marketing, etc. With consistency over eighteen months, you first raise identity resilience, then launch the commercial campaign. Guaranteed sales recovery.

These tests should be conducted periodically to gauge customer willingness to pay, which inversely reflects economic resilience.

6 IDENTITY TIPS, RESULTS AND STRATEGIES
Example Eight: Miriam's Story, 65 Years Old, Her Mantra of Resilience

Do you remember the Holocaust?

Those who managed to defend their identity, overcoming the annihilation imposed by their oppressors, maintained dignity despite everything and survived.

Primo Levi's **"If This is a Man"** is a testament to this; even after his liberation, he struggled with the lasting effects of identity erosion. The identity, it seems, is the "foundation" of personality itself, and attacking its integrity undermines one's future prospects.

Albina recalls a story about a beautiful Jewish woman named Miriam, who survived by holding onto her sense of self amidst unimaginable suffering. Miriam shared that each time she was assaulted, she thanked God, believing that she had escaped even worse abuse. She stayed with an oppressor who, in some twisted way, saved her for his own pleasure and made her feel beautiful. Her mantra was: "Forget it, you are a beautiful person, life will get better tomorrow. Stay prepared."

In the 1970s hospital, Miriam became somewhat of a legend. She was notoriously difficult to treat, especially for minor injections, which led to her running down the hospital corridors. However, when playing cards, she became calm and accepting. Albina spent an entire week playing canasta with her, helping to desensitize her and test resilience-building techniques. Despite losing many times, Miriam continued to repeat her mantra, and it became a source of courage for Albina as well.

Real Threats to Identity Resilience

Certain humiliations can pose real threats to identity resilience and affect your sons' future. For instance, insults related to height ("You're shorter than me") and concerns about masculinity and sexual performance ("You're not as big as me") start appearing at a surprisingly young age—often as early as three years old. These comments might not be obvious since young children cannot always verbalize their feelings, but they leave deep psychological scars.

If you catch these subtle signs early, you can turn them into humorous moments, teaching your child to view the offender as small and ridiculous. This helps reduce the impact of the negative memory. Then, identify and praise one physical attribute of your child—whether it's their hair, legs, lips, eyes, or body shape—to anchor their confidence in a positive and visible trait.

For children aged two to three, these judgments have an even deeper psychological impact. Such trauma can manifest as psychological imbalances in adulthood, leading to fears, insecurities, or behaviors like isolation (NEETs). Identifying and addressing these issues early can prevent long-term harm.

The Connection Between Identity Resilience and Physical Resilience

Lower identity resilience also impacts physical resilience. This is a direct connection between Level 1 (identity) and Level 4 (physical well-being). When identity resilience is compromised, physical health often follows—leading to more susceptibility to stress, illness, and other related issues.

By enhancing identity resilience, you simultaneously strengthen the physical and emotional well-being of yourself and your children.

EXAMPLE NINE: THE STORY OF LITTLE LUCE, 5 YEARS OLD, AND HER DIAPER

We share an educational incident many mothers face: chronic constipation in young children and the struggle to remove diapers. Childhood constipation isn't typically a physical condition unless related to anatomical issues or restrictive diets—it often stems from psychological or identity-related causes. It's a sign of fear of self, with the enteric brain (gut-brain connection) resisting. For Luce, holding back her bowel movements became a natural defense, a sense of control—especially in comparison to her siblings. A psychologist identified and resolved this issue within three months by giving her security and value, helping her understand that she was important just as much as her siblings. Once she regained control and confidence, her fear subsided, and she naturally released what was no longer needed.

Life offers many emotional experiences—ensure your child has mostly positive ones. By fostering perceptions of self-worth, the fear will diminish, and your child will feel empowered, capable of mastering their body, including their bowels and sphincters. This approach can resolve issues like nocturnal enuresis and incontinence in preschool-age children, provided no organic imbalances exist. Functional problems are often rooted in low identity resilience, stemming from strained relationships and the perception of being "left behind"—whether in preschool, school, or due to absent parents. The absence is perceived as a lack of importance, contributing to low resilience.

Addressing Social Comparisons and Low Resilience in Childhood

In elementary school, some children from less affluent backgrounds may feel embarrassed by differences in social status, often reflected in clothing choices. For instance, their clothes might be out of fashion compared to wealthier classmates. The solution remains the same: boosting self-esteem, providing clear explanations of core values, and creating supportive, empathetic social networks.

Encouraging group activities that align with their interests—like sports teams or matching uniforms—can help mitigate feelings of inadequacy and foster a sense of belonging.

SIMILARITIES IN YOUR BUSINESS STRATEGIES

The strategies for minimizing attacks on your brand are strikingly similar to those recommended for children:

- **Brand Image Defense**: Just as boosting self-esteem is a long-term personal goal, defending and enhancing the brand image is a long-term corporate strategy. Both require nurturing and persistence.

- **Advertising and Marketing for Brand Strength**: Strategies that strengthen a brand's image—such as campaigns, testimonials, and customer engagement—are akin to praising and rewarding children. Recognition, awards, or even physical tokens like samples or promotional items serve as visible, tangible boosts to self-esteem.

- **Partnerships and Collaborative Networks**: Building partnerships along the supply chain with other companies mirrors the social bonds and friendships formed by children. Collaborations foster trust, sharing of values, and collective growth.

- **Company History and Storytelling**: Highlighting the company's history, traditions, and milestones parallels the personal storytelling and keepsake collections (like photo books and journals) that help reinforce identity and belonging in children.

These strategies ensure that both children and businesses alike can build resilience, foster positive self-perception, and strengthen their social or market presence.

LET'S REMEMBER

1. Gratify small successes (praise, acknowledge immediately) as they lay the foundation for growth. Each compliment is a seed that will bloom over time. Stop criticizing and let go of mistakes, including those made by yourself.
2. Encourage children to participate in social activities to help them confront, measure, support, and earn respect. Socialization builds resilience and strengthens personal identity.
3. Host contests and competitions at school or work to promote healthy competition and recognition, fostering a sense of belonging and personal growth.
4. Don't practice false humility—social recognition and external rewards aren't empty ambitions but signs of self-love and commitment to your business. If given the opportunity, accept and celebrate success. For children, seeing a rewarded parent serves as a powerful model for motivation and success through modeling and copying.

1 IDENTITY

LEVEL 1 SPIRITUAL

Questionnaire to draw inspiration on identity (sample) that you need for:

a) mapping character traits, personality, visual tools of the journey
b) identifying which roles they would like to play in life
c) setting up a coaching plan, personal growth
d) Assets already acquired, riches derived from roots, origins, relationships, epigenetics, positive experiences to replicate, and negative ones to transform

How can your child take pride in their origins and leverage them for visibility? Write or have them list their best parental and local connections that they see as beneficial and worthy of pride. Observe grandparents, uncles. Find the similarities.

1 _____

2 _____

3 _____

IDENTITY Basic Elements.

Write or have them list their best attitudes, skills, tendencies, character traits, abilities, and attitudes to create their Best Image according to their own opinion.

Also, list the advantages of these traits.

1 _____

2 _____

3 _____

IDENTITY Technique to Replicate Success.

Write down what you were thinking and how you felt when you received awards, praise, or recognition. Can you recreate the same conditions? Apply them to your current image, it will strengthen you. Build for your child an image around the positive events they have experienced.

Alternatively, first create different situations for them where they are praised, appreciated, and chosen, and repeat this "copying" process several times until the imprinting (memory formation) is complete. It will strengthen them.

1 _____

2 _____

3 _____

IDENTITY Technique to Modify a Failure.

Have you overcome obstacles to your identity? Describe the elements that offended you and how you felt. Help your child overcome those moments by turning them into valuable learning experiences, finding the positive side often hidden behind the difficulties.

1 _____

2 _____

3 _____

b) *Strengthening training and required formative needs (it's a process).*

IDENTITY Today, how can you improve the basic elements? Describe the procedures, focusing on the manual, especially resilience and areas of strength and weakness.

1 _____

2 _____

3 _____

Help your child identify the goal of their identity. Work together to create a plan with imagined solutions. A leader, a follower, a champion, a professional? What do they want to be when they grow up?

1 _____

2 _____

3 _____

Have him compare with their peers, classmates, or siblings, and write down his next actions to project his identity to the world (to be recorded in his journal).

1 _____

2 _____

3 _____

For constant and effective personal growth training to develop an excellent personality, have them check their initial character tendencies and plan any necessary formative steps to strengthen their identity, moving from tendencies to skills, abilities, and then competence.

For example, cultivating expansiveness, improving shyness, achieving high self-esteem.

List the sources of support that can enhance their value as a unique and irreplaceable person. Who can help? Mother, grandparents, uncles, coaches, peers, family collaborators. Collaboration helps them compare and clarify aspects.

1 _____

2 _____

3 _____

c) Goals

What do you/s/he want to improve in your/their identity? Where do you/they want to reach? Prestige, promotion, visibility, fame? Write down 3 aspects of their identity that you/they will work on. Note the related advantages and benefits gained.

1 _____

2 _____

3 _____

Witness of progress. Write down who measures the transformation of your child in the 3 chosen aspects with you.

1 _____

2 _____

3 _____

Imagine and help him visualize his goal as achieved and fulfilling. Train him in Transcendental Meditation (go and learn it) by visualizing his image with confidence and pride.

1 _____

2 _____

3 _____

d) Results - Control of results - Goal achieved confirmed by the witness

Goal achieved on date _____ from _____.
Congratulate, reward at every step.
Update the form with date, signature of buddy, tutor, mentor, coach.
Location, date, signature.

1 _____

2 _____

3 _____

WHO HAD SUCCESS

Example ten: The story of Bob Marley

We present an example of someone who achieved success by creating his identity from scratch, even from below zero, given the context of racism. The analysis will go into detail to understand the method. Subsequent examples in the book will be simplified for your enjoyment in further developing them.

Let's analyze the character using our model as an interpretive tool to understand how a singer—a legend—defended his identity.

Bob Marley's story, from nothing to greatness as an artist, from poverty to stardom.

"Find out the pieces and reassemble the puzzle of your life."

"How BM has become the number ONE: from rags to riches step-by-step."

He is a singer who fascinates today's youth as well. His legacy is still appreciated as a legend. I imagine you know the great Jamaican singer, creator of reggae, who died in 1981 at the age of 36 from cancer. Here's what he did according to the 10 levels model.

Behavioral Analysis Model Applied to 10 Levels

Level	Estimated value	Value Invested	Result
3 Areas	Average Weight in life	Real Weight on Bob M's Life	
a) Being	30%	45%	Motivated by the religion of Rastafarianism
1. Spiritual	10	30	Leader Philosopher Benefactor
2. Cognitive	10	5	Not very cultured
3. Emotional	10	10	Emotions against injustice
b) Having	30%	25%	
4. Physiologic	10	0	He lost his life for not seeking treatment
5. Financial	10	20	Lots of money but indifferent
6. Logistic	10	5	Messy
c) Doing	40%	30%	
7. Relational	10	10	Lots of women but superficial relationships
8. Environmental	10	20	Very interested
9. Behavioral	10	0	Indifferent
10. Social Proof	10	0	Non-existent
Total	100%	100%	

Please Note: How to Assign the Score

The evaluations you assign to the 10 levels are your personal assessments. Their absolute value is not important; they are only meant to indicate trends, the dominance of one area over another, or the prevalence of one level compared to others.

As you will notice in **Column 1, "Estimated Average Value,"** the 100% weight is divided among three average areas and 10 levels. These percentages reflect the equal distribution across all levels. In **Column 2, "Invested Value (Real Weight),"** we provide our opinion. (We apologize for any methodological errors in terms of statistical rules and proper sampling techniques.)

The **"Doing"** area is given slightly more weight (40%) compared to **"Being"** and **"Having"** because actions determine results. For this reason, we have categorized **Level 7, "Relationships,"** under the "Doing" area, understood as "acting with or in the company of others."

It could also be argued, reasonably, that relationships are a form of wealth and should belong to the "Having" area. (Indeed, statistics suggest that behind our successes lie friends, family, and close relationships, which conceptually represent resources.) However, in our map, actions carry greater weight.

The Story of Bob Marley

- **Place and Date of Birth:** Jamaica, February 6, 1945
- **Parents:** British father, Norval Sinclair Marley, and Jamaican mother, Cedella Booker
- **Ethnicity:** Mixed-race
- **Height:** 1.63 m (5'4")

Level 1 - IDENTITY

He saw himself as a political and religious leader and used his artistic ability to spread humanitarian principles and values faithful to Rastafarianism. This religion, originating from Ethiopia and led by Emperor Haile Selassie I, has about 10 million followers. He embraced its political aspect, actively fighting against racism to defend Black populations, spreading these ideals worldwide. It influenced his entire life until his premature death at the age of 36.

Level 1 - MISSION

"His music is strongly dedicated to the fight against political and racial oppression and to the call for the unification of people of color as the only way to achieve freedom and equality," according to Wikipedia.

A marvelous moment was when he orchestrated, on his stage, the meeting of two opposing Jamaican political leaders and made them shake hands!

Level 1 - MOTIVATION

"In addition to being a musician, Marley became a political, spiritual, and religious leader, always at the forefront of spreading ideas of equality, peace, brotherhood, and respect.

For this, in 1978, he was awarded the Peace Medal by the United Nations on behalf of 500 million Africans.

Level 1 - ROOTS

He considered his roots to be Black and Jamaican, less so British, and was never forgiving of his father's abandonment, who, pressured by his family and societal norms, did not marry his mother. He never forgave him.

"I didn't have a father. Never knew him... My father was like those stories you read, slave stories: the white man takes the Black woman and gets her pregnant."

He was a victim of racial prejudice due to his mixed origins and turned this into the manifesto of his life. Humiliation became a strong motivation. It gave rise to a tremendous drive for redemption, and he devoted his entire life to his racial identity.

"I have no prejudice against myself. My father was white, and my mother was Black. They call me mixed race or something like that. But I don't side with anyone—neither the white man nor the Black man. I stand with God, the one who created me and made it so that I was born both Black and white. Trenchtown isn't in Jamaica; Trenchtown is everywhere because it's where all the dispossessed, all the desperate people come from. Trenchtown is the ghetto, any ghetto in any city. And if you're born in Trenchtown, you don't stand a chance."

He was a victim of bullying, with the humiliation tied to his short stature. His motivation led him to exercise intensely, building a significant muscular physique, earning him the nickname "Tuff Gong." As a child, he fought against poverty and misery—another source of motivation.

This also explains his idea of an open marriage with his wife, Rita Marley, fathering 13 children with 8 other women.

He survived an attempted political assassination but still performed at his concert on the scheduled date despite the threat.

"Because the people trying to make this world worse don't take a day off... How can I?!"

And then, his death: he could have reduced the risk of melanoma, but it required amputating his toe, which his religion forbade.

Meanwhile, international success and wealth enriched him, and he helped everyone without reservation. He even came to Italy, performing in Milan on June 28, 1980. It was a success.

Level 1 - THE MESSAGE

"Emancipate yourselves from mental slavery; no one but ourselves can free our minds..." He was terminally ill and knew it. He tried to heal in the end, but it was too late. He gathered all his children and, on his deathbed, told his son Ziggy Marley: "Money can't buy life."

Level 1 - MESSAGE

"Money can't buy life."

In the summer of 2006, the city of New York named a portion of Church Avenue, from Ramsen Avenue to 98th Street in East Flatbush, Brooklyn, as Bob Marley Boulevard.

LET'S REMEMBER

1. Never let anyone undermine your identity—your height, the color of your skin, the shape of your nose, or any other aspect of yourself.
2. Turn your humiliations into motivations for redemption (your "why" for taking action), especially if you're of small stature, and teach this to your child.
3. Money can't buy life, so take care of your body! Neglecting it won't save you, not even if your name is Bob Marley!

Summary of Strategy 1: Define Identity

1. **Empower Your Child's Identity**
   - Understand your child's aspirations.
   - Recognize the context they are born into: family, ethnicity, city, nation, culture, and school, all rich with traditions and history that can inspire them.

2. **Connect Them to Their Roots**
   - Begin an **Epigenetic Journal** by narrating their grandparents' stories and your coaching experiences. Over time, they will continue it themselves.
   - This journal is a priceless gift, far more valuable than toys. While it requires time, the long-term benefits are immense. When they grow up, it will become a cherished relic.

3. **Celebrate Their Achievements**
   - Highlight their victories to boost their confidence.
   - Emphasize their right to belong in the world, nurturing their evolving personality.
   - Expose them to varied experiences to broaden their choices about who they are and what they wish to become.

Important Note: Gender Identity

We intentionally omitted gender identity from this strategy, as it's a topic often in the public spotlight.

Examples include children of Hollywood actors like Angelina Jolie and Jodie Foster.

We address this issue comprehensively in a book titled *"The Gender of Children: How to Address Homosexual Tendencies,"* expected publication in September 2017. For preorders, contact info@gsm-online.it.

Key Concerns:

- **Lack of Information**: Many young people and families struggle with ignorance about gender orientation, leading to doubts, conflicts, and trust breakdowns.
- **Support from Experts**: We consulted medical professionals who provided practical solutions for navigating these experiences.

INSIGHTS ON GENDER EVOLUTION:

For centuries, humanity has witnessed a blending of traditionally male and female roles:

- Women can now lead wars, work in workshops, transport goods, drive trucks and airplanes, and even go to space.
- Physical labor and strength, once a male domain, are now replaced by machines, erasing traditional boundaries.

Future Questions:

Will technology advance to the point where surrogacy occurs in male wombs? Possibly, as science heads in that direction.

SUPPORTING CHILDREN WITH GENDER CHALLENGES:

If children exhibit signs of gender discomfort, avoid judgment and obstacles. Instead, aim for an **integrated and harmonious development** by focusing on:

- **Identity Unity**: Align heart, mind, spirit, and body.
- **Social Beliefs**: Foster respect for their individuality.
- **Emotional Growth**: Encourage interpersonal challenges to be experienced as emotions rather than purely sexual impulses.

Adolescence and Beyond:

By developing self-awareness, gaining societal respect, and interpreting their emotions correctly, adolescents often find their authentic selves during youth without trauma.

If Gender Identity Becomes Definitive:

When recognition and coming out occur, let **Love** guide your reactions. Provide respect instead of shame, guilt, or resentment.

Help them tackle "Level 10" challenges, like social validation, by offering strong positive feedback to build their self-esteem.

2 MISSION

LEVEL 1 SPIRITUAL

Revised by Prof.ssa Laura Mazza

"The true vocation of every individual is to know themselves."
— *Hermann Hesse*

Definition	Goal	Aptitudes, Skills, Capacities, Competencies	Maximum Excellency	Minimum
Mission	Finding the role, the place in life	Personality Passion Clarity Harmony	Great Vision High Values Principles Certain References Powerful Beliefs	Darkness False myths Negative beliefs

1 Definition and Purpose of a Mission

A mission is the inner voice that calls you to fulfill a role in life. It manifests as a tendency, passion, love for something, instinct to help, or an often unconscious drive to achieve long-term goals.

The ultimate purpose of a mission is to serve humanity. It acts as a command, a direction to follow, a conscious acknowledgment of the profound messages of the self—a calling, as Saint Mother Teresa of Calcutta described it.

When we align with these messages, we uncover unexpected energy. A deep joy emerges from participating in the flow of the world.

It's a powerful love, urging you forward with an urgency to arrive at your goal.

Conversely, straying from this path brings an unpleasant sense of purposelessness and futility, leading to sadness and discontent.

Think of Saint Francis, Saint Joan of Arc, or, in the business world, Bill Gates and Steve Jobs.

LET'S REMEMBER

The second step to success is clarity about your mission.

Immediate Action: Recovery
We begin by asking questions to uncover passions. Start small, taking steps to exercise your impact. By pursuing this purpose, we honor both our mission and that of others.

What keeps us awake, engaged? What do children ask for?
A mission, rather than being a message, is a force. It connects us to a Value so vital to us that we dedicate our lives to it.

Typically, the purpose or allure of a mission is the hope of improving a flawed situation in the world or achieving excellence in private matters (e.g., solving world hunger, educating children).

The most significant challenge is identifying and genuinely understanding a child's mission, even when they explain it themselves. This understanding is influenced by:

- **Their worldview**
- **Values, principles, and points of reference**
- **Epigenetic and genetic heritage**
- **Their perception of inner drive**
- **Education**
- **Social context in which they operate**
- **The unique opportunities of the moment, which will never be identical in the future**

2. Skills and Aptitudes That Shape the Mission

The natural inclinations of a mission, which deserve attention, emerge over time and are not apparent from birth. Their development depends on proper education and, for adults, is often triggered by a life-changing trauma (e.g., parents who become anti-drug advocates in schools after losing a child).

Parental imposition of rigid models can hinder the process of identifying one's life purpose.

In conditions of poverty, the urgency of survival may overshadow the mission, prioritizing a more practical purpose where financial needs often take precedence.

2 MISSION Steps of "know-how"	Signals	Benefits
Attitude	Inner voice, discomfort, dream, interest in a "word" as an artist, actor, doctor	Clarity, call initiation, message selection, pleasure in hearing the "word"
Ability	Alternation of roles, changes of job, of professional figure, attempts to understand, to verify what one wants to be	Sensation of coherence of purpose and energetic phase, the word resonates inside giving greater serenity, joy
Capacity	Verbalization of one's purpose in life, intention to continue on the chosen path, dedication	Strong energy, union of purpose and means, focused orientation towards the chosen goal in the long term throughout life
Competence	Strength, seducing others of one's purpose and value, teaching others	Excellence Automatic attraction as a guide, mentor, leader. Example SOLITARY PURPOSE SUCCESS IN MATURE AGE or rare precocity

EXAMPLE ELEVEN: THE STORY OF MARIETTA, 40 YEARS OLD, GRANDMOTHER

The stories of older generations often reflect a sense of sacrifice and regret. Marietta is a clear example of how life can take unexpected turns, transforming pain and loss into opportunities for personal fulfillment.

- **The Story of Marietta:**
  Marietta, originally from the south of Italy, was a talented dancer in waltz and tango. After marrying at a young age and raising twins, she had to sacrifice her dreams. By the age of 40, with her children grown and the loss of her beloved husband in an accident, Marietta moved to Rome, resumed studying dance, and finally realized her dream of becoming a professional dancer.

  Today, Marietta is a sought-after artist, and with her new partner, they radiate energy and joy.

- **Reflection and Questions for Parents**:

  Marietta serves as an example of how difficult experiences can transform into opportunities for realizing one's mission.

  We ask ourselves:

  Are we truly helping our children discover what they desire in their hearts?

  Or are we simply trying to have them follow our expectations?

  Are we focusing too much on academic education, without exploring their authentic passions and talents?

  Allowing them to discover their own direction might be more beneficial, even if it means letting go of the dreams we have for them.

- **Examples of Successful Individuals from Challenging Backgrounds**:

  Stories like Marietta's remind us of the importance of recognizing and honoring unique vocations.

  For instance, Alex Zanardi, who found his mission despite the tragic loss of his legs. His determination and resilience led to success in motor sport without a car, redefining success and mission.

  The message? There are no rigid scales for mission: a reserved person can excel as a researcher, and an outgoing person can thrive as a salesperson. Every vocation is unique.

- **The Price of Imposition**:

  Insisting on having children follow our models can lead them to be divided between two identities: the imposed one and their authentic self. This conflict can result in suffering or illness.

  Our role as parents is to support them in listening to their inner voice, avoiding the imposition of our expectations.

In conclusion, **supporting and respecting our children's true vocation** is essential. Allowing them to follow what they feel in their hearts can lead to a more authentic and fulfilling life.

3 THE HIGHEST SITUATION OF THE MISSION: EXCELLENCE
(The benefits you gain if... the pleasurable state you aspire toward)

Discover your mission, your opportunity: "There are two things that never return: an arrow shot and a lost opportunity" (Jim Rohn)

The ultimate aspiration of the mission is the realization of life's purpose.

It is built upon a solid vision, faith in values, which are anchored in universal reference points.

The highest form of mission is missionary in nature, aiming to "Act for the greater good of humanity." A deep sense of satisfaction arises from fulfilling this duty, this calling. Every human contribution matters. In fact, if we believe in the morphogenetic field, as quantum science affirms, we understand that even small actions yield great results.

Educate your children's mission, anchoring it to grand principles.

Explain and convey values using simple language, and clarify them with your child. No one engages them emotionally, so they often perceive these concepts as abstract. Use metaphors, objects, or personal experiences to make values visible and relatable.

Realizing a Mission

The mission is the result of a long journey, facilitated by a tendency. To transform it into an excellent life mission, there are several steps:

Coaching phases to transform a person's life, with the inner voice that pushes towards a great purpose	
Passages	Some mini strategies that cultivate ambitions, attitudes, actions
A Attitude	Loving yourself, being introverted, caring for a theme of humanity
B Ability	Deepen your listening to your soul, take a definitive attitude of the chosen role, clarify the fields of action, the concepts, the challenges
C Capacity	Communicate your mission to the world. Internal conviction to convey to others.
D Competence	Study the life of models, expose theories, defend your choice
E Excellence	Transform ourselves into the best Exemplary Guide who offers a path to others and encourages them to share the purpose while also exercising a missionary function
F Accelerating Techniques of the "Flow"	Psycho-physiological accelerators, by putting us in a particular mental disposition in which the final result is anticipated, can put us into the "flow" even if often those who are mature for their mission, feel the call without resorting to further techniques.

There are at least 6 steps to identity excellence. The gifted person must be trained in the various steps as the muscles of a sports player are trained.

Example number twelve: the story of Saint Teresa of Calcutta

Small in stature, poor, not beautiful. Yet when you saw her, she seemed very big.

She spent her life helping the underprivileged in India. You heard her voice very early.

She was happy and cheerful. She spoke in a hieratic tone. She acted immediately like lightning.

Children love stories. The story of water is one of the most favorite.

If you point out to children the mission of water, telling the story of how it is necessary for plants, animals, the earth and for themselves, you will see that they will not waste it anymore!

We played a game with four girls using eight very small balls.

To one girl, we gave only one, instead of two! She noticed it immediately and began to complain about the difference in treatment!

Injustice is a strong feeling and you can easily arouse it in every experience.

We immediately apologized, gave her back the missing ball and told her how beings must divide water into equal parts, how animals cry if humans take it all for themselves and so we continued with plants, which suffer if they no longer have water, just like her, who had had one ball less than her other companions. With these examples, girls as young as five learn to turn off the taps and save water even when brushing their teeth.

A mother told us, surprised, how seriously her little girl observed this rule, inviting her to do the same! You can repeat this game with each Value, with each Mission to induce respect for the environment.

4 MINIMAL SITUATION of the Mission
(The price you pay if you don't... The painful situation you want to escape from)

This is the condition where trust is lost, the desire to fight diminishes – this is the state of NEETs. Realizing they have a high mission to fulfill on this earth could be a lifeline.

We must give importance to their lives, asking for their help from as early as age three, making them feel they are contributing to the important plan of "helping" humanity, the planet, and the universe, stating that these things depend on them. If the game is played well, you will have beautiful surprises. The kids will take their piggy banks and offer them to you, ready to set out immediately to help. Some, in our example, put on their coats ready for their mission! (So sweet! They don't yet have the concept of later, only of here and now.)

Caution: The lack of identification of a personal purpose leads first to negligence, low self-esteem, and eventually to more serious issues.

A secret to help the mission emerge is to give your child a constant message that says, "Everything has a purpose. What is yours?"

This gives them space to naturally discover it!

The mission carries with it the concept of sacrifice and dedication to a cause.

If a child has everything, their imagination of "their dream" is reduced. What reason would they have to fight for?

Example Thirteen: Carlo's Story, 12 Years Old, Disillusioned by Sports

Carlo suffered a "setback" (trusted the wrong people) in the sport he was truly passionate about. He believed it was his mission.

He was excluded from an important game for him. To avoid further pain, he suppressed his inner Voice.

The following week, he told us that perhaps it was the wrong sport.

He also distanced himself from friends, becoming excessively anxious and nervous. Level 1 blocked Level 7 and vice versa.

Those managers who work only for money—though necessary—empties their spirit, drying up their mission. They will find themselves dissatisfied, lacking love and purpose. In the process, they will have extinguished many missions in the youth.

Carlo was rescued. Today, he is a promise. He changed both the coach and the youth team.

Caution against the opposite:
Cultural narrowness, obscurantism, create false myths of a Negative Mission. When a cursed leader promotes these, we reach Nazism.

Mastering the sentiment of mission creates a force of cohesion and blind loyalty within the individual toward the community, among the most powerful and free.

Fortunately, religions have claimed the right to a positive mission.

Hiding behind a religion makes everything easier. It's a choice. We could also reclaim it for our own freedom and commitment (though a difficult path).

Example fourteen: the story of the salespeople from Company B.

At one point, the indirect sales network of this company lost direction, purpose, and the attraction tied to the company's mission. Sales plummeted. The management team didn't notice this decline immediately; they were too focused on the internal power struggle among the heirs and assumed the company's market leadership would carry them.

Let's be clear: by working on rebuilding the mission with this goal, they recovered performance within six months and achieved the best results of recent years—excellence.

Every employee should feel connected to and act in accordance with the company's Mission. A company that loses respect for its people disperses a common purpose and offends their Mission. A lack of mission creates confusion about identity and difficulties in adapting to market changes.

If you don't know the company's purpose, what are you fighting for? The result is a clash between commercial policies and marketing objectives.

Marketing's mission is to present products in their best light, emphasizing quality. The sales division relies on external distributors whose mission is profit-driven—selling. They don't share the same Mission. A conflict is inevitable: marketers aim for high prices supporting product quality, while salespeople prioritize low prices to maximize sales quantity. This gap had weakened the company.

Consider the school system and mission divergence:

Teachers have the mission of conveying as much information as possible, ensuring students are informed about the subject and completing the pre-set curriculum.

Students aim to understand topics deeply and at their own pace. The teaching approach is based on quantity and speed, while students often seek quality and slower learning (different personal paces often clash with the teacher's approach).

5 RESILIENCE OF THE MISSION

The resilience of the mission is an internal force that attracts and drives you to act. It fills you with energy, freely and abundantly, and compels you to channel it.

There has long been debate about whether this energy is vital or metabolic. What is the difference?

Vital energy is a finite quantity, fixed from birth, consumed throughout life. When it runs out, life ends—just as an individual's mission can end.

There are analogies between the two: both are long-term, lasting a lifetime; both are unique and irreplaceable.

Metabolic energy, on the other hand, comes from the food, emotions, and acceptance we consume and expend daily. It aligns with the efforts we make daily, driven by temporary motivations.

The resilience of the mission is a celebration of life.

We perceive its signals—spiritual and operational—in two ways:

- **Optimism regardless of rational support**
  When we are aligned with our mission, we feel as though we are participating in a greater flow, one of purpose far superior to any other task, greater than ourselves. It brings intense joy, akin to falling in love, stronger even than love itself.

- **Great faith**

  This is the drive toward the survival of the idea that has captured us because it resonates deeply within us. It demands complete dedication.

  Such unwavering belief gives us a sense of well-being, prevents suffering, and makes the purpose seem attainable, even in difficult circumstances.

We express it physically:

- **Eyes and vision**

  The singular, compelling, exclusive reason for life to which we devote our entire being is often expressed through eyes that look toward the sky. We may not even know the reason for this gaze. Look at the portraits of saints!

- **Seductive, vibrant, sensual voice**

  High resilience is capable of gathering all resources, concentrating emotions, and removing rational clarity in this focused state. People adopt fervent, almost possessed attitudes, with unnatural, solemn tones, often preceding religious conversions.

- **Sense of alertness is nullified**

  The resilience of the "mandate received" provides an overwhelming determination that breaks down all barriers, scruples, and fears. You become willing to risk life itself, defying common sense, in acts of apostolate and evangelization.

  It produces martyrs.

Recovery

Recovering mission resilience is slow because losing a mission feels like losing a love. It takes time to heal from disappointments.

An old mission is not easily replaced or forgotten. It leaves deep emotional traces like a sense of emptiness, ineffectiveness, and defeat, which can lead to severe consequences, especially among adolescents who feel ashamed of social validation.

Losing a mission is like erasing the reason for existence. The person feels fragmented and attempts to rebuild their sense of unity, but this requires significant energy.

For example, if an adolescent has already identified themselves with their vital purpose, believing they know who they are and what they want (the ideal scenario), confronting that fragmentation is more painful and perilous. It's crucial to help them regain orientation and purpose as soon as possible.

Recovery can occur by guiding the youth through exercises that promote **self-awareness**, focusing on remaining loyal to their former life ideals, and identifying a new purpose that is better suited and re-attaching that loyalty to a new goal, thereby reducing emotional burden.

Until about thirty years ago, these experiences of urgent mission resilience recovery were common among middle-class adolescents; they coincided with mandatory military service. There was a "life before the military" and "life after." The transition, along with rites of passage, from adolescence to adult responsibility, from school to work. The enforced pursuit of financial independence began the day after the "Oath of Loyalty to the Republic" (a grand celebration), often becoming too heavy a burden for overprotected children.

Conversely, among poorer rural youth (about 7%), those from the countryside who reached military service as adults were already responsible, concerned about the possibility of not being able to work on family farms, often without even the ability to read or write. We provided literacy education for them.

We witnessed touching situations where these youth, whom we could only admire, asked us to send their small daily allowance home to their families, who were often considered elderly by age 45. We collected money at the bar to send more. Their mission was to care for aging parents, often seeing them for the first time as they traveled to military service from places like Sicily or Sardinia.

To help today's youth recover quickly, we can focus on three key areas:

- **Confirming the power of self-control over their environment**, reconnecting them with solid reference points, allowing them to anchor themselves once again to something substantial.
- **Offering or helping them discover a new, higher-profile purpose** than the previous one (recovering their sense of self-value) for greater engagement.
- **Encouraging them with self-messages that challenge them**, providing at least a higher level of eustress, greater emotional involvement than the old mission, creating a sense of greater utility and triumph, whether continuing or changing paths, making them feel like extraordinary individuals (which they rightfully are).

The weakness of mission resilience among girls, who tend to be more adaptable, often leads to internal conflict that can be resolved more easily when faced with contrasting alternatives. Sometimes they are unsure of what to choose. Their mission may lead in one direction, while behavior and strategies move in another.

Attention

If girls are inexperienced, naive, and defenseless, lacking love and the new mission rooted in cognitive and emotional foundations, they may become easy prey for false gurus who exploit this void. In confusion, girls may fall into illusion and become victims easily manipulated (see here).

Example Fifteen: The Occult Movements

Let's explore the case of NEETs (Not in Education, Employment, or Training) who suddenly become drawn to secretive satanic cults, often hidden from their parents.

They find joy in embracing a distorted yet stimulating mission. Think about how often we chase after false prophets and empty promises, seeking a path that seems meaningful but leads to nowhere. Has this ever happened to you? If not, consider yourself lucky!

Astrologers, psychics, and charlatans thrive on these vulnerabilities. These individuals tend to erode mission resilience and distort the orientation provided by a true mission.

If your child still believes in themselves but is directing their energy toward false leaders who make them feel part of a prestigious mission, it's crucial to redirect them physically from this environment. A stimulating journey is ideal.

Warning: High resilience, if prolonged, can become dangerous, akin to a form of addiction, living in heightened tension that could lead to exhaustion.

Signs of low mission resilience include:

- Becoming more inattentive to dangers, more disorganized.
- Losing sight of healthy pride.
- Neglecting old goals, distancing from friends who once provided support and connection.

Living with low mission resilience is a creeping affliction of the soul. Often, we ourselves (especially mothers) serve as poor examples. Women in their forties become harsh self-judges of their own shortcomings, questioning their roles in family and work.

Children perceive this mid-life discomfort and enter into their own crises. The proper path is to become aware of this, discuss it openly within the family, and address it with care.

Example Sixteen: The Story of the French Twin Sisters

We had the opportunity to interview two French twin sisters—raised in an extremely wealthy family, yet estranged from their social privileges—who had abandoned their affluent lifestyle to join a cult. Their convictions were deeply rooted. They exhibited the posture of prophets, with direct gazes either at us or toward the sky, heads held high, shoulders straight, speaking in hypnotic cadences, attempting to persuade and seduce everyone around them.

"They carried their mission embodied in their very bodies," the deep faith radiating from their eyes.

When we asked questions—requested by their parents—reminiscing about the beautiful travels in Africa we had shared, there was no emotional response. For them, the mission of the cult was an extreme calling, even to the point of sacrificing their lives—a life once full of luxury and pleasures now replaced by hardships and privations.

They had fortified their mission resilience with false goals.

A mission can truly move mountains, especially when rooted in religious belief.

The task of parents is to discover a child's mission that is built on positive values.

These girls, still minors at the time, were consumed, enslaved, unwilling to recognize the danger of their situation. They were happy with this, to the great sorrow of their parents with whom they had severed all ties.

After the interviews, they again became unreachable. Since they had reached adulthood, the police could no longer search for them. We had no success.

6 TIPS, RESULTS, AND STRATEGIES FOR THE MISSION. VALUES AND BELIEFS

The mission will eventually emerge from within you. Why wait? Let it come to the surface as soon as possible. Take the time to reflect. If you've gone through disappointment or defeat, try to understand what you truly want to do, realign yourself, seek direction, and overcome your battles.

For example, an initial test might contain these questions

Questions and Possible Answers	Yes/no	% of Risk	Answers
Level 1 Have no direction to aim for? Goals to achieve?			
Level 2 Is your nature at odds with the euphoria of easy gains?			
Level 3 Does everything weigh on you? Are you always sad, dissatisfied? Do you feel useless?			
Level 4 Are you feeling sick for no reason?			
Level 5 Have you made any wrong income plans?			
Level 6 Do you feel incompetent everywhere?			
Level 7 Have you accepted too many compromises?			
Level 8 Have you become selfish, indifferent to animals and plants?			
Level 9 Are you stuck in old habits?			
Level 10 Are moral slaps and criticisms ruining your vision? You are arguing.			

Pause, reflect, explore, and then choose a direction. You'll feel better.

All these difficulties could be your mission (implicitly) asking for space. A painful corridor through which to "pass through" to improve yourself.

LET'S REMEMBER

To understand the purpose, the mission of your life, Transcendental Meditation is effective

Better to anticipate the times by sharing. Resilience is strengthened first, if you share the same mission with others.

About social proof, many coaches give this advice: "Do not consider other people's judgments, go straight on your path" Right, with the exception of resilience. In this case, positive social judgment, encouragement, gives you energy that multiplies yours exponentially, (more than the sum) and you will increase resilience quickly.

The reason: you better highlight the efficient aspects, you consistently practice the useful ones, being under the cross-check of others.

Observe the failures, the discomfort, that you have experienced up to now: are they a sign that you are far from your mission? If so, look for it, get back oriented as a person and as a parent.

Example seventeen: the story of Marty, in Paris, a drama

Sometimes the mission comes to you suddenly, like a punch in the face. With great pain.

This is the case of Mrs. Marty, with the death of her two children from drugs, 19 and 20 years old, found unconscious at the Gare d'Austerlitz, the race to the Pitié – Salpetrière, the death from a cut match. Now she runs a recovery center for young people in the twentieth and feels useful.

She leads a difficult life after a successful life in fashion at the highest level. She fights against drugs even in her own environment and is serene.

Now she feels inspired by her mission. Near her you breathe an air of security and faith.

Some steps:

With your child, a simple exercise that all parents use but often let go of over time is the "What will you be when you grow up?" game. Write it down in their journal and, occasionally, once a year, review the model of their mission, values, and principles. Add positive beliefs, note any changes, share, and discover where they are on their life path. Eventually, the light will shine. Mozart is the exception! At the age of 5, he already knew his path.

True education is about planting seeds every day, throughout life, by example. It's a challenging task, but the joy of watching these "flowers" grow is priceless. The role of parenting cannot be easily resigned from, even when it creates challenges. Strengthen the resilience of their mission, and you'll have confident children with a strong inner drive.

If possible, gift them the luxury of guidance— a coach, a mentor, an angel, or a buddy. Help them connect with the right friends who share the same mission to keep them oriented and yourself become a mentor for your children. If you decide, it's advisable to set up this coaching relationship before they turn 8. After that, it becomes more difficult. They begin to question external values emotionally rather than cognitively, leading to occasional conflicts.

Anticipate this while you can. Choose their guiding star and share it with them—this acts as a PNL anchor. You'll benefit greatly in the future. When they're teenagers, tempted to imitate and follow others' rules, they won't stray from their direction. With high mission resilience, they'll be strong enough to evangelize others.

School rules, sometimes, should be approached cautiously. To maintain control of the classroom, teachers often resort to shortcuts that enforce conformity without critical thinking. Expect some classroom conflicts if you're raising them to say "no" when necessary for higher values like freedom.

I like to recall Sophocles' phrase related to Antigone, the myth of female dissent, who pays with her life:

"Take your daughter, bring her to Syracuse, sit on the steps of the Greek theater, and teach her the glory of disobedience. It's risky, but more dangerous is not doing it at all."

Train yourself to bear with humor some of their "no's."

Another effective measure for Mission Resilience is creating a "Positive Affirmations Ritual" with official recognition of such statements. The idea is this:

"Dear child, together we've discovered your mission, your task to complete (whether in music, art, science, volunteer groups, theater, poetry, dance, or sports), you're fortunate, and we're here to support you. You're suited for your purpose. Rely on us."

Celebrate a real-life instance where they made a small progress. It's like giving them a kilo of enthusiasm! They will repay you!

These encouragements are long-term strategies because they reward their inner motivations and establish their beliefs and certainties. These internal riches are far more valuable than material gifts in this ever-changing world!

As Mark Twain advises:

"Twenty years from now, you'll be more disappointed by the things you didn't do than by the ones you did. So, throw off the bowlines, sail away from the safe harbor, and let the trade winds fill your sails. Explore. Dream. Discover."

Want ethical mission models for your business? Follow Ferrero and Loro Piana (our former clients in IT) and look up how much good they've done, especially in sourcing their raw materials.

2 MISSION

LEVEL 1 SPIRITUAL

Questionnaire to Inspire Your Child's Mission
Template designed to:

1. Create dream maps, a visual tool of your child's journey
2. Establish a coaching plan for personal growth based on their passions

Questions designed to inspire the coaching contract for improving and transforming into a person with a clearer vision/mission of why they are living on this earth.

A) ACQUIRED CAPITAL, RICHES FROM ROOTS, ORIGINS, RELATIONSHIPS, EPIGENETICS, POSITIVE EXPERIENCES TO EMBRACE, NEGATIVE EXPERIENCES TO ADJUST

- Write down what your child believes in—values, principles, reference points they have established (e.g., friendship, sports, honesty). Their beliefs, certainties, and doubts.
- How do they interpret the world? What inner voice do they hear? List the non-negotiable principles they believe in and that guide their behavior.

1 _____

2 _____

3 _____

MISSION Basics. Write or have written his best aptitudes, skills, tendencies, character, abilities, attitudes that lead him towards his passion, to complete his internal message. Also list the advantages.

1 _____

2 _____

3 _____

MISSION Technique to copy a success. Write how he feels when he follows your inner voice. Have him reproduce the same conditions of coherence and unity, of joy many times until he feels his passion and can verbalize it. Build for your child the path to identify his mission.

Write down what you thought and felt when you respected your inner guidance. Can you reproduce the same conditions? Transmit them to your will. It will strengthen you.

1 _____

2 _____

3 _____

MISSION Technique to change a failure into an experience. Have you overcome obstacles against your mission? Describe the elements that blocked you or made you do things differently than you should have done, how you felt. Help your child overcome those moments, turning them into very educational lessons.

1 _____

2 _____

3 _____

b) Reinforcement training and training needs It is a process

Help your child identify the goal of his mission. What do you like? Observe his actions and see which ones he does with greater ease or passion. Find his path that is different from yours. Everyone has their own reason for living. Make a plan with solutions together. After disappointments, rewrite the reference points to anchor yourself on and start again. Who are the ones who inspire him? Who does he trust and want to emulate? Is your mission in line with your Passion?

Write where he is today, from where you want to continue. How can you clarify his mission better

1 _____

2 _____

3 _____

Have him compare himself with his peers and write down his next actions to impose his will on the world as an expression of his passions (to be reported in his diary). This is a delicate step, listen, observe, do not judge a priori and accept. Let him experiment.

1 _____

2 _____

3 _____

For Continuous Training, check the skills on the market and follow up on his possible training needs to enhance the clarity of his Vision and callings. (Buddying)

What are the sources that can support him? Who can help him? Books, courses, mother, grandparents, uncles, coaches, peers, friends, family collaborators.

1 _____

2 _____

3 _____

c) Goals

What do you want to improve in his mission? Where does he want to go? Help the world, the poor, the defenseless? Deal with art? Raise a family? It's up to him.

Write 3 aspects of the mission, relative advantages and benefits he gets from it (also for you).

1 _____

2 _____

3 _____

Witness of progress. Write who measures his transformation with you

1 _____

2 _____

3 _____

Imagine and make him imagine his goal as achieved and satisfactory

1 _____

2 _____

3 _____

d) Control of Results Objective Achieved confirmation of witness.

Goal achieved on....................by ....
Congratulate and reward yourself at every step.

Update the card with the date, signature of buddy, tutor, mentor, coach

Place, date, signature

1 _____

2 _____

3 _____

7 Who Achieved Success Following Their Mission

Life is 10% what happens to you and 90% how you react. (Anonymous)

So, let's interpret and decode the lessons of your life that align with your mission. In Italian history, all our artists and heroes followed their inner voices. There are countless examples. In childhood coaching sessions, we love to tell children the memorable stories of our national heroes, helping to balance the modern trash of dragons, bees, violent models, and TV monsters. It's wonderful to hear them speak with competence and emotion about Dante, Paolo and Francesca.

Lauretta tells her parents, "Do you know that Gianciotto was evil?" and about Petrarch, "Did you know he didn't want to be a notary, like his father?"

Elisa talks about Giotto, "He made a circle with his hands." So sweet.

Children listen, understand, and comment. When we tell the life of Saint Francis, they're excited. Their logical questions are delightful.

Giuseppe: "At La Verna, how could he sleep on such a small rock? It was hard! Was there water? So cold."

We are building a format and a series of eBooks for children in English to begin selling our wonderful Italian culture to children around the world. If you'd like to participate, contact us at info@gsm-online.it.

We'll be ready by December 2017.

Children also love stories of scientists. Newton, Galileo are their favorites! A particularly funny scene happened recently. The children were dropping apples like Newton, but they wanted to be Galileo Galilei in front of the tribunal! We had described it with more passion: a bit of confusion!

Gioia shows us her hand:

"Look, I opened my hand and the Earth stole my apple! She has the force, glavi… glavitaziooo… ahahah! Gravitation!"

Example 18: Caravaggio and Mission

Returning to our great ancestors, a painter with a clear mission was Caravaggio. Michelangelo Merisi was born in Milan on September 29, 1591; he died in Porto Ercole at just 39 years old. Let's analyze his character using our model, which helps us understand how his discovered mission shaped his life.

The story of Caravaggio, from childhood to his future greatness as an artist, from Milan to Rome (then the center of the world), is very tumultuous. Let's only focus on the first part of his life, from childhood to the age of 21, when he decided to go to Rome toward success.

"Without energy, there is no color, no form, no life," Caravaggio said, absolutely in line with today's times.

As we can observe from the levels, he was someone who placed so much energy into his realization as a man and an artist, neglecting his well-being and peace, which led to his premature death. Bad behaviors, poor management of relationships, but he was a great artist. Master of painting techniques using light and contrast, with realistic depictions of the world, imitated throughout Europe, he would be a social failure, a bully, not loved, and forgotten for many centuries.

Level	Estimated value	Value Invested	Result
Areas	Average weight in life	Weight on Caravaggio's life	
a) Being	30%	50%	Strong personality. Pride High self-esteem.
1. Spiritual	10	20	Selfishness Arrogance Ego
2. Cognitive	10	10	Only the technique mattered School of Costanza Colonna
3. Emotional	10	20	Violent emotions
b) Having	30%	20%	He cared about money and his technique
4. Physiological	10	0	No respect for his health
5. Financial	10	5	Search for orders
6. Logistic	10	15	Innovator, many masters of Technique
c) Doing	40%	30%	Exuberant quarrelsome
7. Relational	10	20	No family Trouble with the law
8. Environmental	10	0	Zero interest
9. Behavioral	10	5	Violent in defense
10. Social Proof	10	5	Indifference, appreciated, criticized
Total	100%	100%	

From zero to 24 years old, Caravaggio prepared himself, dedicating energy and passion. He invested in the big day, spending money, attention, and time. His life was marked by violent behavior to be avoided (level 9). It is important to highlight how a vocation can be developed from a young age.

"The year 1595 was a turning point. Caravaggio's life changed when he met Cardinal Francesco Maria del Monte, the first to recognize the great talent of the painter. Under his protection, Caravaggio obtained numerous commissions, and his fame spread throughout the capital. Del Monte also secured his first public commissions."

Level 1 IDENTITY

He was a child, born in Milan and raised in Caravaggio, educated by his surveyor grandfather. In his grandfather's palace, he saw the great images on the ceiling every night, and his imagination soared. He was surrounded by illustrious figures. His strong sense of self-esteem came from his social status, belonging to a respected family. By nature, he was dominant, feeling like a privileged figure who commanded respect, even though he spent his days among the common people.

Level 7 RELATIONSHIPS reinforced his pride. He was protected by Marchesa Costanza Colonna throughout his life. His aunt was the wet nurse to the Colonna children.

"I borrow bodies and objects, paint them to remind myself of the magic of the balance that governs the entire universe. In this magic, my soul resonates with the Unique Sound that leads me back to God." It seems written today!

Level 1 MISSION
Level 1 Sub 2

Impulsive and lively, he always knew he had a mission to accomplish. His mother reminded him of this regularly. His father was a mason architect, a trusted man of the Marquis.

Level 7 family and epigenetic influence. Following his grandfather and father, he traveled throughout Lombardy from the age of 6 with his father, and after his father's death, he continued with his grandfather, a promise to be fulfilled.

Level 6 logistical

He was introduced to drawing by a mason worker employed by his father, who challenged him. This competition strengthened his self-esteem.

Level 2 cognitive knowledge

From a young age, he had a clear reference framework: walls, paintings, glue, lime, and examples.

Level 2 Sub 2 memory

His father was passionate about paintings, leaving him six that he knew by heart.

Level 1 MOTIVATION

Level 1 Sub 3

He had studied, paying a high tuition fee, and had to maintain a prestigious reputation. Level 10 social proof. Everyone knew he was destined to become a painter. His dream, like that of artists of his time, was to go to Rome. He dreamed of it and went there, thanks to the help of the Colonna family.

Level 3 emotion

His entire emotional focus was concentrated in his works.

Level 1 ROOTS

The education from his grandfather and family was the foundation of his profession. He invested all his land to attend the school of Simone Peterzano. What did he learn, and what did the great Venetian painting of Titian and Giorgione, conveyed through Peterzano, give him? The painting technique and the confrontation gave him credibility in his vocation to "paint from life," understanding the true nature of men and things.

When did Caravaggio realize he was in the flow of his inner mission? At the age of thirteen.

Michelangelo, Leonardo da Vinci, Saint Catherine of Siena, Joan of Arc, and Saint Francis often felt their calling in conflict with their parents and families. However, for Caravaggio, it was a shared understanding. At twenty-one, after his mother's death and with no money, he was left only with the Marchesa Colonna.

His logistics, Level 6, and his method were innovative and a major factor in his success—his expertise. For example, using a mirror, an optical tool, he could cut out a piece of nature and lock it onto the canvas. As seen in his self-portrait in 1593 as Bacchus or in the "Boy with a Basket of Fruit," found in the Galleria.

Physically, Level 4, he was an ordinary but unattractive young man. A police report described him as "a chubby, black-dressed, unkempt youth, with little beard."

LET'S REMEMBER

1. A mission can be identified from a very young age. Pay attention to your child's signs of passion and tendencies.
2. Expose your child to various experiences. Surround them with images of great Italian figures as sources of inspiration.
3. Invest in their education. Caravaggio and his mother are modern examples of the effectiveness of this approach. If possible, act as a coach for them or provide one.
4. NEET (Not in Education, Employment, or Training) are young people who have lost their sense of direction, don't feel their mission, or believe they have failed. "Extend them a thread and pull them, helping them gather enough energy to follow their own path."

Technique Bring out the sense of duty. It could be a winning strategy, without do-goodism with severity.

Example nineteen: the story of a teenage entrepreneur with a clear mission.

Moziah Bridges, a boy from Memphis, started selling bow ties and special ties with his own brand at the age of twelve. His dream had been building for years—he had shown his talent as early as six. Moziah wanted to dress stylishly, adhering to strict fashion rules like bow ties and suspenders, aiming to stand out.

By the age of nine, his passion had fully taken shape, driven by a desire to be different. This passion fueled his identity, mission, and motivation, giving him a clear sense of who he was: a fashion creator.

"I wanted to be different from the others. If there were ten red candies and one green one on a table, I always desired to be that green one," Moziah said.

He collaborated with a fashion blogger, Tavi, who was thirteen, and Ava Anderson, who was fifteen, both of whom found success in their own ways. Ava, in particular, created a non-toxic skincare line, attracting praise from renowned designers like Karl Lagerfeld. All three had an exceptional coach: their mothers.

What lessons can be learned?
"Follow your dreams now," Moziah's mother advises.

Seek out the dreams in your children and nurture them. You will begin a 4.0 life—digital and internet-driven.

This is our flagship formula, "Digital Family," which helps families turn their fortunes around. No more fear of debt or lack of funds! See the attached courses or visit our website.

Part Three
The Spiritual Level
Motivation

3 MOTIVATION

LEVEL 1 SPIRITUAL
Revised by Dr. Daniele Giannini

"Begin by doing what is necessary, then what is possible. And suddenly you will find yourself doing the impossible." St. Francis

Definition	Goal	Skills Aptitudes, Abilities, Capacities, Competencies	Maximum Excellency	Minimum
Motivation	Push towards a purpose, a direction	Self-esteem Enthusiasm Courage	Leadership Charisma	Despise Demotivate Mistrust Negative judgments

1 Definition and purpose of motivation.

Motivation is a concentrated force that drives action in the short term, whereas mission attracts and guides us over the long term. Typically, a mission has one central purpose in life, while motivation evolves over time based on the goals we aim to achieve, experiencing highs and lows along the way.

Motivation is also energy—an activating, catalytic, and driving force. Unlike mission, which is intimate, solitary, and requires effort to share, motivation can be cultivated, distributed, and shared among many.

In general, enthusiasm spreads through imitation or healthy competition, and leaders often inspire others through charisma—another motivational quality of the spirit.

In quantum terms, motivation could be seen as the observer's force—without it, nothing happens, nothing materializes. In this view, guidance is essential. You are that guide!

LET'S REMEMBER

The third step of success is the energy of motivation provided to the project

> **Immediate action, recovery**
>
> **If your motivational strength is low, here are the effective steps.**
>
> **This exercise/model is also useful when you want to develop "a new idea".**
>
> **Check your energy and your life priorities. If nothing has changed, then imagine the future, smile, give enthusiasm and find someone who is only trustworthy and reserved to explain your project or your temporary stop. With the Logos you revitalize it.**
>
> **The path of a project has passages from the immaterial to the concrete matter. After having told, do an action, even a small one, it serves as a starting engine. Then do a sensorial awakening with sight, hearing, touch, etc. as if the project were already alive. Share the material operations. Stimulate, support curiosity, interest. If you can, make your temporary tiredness comical!**

The motivation mechanism has a dual function:

- as a cause - force that goes towards, that pushes a person towards a goal in the direction of success, of performance.

- as a cause - force that escapes from a losing situation from the Minimum point. Reverse direction away from the errors towards a new Maximum point.

It is used to "stay connected, attentive" to the initiative you want to undertake. Focus Attention, pushed or pushed in a concrete direction that can be measured.

Unlike the mission, which is abstract by nature, and is considered satisfied by values, motivation is a "desire" for concrete evidence, even small, tangible.

Evidence gives energy, because we are very good at expressing doubts and we need answers and confirmations continuously. The chain of a "desire" towards its realization, is realized only by hearing the real facts.

2 SKILLS AND ATTITUDES THAT SUPPORT MOTIVATION

3 MOTIVATION Steps of "know-how"	Signals	Benefits
Attitude	Hope for a result, desire to act	Enthusiasm, desire to do, beneficial illusion
Ability	Determination, being constant, courage, stubbornness, wanting to continue and not giving up	Contentment, being effervescent, still dedicated to the purpose through ups and downs
Capacity	Clarity of strategies, management of emotions of fatigue	Having a following of people who share your purpose and add energy
Competence	Single Goal Achievement, Focus, Attraction, Convincing	SUCCESS IN MOTIVATING OTHERS Excellence, Being a magnet that attracts groups in the short term with purposeful efforts and being well rewarded for it

Every person is born with the aptitude to act. We can educate children at different paces.

There is no fixed rule to transform the tendency into ability, there are children who are too active, curious, always ready to try, always motivated and others who are too slow. It is an epigenetic and genetic state. There is no need to force it.

Instead, energy can be provided in order to keep the tone high to complete a project. Any system of reward, of attraction can be valid. For our well-being, it is good to alternate cycles of "tensions" limited in time with rest.

Health, esteem, success, money, love are important external attractors that fuel motivation. Survival and love, falling in love are among the most powerful forms of acceleration of motivation. This is followed by that of interest, both psychological and economic: revenge, redemption, revenge or very high earnings. Even passion if it is constant. It revitalizes a tired motivation.

3 MAXIMUM MOTIVATION SITUATION Excellence

**(The benefits you get if... The situation of
pleasure you want to go towards)**

The highest desires of motivation are to achieve a personal, business, or competitive result, such as winning a war.

Since in the last century, even economic life is interpreted as a war against competition, motivation today is stimulated to the maximum in order to obtain Engagement, responsible involvement to stay on track, to invest the objective with a lot of energy.

It's nice to share projects with motivated people. Everything is lighter, more fluid. Smiling, laughing, communicating becomes easy. Above all, the willingness to work without a schedule.

If your child is motivated, it will be easy to explain an unexpected request to him. He will respond with enthusiasm and the mood of the environment will be serene and lively. With his attitude, he will enrich everyone around him through copying, mirror neurons and unconscious imitation.

The classic family reunions, chats at the table, prizes, recognitions, simply checking daily on progress at school are supporting factors. They make the commitment of the children important. It is certainly tiring, after a day of work, but he expects to talk about it. Since he will encounter his difficulties, he is in a hurry for immediate answers, if he receives them at home from people he trusts, he avoids turning to the outside. The lack, the loss of trust and contact, of dialogue produces Neets. The price you pay is very high.

If you can't answer right away, maybe you're in a meeting, today the cell phone is a great help. You can agree on the type of communication. For example, smileys on text messages, so that they feel your presence and respond if they ask for SOS.

The mother carries out this first aid task. In the collective imagination, she is authorized to give priority to her children, if she is working. It is good to make agreements with the family on the procedures to follow with respect to managing emergencies. Each child must be reassured about what to do in the event of an SOS, of danger. It is their right to feel protected by the family. If there is an emergency, this becomes an obligation. You can use Stephen Covey's table game as a basis for risk assessment. What is urgent? What is important? (Look it up on the internet)

Exercising children is fun. They become faster than their parents. They understand the concepts and enjoy putting them in order. They take the table to school, play with it with friends.

They learn what a matrix is: every time they are faced with a crossroads in life, they will use it properly and visualize the alternative solutions in a short time. They will find the order of priorities. Practice it too, it is an intelligent scheme, Einsenhover used it too.

Engagement as one's own and others' commitment

Staying in the flow you feel engaged in without stress is the result of a long preparation, facilitated by the tendency to be optimistic. To transform it into excellent behavior, there are several steps, at least 6. The gifted person must be trained in the various steps as the muscles of a sports player are trained.

Coaching Steps to Transform a Positively-Inclined Person into an Excellent Motivator	
Steps	Some mini strategies that cultivate ambitions, attitudes, actions
A Attitude	Unveiling optimism, cultivating hope, open-mindedness
B Ability	Train your own energy and its distribution, develop attitude and role
C Capacity	Practice self-motivation, copying effective models, empowering different types of people in difficulty and different situations without stress
D Competence	Study key authors, models, theories and practice them. Share successes
E Excellence	Transforming ourselves into the best motivator, with mastery of psychology, Transcendental Meditation, various behaviors, effective techniques in constant updating listening, empathy, encouragement, example
F "Flow" Accelerating Techniques	Psycho-physiological accelerators bring you into the mental state in which you always see yourself as full of energy and enthusiasm to transmit to others.

4 MINIMUM SITUATION of the Mission

(THE PRICE YOU PAY IF YOU DON'T... THE PAINFUL SITUATION YOU WANT TO ESCAPE FROM)

Strengthening motivation is like inflating a balloon. It flies high. If you feel motivated, you unblock and decide. Actions begin and you unleash constructive feelings. If you admit your mistakes and your victories, you will feel like a winner, you will make others explode with the same expectations.

Attitudes lead to appreciation, encouragement, becoming generous and issuing other positive judgments, generating success. When motivation is at its lowest, every project stops. It has surely happened to you.

You need to understand the causes. It could be that the objective is wrong, or secondary.

The boy's disaffection can come from causes external to him, to which he is incapable of reacting. Sometimes the saying "Ubi maior minor cessat" has its own logic. The state of neet can be caused by other boys with stronger character or he is dealing with something unimportant.

If you apply the model to companies, to business, demotivation arises from the lack of rewards for the efforts made, for example, a reduction in turnover. It can itself cause a drop in returns, due to monotony and boredom. It is a recurring mechanism: you sell little, you become demotivated, you lose the enthusiasm to sell and you sell less! A real threat that kills growth, the acquisition of new customers and impoverishes the brand.

If your salespeople are demotivated, this state of mind is contagious, like a rotten apple in the basket. The best ones run away and go to the competition, the mediocre ones stay and save the situation temporarily, in the long term they contribute to the disaster. Without the right leadership skills, ships sink.

Coaching can offer a vital solution, in four steps:

- with immediate tactics
- with the modernization of products at a strategic level
- with the change of commercial policy
- with the improvement of the compensation plan

Example twenty: The story of armies

Motivation is time-sensitive—it must be short-term and often fades over time.

Throughout history, all armies led by Napoleon, Hitler, and Mussolini were driven by motivations for victory, blending identity-based mission drives (patriotism) and short-term motivational drives (gains). However, when these goals persisted longer than expected, they all ultimately failed.

Defeats, in addition to resource scarcity, can largely be attributed to weakening motivations. Motivation focuses on power, leadership, and the ability to seduce large crowds in a short time. It nurtures pride— domination and idolization. In marketing, it's being recognized as authoritative experts due to results achieved.

Children lose interest and abandon activities they initially love if they are engaged for too long. Motivation declines, and so does their interest. Motivation breaks down if stretched too thin—due to perceived cold, hunger, loneliness, fear, exhaustion, boredom, both physical and moral.

5 RESILIENCE OF MOTIVATION

Good motivational resilience is a source of perseverance, while weakness leads to a loss of control over undertaken activities. It is important to distinguish the cause.

If the decline is due to a reduction in energy, it can be easily recovered. However, if it stems from new rational beliefs, the task becomes more difficult and requires tangible proof. Low motivational resilience is contagious because it seeks sharing. People tend to commiserate, tell, and listen to negative stories, which fosters the absorption and spread of pessimism.

According to our statistics, motivating a healthy person to share even a small project requires at least three reinforcements and three repetitions, even using persuasive techniques. In contrast, demotivating a person can be done with just one instance if the Logos (motivational speech) is appropriate and structured at three levels.

We recognize signs of low motivational resilience through:

- Temporary fatigue, often due to a lack of trust in the purpose or perceived insurmountable difficulties.
- Loss of Logos, or the inability to express oneself clearly and convincingly, often caused by a reduction in rewarding stimuli or the emergence of disintegrative forces.
- A decrease in motivational tone, due to poor management of internal and external resources, such as discomfort, doubts, poor organization, or limited competence when initiating an endeavor.

Example twenty-one: The story of Tanzi selling vacuum cleaners

Working door-to-door is not easy. Here's how a "friend" of Tanzi destroyed his motivation.

The repeated question: "What do you struggle with if you think?"

Level 5 financial: **It costs too much**
Level 3 emotional: **It's perceived as low quality**
Level 6 logistical: **Too many contacts needed to get an order**

This is a real example—Tanzi stopped selling vacuum cleaners. This decline spread throughout his network in Milan. The drop in sales occurred in the same week across the entire network (domino effect).

Demotivation is a lethal process for a new project. When doubt sets in, it quickly leads to **operational necrosis**, immobility, and the collapse of still-young, unsteady collaborations. Tanzi struggled to get back on track.

After the desire exercise, he chose a market that was still predominantly female. Today, he successfully sells wellness products and no longer sees his "envious detractor."

Recovery

The recovery of motivational resilience happens through 4 phases. It occurs through Logos, personal and social reinforcement.

a) Reinforcing the Logos—the study of powerful, engaging, and compelling language.

Re-study a new vocabulary, new definitions of the topic. Redefine goals, identify advantages/benefits, and make them more tangible. Reinterpret sales proposals, making them seductive with more captivating concepts. Examine still-valid values and references, anchoring new proposals in an authoritative, credible, and verifiable manner.

Mistakes are allowed; one can restart on new foundations with the right credentials. A key secret that always works is to assimilate rules dynamically, believing they can be adjusted in real-time and there are tools to adapt. In this way, there are no disappointments that lower resilience—only change management. Children love wonderful stories. The mere idea of imitating them strengthens their motivation. Finding new examples and role models to reignite interest.

a) **Personal Reinforcement**

Temporary fatigue:

- Check general health status.
- Strengthen diet, rest, and leisure time.

If there is a decline in tone:

- Reorganize relationships.
- Redefine the strengths and weaknesses of the topic.
- Improve skills to rebuild trust among those involved.
- Define roles—who leads, who follows, and procedures.

b) Social Reinforcement

The best social reinforcement is dialogue—friends, family, colleagues. Talking about it provides energy when encouragement is done without excess.

Dialogue must occur on three levels:

- Reaffirming trust and confidence.
- Providing and receiving more precise information for better understanding and communication.
- Offering love, affection, attention, and care to compensate for the drop in resilience.

To quickly boost resilience, both the quality and number of relationships—trust-based connections formed prior to the issue—are essential. By broadening the perspective and approach to obstacles, we suffer less because motivational suffering is the key factor in reducing resilience.

c) Physiological and Body-Based Reinforcements

Negative feelings like discouragement, disinterest, disappointment, and apathy reduce resilience, which in turn lowers immune defenses. This also impacts level 4 health, contributing to the rise of NEETs (Not in Education, Employment, or Training).

In coaching, to quickly boost motivation, shortcuts such as anchoring or hypnosis are used. By visualizing people, events, loved ones, spouses, mothers, or experiences that evoke emotion, we connect them to the desired outcomes. Joyful success—winning a gold medal, a Nobel Prize—is anchored to those emotions.

These pairings become like Pavlov's dog—every time we think of success, we visualize the happy person or ourselves enjoying the glory, triggering the drive to achieve it. When you think about your happiness or the motivation for success you've envisioned, you'll feel energized and uplifted, boosting your defenses.

The pairing becomes a monomyth—a miracle. To solidify this, supplements like papaya can be used to enhance immune defenses.

An additional skill for a coach to maintain high motivational drive is teaching or providing the coachee with the ability to mediate between maximum and minimum points of resilience. This helps prevent the coachee from becoming overly discouraged or feeling weak. This skill can be learned.

(If you've already read and followed our courses, you may skip this section, although repetition always helps illuminate concepts more clearly.)

A coach with this orientation should know this part by heart and apply it in sessions.

Resilience is the capacity of any isolable system to react to attacks on its position of stability autonomously. Resilience is not an absolute value but a relative function tied to specific spaces and time intervals. It's calculated within a range of minimum and maximum values, known as tolerance thresholds. Above or below these thresholds, abnormal phenomena occur, or we are no longer discussing the same system. The tolerance thresholds are bio-physical, sensory phenomena crucial for survival. They signal limits beyond which the system can no longer maintain its state.

6 TIPS, RESULTS, AND STRATEGIES OF MOTIVATION

Don't let demotivation erode your child's health, prospects, and expectations—it's a virus of the mind and heart.

From a young age, dedicate time to your child so they develop interests, friendships, and hobbies. It's exhausting, but the rewards are immense as they'll channel their energy and won't become hyperactive or depressed.

When they face their first disappointments, commitments will keep them occupied, reducing rumination and supporting their mental health.

For short-term tactics, small, achievable activities are sufficient to protect motivation. For example, creating a simple, low-effort activity plan ensures they meet these expectations.

If a romantic relationship ends in adolescent disappointment, distraction is the best tactic to shift focus from painful experiences. Small, repeated efforts will introduce alternative concepts.

If you've played the "What if" game with your child—asking, "What else can you do if that happens?"—you'll know how creative their solutions can be. They'll find imaginative ways that you might not consider due to your more immediate responsibilities (like work, bills, mortgages). They'll come up with self-sufficient solutions.

This is a powerful exercise, often used in coaching.

A journey of study, sports, or exploration for adolescents is the most effective tool for restoring motivation. They'll forget romantic disappointments, finding new interests and relationships. The goal is to shift their focus to new environments that require mental engagement. For instance, navigating a new city means they'll focus on establishing landmarks, transportation, cultural centers, restaurants, and other immediate needs, which will overshadow their past heartbreak.

If you've recently suffered any kind of setback and are feeling demotivated, tired, or discouraged, apply these tactics:

- **Self-help**: Immediately set new goals to pursue. Don't dwell in bed, ruminating on your losses. Cry, move forward. The mantra "I had nothing, I have nothing, I'll try again" works well for losses. For pain, use "No bastard can bring me down, I'm a rock, an oak" (from an American saying). Mantras work subliminally, making a real difference. They provide consolation, courage, and hope. You can create mantras with your child like: "I'm alive, I'm fine, who cares!" or "Tomorrow is another day" from *Gone with the Wind*.

- **Seek professional support** if you lack the strength. Attend courses, connect with motivation groups, or find a coach or mentor.
- **Engage with art and theater** for emotional release and growth.

If your child remains demotivated despite your efforts, prevention and reinforcement are key. The long-term strategy is to plant seeds of motivation early. Concrete visualization exercises work well if practiced regularly. Encourage their dreams by exposing them to events related to their goals, fostering self-assessment and growth.

In the short term, instead of getting frustrated when children appear indifferent to school participation, homework, or responsibilities, set clear rules. As a form of discipline, temporarily deny them a fun activity for a single day (no more than that).

- **Coaching becomes a negotiation with children**, just like working with clients on shared goals, broken down into small steps. The funnel system works well here—a narrowing process where from a wide range of options, the child chooses up to three possibilities.
- **Monitor their energy and health status** regularly.

To Strengthen Motivation

(Remember: one bad apple can spoil the whole basket)

1. **Select, isolate, and clean up the environment**: Surround your child with people who provide attention and energy, as energy doesn't just add up—it multiplies.
2. **Set goals, frequently review them, and reward small progress.**

3. **Reset mistakes and correct deviations toward the final goal**: Mistakes happen, experiences are learned, and content and methods improve over time.

The good news about motivation is that it can be quickly recovered through association and shared goals. Always keep **supportive buddies (facilitators)** on hand to boost morale.

3 MOTIVATION

LEVEL 1 SPIRITUAL

Questionnaire to find inspiration on the ability to create motivation and stay focused

Sample questions to inspire you to:

a) **identify the strengths and weaknesses of motivation**
b) **sign the contract/commitment, to transform a person into a highly motivated, never bored person who knows how to motivate others.**

a) Capital already acquired, riches that come from roots, origins, relationships, epigenetics, positive experiences to be copied and negative ones to be modified

The best attitudes for motivation you want to cultivate are aspects of personality: Will, Determination, and Optimism.

The best skills involve managing short-term reasons that motivate you in life, school, or business—such as appearance, earning potential, survival, enjoyment, distractions, travel, and rewards.

The best capabilities are the secrets that fuel the fire of attention.

The best competencies of motivators are expertise in keeping attention high, connecting people within groups, and pushing forward like a gentle but consistent breeze (a modern model being Brendon Burchard).

Excellence is tied to leadership, even if effective over short periods of time.

Examine your situation or your child's, and list the benefits and advantages. Write down their dreams, hopes, and trust, motivating their loves, friends, hopes, and expectations.

1 _____

2 _____

3 _____

MOTIVATION Basics. Write or have someone write down his best aptitudes, abilities, tendencies, character, skills, attitudes that make him feel committed, that guide him towards the achievement of short-term goals. Look for the source of energy to draw from. Monitor his rest.

1 _____

2 _____

3 _____

MOTIVATION Technique to copy a success. Write how he feels when he reaches his goal. Make him reproduce the same conditions of strength, enthusiasm, his laughter, his shouts of joy. Make him repeat it many times until he feels the energy and can verbalize it. Build for your child the path to reproduce his motivation.

Write what you thought and how you felt when you achieved 100% of your goal - Can you reproduce the same conditions? Pass them on to your determination, perseverance. It will strengthen you. Make your child follow his rewarding path.

1 _____

2 _____

3 _____

MOTIVATION Technique to change a failure, such as losing interest in a project.

What obstacles have you overcome against your mission? Describe the elements that tired you, made you disenchanted, how you felt. Help your child to overcome those moments, transforming them into very educational lessons, find the disappointments do not scold, make them consider failure as an surmountable aspect. Children easily change their opinion and interest. Cultivate their consistency, focus, concentration

1 _____

2 _____

3 _____

b) Reinforcement training and training needs. It is a process

Help your child identifying the immediate goal of his motivation. What does he like, what attracts him, what does he want to do? Observe his actions and see which ones he does with greater ease or passion.

Make a plan with solutions together. After abandoning his projects, rewrite new dates. Redefine tasks, deadlines, rewards and small pains. Write down where he is today, where you want to continue. How can you improve his concentration?

1 _____

2 _____

3 _____

Have him compare himself with his peers and write down his next actions to achieve the goal he has set himself. Children get tired. This is a delicate step, listen, observe, do not judge a priori and accept. Let him experiment.

1 _____

2 _____

3 _____

For Continuous Training, check the skills on the market and follow his possible training needs to enhance the strength of his enthusiasm. (Family help, buddying)

What are the sources that can support him? Who can help him? Books, courses, mother, grandparents, uncles, coaches, peers, friends, family collaborators.

1 _____

2 _____

3 _____

c) *Goals.*

What do you want to improve in his motivation? How does he want to get there? Enthusiasm, cheerfulness, lightheartedness, commitment? Write 3 aspects of motivation, related advantages and benefits you get for him and for others.

1 _____

2 _____

3 _____

Witness to progress. Write who measures his transformation with you.

1 _____

2 _____

3 _____

Imagine and make him imagine his goal as achieved and satisfactory.

1 _____

2 _____

3 _____

d) Control of Results Objective Achieved with witness confirmation.

Goal achieved on……………………….. From…………….Congratulate and reward yourself at every step.

Update the card with the date, signature of buddy, tutor. Mentor. coach

Place. Date. signature

1 _____

2 _____

3 _____

7 Successful People With Strong Motivation

Motivation is the basis of action. It is ignited by a reason, a cause, a desire. Here are two examples explained with the various whys.

Example Twenty-Two: Dario's Story from a Steady Job to Starting His Own Business
We asked Dario what motivated him to leave a steady job and start a risky business. Here are his responses:

- "To feel my identity realized."
- "For the love of success and benefits."
- "The respect of my children, my family, and society."
- "To have a new life full of challenges and stimulation."
- "To depend solely on myself."

Dario found motivation in personal fulfillment, the drive for success, and a desire for independence. These motivations helped him overcome challenges and bring his idea to life.

Example Twenty-Three: Dr. Paolo P.'s
Story on Saving and Sacrifices

During a financial seminar, we asked Dr. Paolo about the sacrifices he makes and for whom. Here are his responses:

- "Why do many entrepreneurs invest their savings in long-term plans managed by insurance companies instead of doing it personally?"

- "I'm motivated to protect my three children 100% from any risk. I believe insurance companies are more competent than I am!"
- "We all love our children and family, which is the highest purpose when you are a parent. I work for them."
- "I motivate myself every morning by kissing my children as they go to school."
- "Risk coverage provides me with significant security."

Dr. Paolo finds motivation in protecting and providing for his family, reflecting a deep connection between saving, security, and his children. Find your own motivational drivers and update them frequently.

Example Twenty-Four: Farrhad Acidwalla's Story of Triumph and Motivation

Farrhad Acidwalla, born on November 16, 1993, is an Indian entrepreneur from Pune, aged 23. In 2009, with just $400, he founded Rockstah Media, a thriving international web marketing agency employing nearly 100 people.

Widely recognized as a promising figure by renowned sources like CNN Money and The Telegraph, Farrhad has been invited as a guest speaker by The Telegraph and featured at events like Tex, the hub for successful individuals. He is considered one of the world's youngest entrepreneurs. Today, he holds a degree in Economics and Commerce from Mumbai.

At the age of 12, Farrhad launched an aviation modeling site with just $10, which he later sold for $1,200. This experience helped him understand that he could succeed even without completing formal education. His first successful sale reinforced his belief in aiming high.

Passionate about travel, nature, and wide-open spaces, Farrhad credits his success to traits such as passion, initiative, impatience, perseverance, and a sense of responsibility. He lives with his laptop, having transformed both himself and his city—less prominent than Mumbai—into a hub of entrepreneurial activity. His motivation goes beyond financial and geographical factors; it's deeply tied to identity and personal achievement.

Farrhad is ambitious, confident, and values his appearance as a reflection of his self-esteem and the status he has earned.

What can we learn from Farrhad Acidwalla?

Take the leap, pursue web-based initiatives with minimal financial investment, and continue to take risks. His motto is: "High risk equals high rewards." Farrhad's story is a testament to the potential within every young person like your child. This is the second example in embracing the "DIGITAL FAMILY." Courageously take the leap and free yourself from worries.

OTHER EXEMPLARS OF STRONG MOTIVATION IN THE ARTS

Why Maria Callas Became the Greatest Opera Singer

Maria Callas didn't rise to become the greatest opera singer driven solely by mission but by the motivation of redemption—to prove her worth to her family. Her greatest ability? Perseverance and determination. Her love, though initially a driving force, ultimately became her downfall. Even she had a coach to guide her journey.

Success Stories of Modern Managers

Many successful managers today come from humble beginnings. The common motivation is the affirmation of self-worth. Consider Steve Jobs of Apple, who came from Syrian roots and had little interest in formal education. His motivation? To prove he was the best. His greatest ability? The courage to embrace the new and risk everything.

Leonardo Del Vecchio: A Story of Overcoming Adversity

Leonardo Del Vecchio, the owner of Luxottica, one of the world's most influential entrepreneurs, was motivated by the need to emerge from his roots as an orphan, raised in an orphanage. His motivation was driven by the quest for love, to feel sought after, valued, and desired—something he had long been deprived of as a child.

PHIL FALCONE, FOUNDER OF HARBINGER CAPITAL

Phil Falcone, with a net worth of two billion dollars, reflects:
"Not all the biggest names in finance are born on Fifth Avenue."
His response:
"Commitment, talent, and luck."

CHRIS GARDNER – THE INSPIRATION BEHIND
THE PURSUIT OF HAPPYNESS

Chris Gardner, the inspiration behind the film *The Pursuit of Happyness*, became the CEO of his own investment firm, Gardner Rich & Co, founded in 2006. Starting from nothing, homeless with a child to support in San Francisco, he fought and triumphed, believing in himself and his ability to succeed.

His key lessons from his journey:

- **Resilience and determination**
- **High expectations to uphold for his son**
- **Maternal imprinting of self-belief**
- **Trusting in one's own abilities**
- **"You can only count on yourself, the cavalry won't come to rescue you."**

SUMMARY OF LEVEL 1 SPIRITUAL

Attach this module, linking it to the other two, identity and mission. You will have the entire map, the answers of the spiritual level in its sub-levels.

You will have a picture of your current situation, your being as a person, and the synthesis of the strategy.

Complete this module for your child if they are young.

Let's summarize all the benefits of the Level 1 SPIRITUAL

You have learned who you are, what you want, how to be, how to believe in yourself, and how to earn respect. You are a unique and unrepeatable asset to yourself. Your self-esteem must be kept high, just like your resilience, across all three levels.

(You still need to understand how your mind works and how your heart beats—this will be covered in the next levels).

This model can also be applied to your child.

Gaining awareness and confidence in oneself at an early age means having a significant competitive advantage in every field.

I believe in my worth. I value myself.

1 _____

2 _____

3 _____

My identity is perceived by others correctly. They see me as a...

1 _____

2 _____

3 _____

My mission, my passion is

1 _____

2 _____

3 _____

My motivation helps me to

1 _____

2 _____

3 _____

I can excel in...

1 _____

2 _____

3 _____

I lack training in...

1 _____

2 _____

3 _____

The 3 spiritual objectives are...

1 _____

2 _____

3 _____

E.g. The actions to take. How will you use your personality, character, qualities, and talent? How much time will you take to further improve your skills? Record your reflections in the journal to share them with your peer, coach, or child.

Always remember to write concise sentences with a maximum of 9 words.

THEME	**STRATEGIES**	**RESULTS**
IDENTITY' **MISSION** **MOTIVATION** **ACTIONS** **By** **Signature and date**		

Summary of strategy one, two and three of the spiritual level

Strategy #1 - Define your identity

Strategy #2 - Find the mission

Strategy #3 - Always motivate your kids, your clients, yourself

LET'S REMEMBER

1. Your child has the right to become a great person.

Encourage their dreams and respect their own pace. Seeing your children grow into roles—professionals, parents, and eventually grandparents—is a joy that rewards all your sacrifices!

Follow great examples and seek environments rich in stimulation and valuable role models. Leaders and coaches like Brendon Burchard, Jeff Walker, Anthony Robbins, and Richard Bandler all emphasize this.

Study the info-product market to gain valuable knowledge, become an expert, and ensure your children excel. This will boost their self-esteem and financial value.

Heroes and champions shape the collective imagination, and your children absorb these ideals. As a wonderful coach, guide them toward the role and identity they have chosen freely. Balancing profession and love is possible—discover your own role and value, as well as that of your children.

Attend courses, read books, and explore profitable markets. Engage your children in the search, challenge them, and enjoy the journey together.

2. To discover your mission, practice by filling out experience sheets.

Don't worry about mistakes—trial and error are part of the process. Fill out and have your children complete the questionnaires. It requires patience.

These will become your personal "books" of development, like those of fashion designers or architects. Every experience will grow both your competence and your children's value.

3. Motivate yourself and others, aiming high with enthusiasm.

Study these models and improve upon them. Share your successes by emailing info@gsm-online.it—we will publish them in the Facebook Group "Parents as Coaches."

End of Level 1

COACHING THAT IMPROVES
THE SPIRITUAL LEVEL

OUR MOTTO IS
LEARN, TEACH, WORK
"IMPARA, INSEGNA E LAVORA"
The oriented family

Let's take our dashboard again. With a simple glance at the 10 levels you have under control the topics of Being to develop spiritual abilities, personality, your "I" and that of your child.

What new training do you need?

LET'S REMEMBER

The 3 spiritual areas involved are:

- Identity
- Mission
- Motivation

After analyzing the themes on the spiritual level, we know that to transform your Being or grow that of your child, in addition to the Gabellini model, we need the most advanced tools on the market that use new disciplines.

Let's start with the first one, the most recent one:

Epigenetic Map

Create a genealogical map of your family, highlighting traits from grandparents, ancestors, to understand the tendencies in your character (and your child's) and to define your true identity.

Complete this as soon as possible while your parents and grandparents are still present. The memories of your family will fade with them.

Example Twenty-Five: Angelica, 6 Years Old, and Her Fear of the Dark

At 3 years old, Angelica began expressing fear of the dark. Her parents had never experienced such fear nor allowed her to feel it. By investigating the epigenetic map, we discovered that in her maternal line, both her grandmother and great-grandmother had suffered from the same fear. During times of war, bombings, and curfews, they hid in basements, in the dark, and lived the rest of their lives sleeping with the lights on. Once we identified the origin of the fear, we respected Angelica's request to keep the lights on while gently desensitizing her to this limitation.

Many parents might have dismissed her fear as a whim or an excuse to avoid bedtime, potentially leaving Angelica with the belief that she was weak or incapable. Do you see the price paid down the line? Epigenetics aids the spiritual level and clarifies character tendencies. It will also be valuable for the emotional level.

When we reach Level 7 and fill out the models, we will have the proper responses to the question "What are your roots?" This will help us build your development plan effectively.

Let's examine new tools to add to school curricula in Italy

- **Map of Your Needs and Those of Your Children**
Study the fundamental elements, identify sources like books, courses, webinars, and events, and draw the map, adding colors if you like. Create a list of your training needs.

    Training is a valuable tool for you, but essential for your child. The more they apply it, the richer their thoughts will become, generating the reality as St. Francis said:

"Be mindful of how you think and speak, as they may become the Prophecy of your life." - St. Francis

- **Lateral Thinking Model (E. De Bono)**

    This discipline can be linked to Level 2, cognitive development. However, the best results are achieved at the spiritual level—fostering intuition, creativity, and problem-solving.

    It's effective for conducting brainstorming sessions and creating mental maps of identity.

    This skill is a survival tool, helping people observe situations from multiple perspectives and invent new solutions not stored in our hippocampus.

    Often, we work with leaders who, after achieving success in one area or operation, tend to replicate the same approach without considering the changing world. Lateral thinking could save their position, making them more flexible and innovative.

    At the spiritual level, we use lateral thinking maps to cultivate intuition in young people, making them more insightful, reactive, and prepared—"with a step ahead."

    These skills can save lives in extreme situations, allowing them to think outside the box, create unexpected solutions, and adopt alternative paths.

THE COACHING EXPERIENCE CARD

A useful form/track for:

a) managing sessions with clients, partners, prospects, children, activities, projects.
b) sample contract/commitment with ourselves, the coach, verifiers and witnesses.

Name

1 _____

2 _____

3 _____

Activities/ Business

1 _____

2 _____

3 _____

Personal data

1 _____

2 _____

3 _____

Challenges

1 _____

2 _____

3 _____

Start Date _____ **End Date** _____

Client Signature, Coach Signature, Witness Signature

LEVEL	BENEFITS	DIFFICULTY	IMPORTANCE FROM 0 TO 100 %
A) BEING			
SPIRITUAL			
COGNITIVE			
EMOTIVE			
B) HAVING			
PHYSIOLOGICAL			
FINANCIAL			
LOGISTIC			
C) DOING			
RELATIONAL			
ENVIRONMENTAL			
BEHAVIORAL			
SOCIAL FEEDBACK			

What benefits will each level bring to your child?

1 _____

2 _____

3 _____

What threats will it have to address?

1 _____

2 _____

3 _____

How to transform them into performance challenges, into lessons learned?

1 _____

2 _____

3 _____

These questions are tracks, you can customize them according to your needs. For example, for children, after describing their character, tendencies, we can summarize the challenges of the month, of the year in relation to levels, with themselves and with others.

1 _____

2 _____

3 _____

Each card forms the Feedback Database.

This is useful information during the transformation. The bank of experience cards is the value of your expertise. Although it will always remain anonymous, it bears witness to your personal journey of "helping people". We are close to 10,000 units. Today it is fashionable to use references, back then it was absolutely a violation of ethics.

What do they say about you? Your child? Your coachee? What do people who have taken the time to judge the results think? (Social proof will highlight areas that are easier or harder to address) How did you overcome the sticking points?

Lessons learned

1 _____
2 _____
3 _____

Transformations that have taken place: yours, your child's, your coachee's, your company's.

What are they?

1 _____
2 _____
3 _____

Write the comments, observations of the witnesses of the transformation where they noticed the improvement in the 3 areas or for each level

People other than the coach
friend nr 1 _____
friend nr 2 _____
colleague _____
wife husband _____

Note: How to handle social proof (preview from level 12 of the Doing area).

When you interact with people, they react and if your interests are conflicting, they will try to block your path.

You go your own way for yourself, for your child or for the client, you can do it!

Listen to the right needs, the right criticisms, minimize risks, be sure of your choices! Update, adapt, change and follow your path.

They will put obstacles in your way and you will put obstacles in your way:

- a series of questions/answers
- a list of challenges/solutions

Every day, someone or something challenges you, and you must respond. How? By reacting, you leave your mark, and you can't go back. Your response is public.

Often, this involves multiple parties, leaving you with little time to reflect. You respond impulsively.

How many times has this happened to you? How often do you regret it later? For children, this happens almost daily.

With this framework, they can quickly prioritize, understand the importance of involved levels, and figure out how to move forward. Their responses will be more appropriate, and they will be happier.

Everyone should follow this protocol—so many misunderstandings, wasted time, suffering, and incorrect calculations can be avoided! Children will learn to ask relevant questions because the mind naturally proceeds by asking. In NLP, we emphasize the value of powerful and restructuring questions, which remains a key aspect of NLP even today.

But what about new experiences? They aren't cataloged in memory. These need to be added.

By using this model, kids will efficiently accumulate their experiences, learn to consider situations, and have their own personal database with necessary coordinates.

"Ask the right questions, and you'll get the right answers."

A good database is an internal wealth for the child—something no one can take away from them! It's a step ahead.

LET'S REMEMBER

1. Create the epigenetic charts and maps while the grandparents are present. Your identity will become clearer.
2. Teach children to reflect on their character and behaviors from different perspectives. Encourage them to observe analogies with their grandparents.
3. Have children describe their behaviors with 'awareness.'
4. Ask grandparents to share their experiences and update the map accordingly.

PART FOUR –
THE COGNITIVE LEVEL

It keeps the wolf of insignificance at the door. (Saul Bellow)

As cognitive mind, we refer to the human capacity to accumulate knowledge. These processes are called cognitive.

Thus, the cognitive mind encompasses all faculties that allow us to reason, the steps between thoughts, the organization of calculations, and memory.

The noblest faculty of humans is constructive thinking.

The mind uses different thinking approaches, such as:

- **Logical, Analytical, and Synthetic Thinking**: rooted in figures like Aristotle, Kant, Hegel, and mathematicians up to the early 20th century.
- **Lateral Thinking (E. De Bono)**: an approach to questions from various angles—towards the end of the last century, incorporating a logical sequence, influenced by Plato and Buddhism.
- **Imaginary Thinking, Mental Maps**: (spatial visualizations, entanglement) After the rise of quantum physics, we realized that thought emerges from multiple non-sequential planes, interconnected with relative space-time in a dynamic regime, not static. Organization is necessary.

Here's what this means:

- **Every thought has its truth**, but verification depends on the approach.
  - Stay within the classical tradition with static phenomena? Use Aristotelian logical thinking.
  - Broaden your horizons? Use creative lateral thinking.
  - Aim for high performance? Use quantum thinking.

Cognitive Level 2 Concepts

Definition	Goal	Aptitudes, Skills, Capabilities, Skills	Maximum Excellency	Minimum
Thought	Open your mind Express yourself Clarity	Intelligence Speed	Logical Speculation Philosophical Scientific	Stupidity Unconsciousness
Calculation	Know how to evaluate Measure	Calculative skills Intuition of trends	Understanding Phenomena with Physical, Mathematical, Chemical Languages etc.	Superficiality Imprecision
Memory	Archive Remember	Archive Remember	Pico della Mirandola	Empty confusion

4 THOUGHT

LEVEL 2 COGNITIVE

Revised by Arch. Lorella Pucci

Thought

Definition	Goal	Aptitudes, Skills, Capacities, Competencies	Massimo Excellencies	Minimum
Thought	Open your mind Communicate Clarity	Intelligence Speed	Logical Speculation Philosophical Scientific	Stupidity Unconsciousness

1 DEFINITION AND PURPOSE OF THOUGHT

Thought is a word we use with different meanings:

As function: it is the faculty of the mind that creates the contents.

- **As content**: these are the information that arise in our minds and that we can communicate.
- **As a field of knowledge**: it is a system, a set of theories that define a global view on a topic by an individual, philosopher, scientist, or religion.

The product of cognitive activity is an idea, which does not reside in the brain as such, although it is formed there. It can follow energy procedures: the idea is created by the collaboration of the two hemispheres of the brain and is controlled by the frontal part. Physically, it is the result of electrical stimulation of billions of neurons. It is an electrical impulse (EEG).

Thought can use imagination, senses, and memory. As the creative activity of the mind, ideas emerge from this complex system, whose processes can be expressed through variations in electromagnetic frequencies. To achieve this, it has an electromagnetic coding, a frequency variation that allows us to express a concept through speech, even though it remains embodied in nerve cells and transmitted by nerves and glial cells.

We are interested in thought as information that must propagate throughout every cell and is the subject of education and communication. Current research allows us to capture these impulses, "transduce" them onto electromagnetic devices, and make them understandable to others. A miracle. It is a major technological advancement that helps those with brain injuries who cannot communicate through speech.

"Transducers are devices that manipulate micro-energy, taking signals 'with or without conversion into a different form' and making them capturable, often with an amplifier. Reading thoughts is now possible by detecting eye movements. These electronic devices can capture 'sensory cellular elements capable of transmitting a physical stimulus to the central nervous system' and transmit them to a healthy nervous system, which decodes them – it is wonderful.

The main task of thought is to build ideas and store them in memory for retrieval when needed. We verbalize these ideas through language and, with the help of voice and body, communicate them in a way that is understandable to others.

Continuously, cognitive activity creates new synapses, neural connections, and processes input that arrives at the brain through sensory pathways, which are then stored in memory (thalamus, hypothalamus). This function is crucial because it contributes to the child's growing knowledge. Brain activity is immense even during sleep. In the REM phase, for example, the brain reworks thoughts and organizes them in a wholly personal order. This process, as mentioned before, is still not fully deciphered.

In the future, we will transmit complex thoughts directly from mind to device and from device to mind – another frontier will be overcome. The brain is the instrument. A frontier pedagogy.

But there is another step to share: if cells can communicate at a distance, we will need to invent a system to intercept these communications. A connected world, transparent and in real-time, would prevent lies, fraud, and conflicts – too ambitious? No. We will get there. Frontier pedagogy."

LET'S REMEMBER

The fourth step to success is originality of thought

"**Immediate action, recovery:**
If you experience confusion, emptiness, or mental dryness, the quick steps are:

Rest and restorative sleep, a rejuvenating pause, and a 16-hour mini-fast.

Thought continues to function even without the light of consciousness. In the darkness, the unconscious produces instinctive, impulsive, automatic behaviors.
The use of Transcendental Meditation as a means of calm and serenity.

This dialogue of peace, calm, and rest provides additional energy, which can manifest the next day in verbalized thought.

It is this verbalization function that young children have not yet developed. We cannot expect too many explanations from them for their actions until around the age of 6. Adults sometimes fail to use it as well when the overpowering nature of emotion is too strong. For us, thought production can follow not only imagination but also logic, one of the modes of functioning, which we will discuss further."

---

2 SKILLS, ATTITUDES THAT DETERMINE THINKING

4 THOUGHT Steps of "know-how"

4 THOUGHT Steps of "know-how"	Signals	Benefits
Attitude	Having one's own ideas, curiosity, using one's imagination, asking questions, loving reading, studying, being petulant, indiscreet, interrupting other people's conversations impulsively (alas)	Trained intuition (even with scolding)
Ability	Cognitive, knowledge of methods of analysis and reasoning	Measuring the value of your ideas
Capacity	Capacity IQ possession and information processing content creation	Esteem, admiration of others, listening to the contents, glory and vainglory
Competence	Abstraction of contents and paths, simplification of concepts, clarity of exposition of times towards the operators	Excellence, recognition of the value of one's thoughts, SUCCESS OF A UNIQUE STYLE of knowledge, in creation (patents, works of art, music, languages)

Intelligence is the natural ability to understand events from birth.

"We could also say that it is the primary faculty of the mind. It understands phenomena, analyzes information, explains, and communicates through language, and moves the body.

There are various types of intelligence. From a theoretical perspective, imagination—the action of fantasy—could also be considered a form of spiritual intelligence. However, we categorize it as cognitive purely for organizational purposes because, in reality, it is interconnected with emotional and physiological aspects, and cannot be separated.

Is cogitation truly a distinctive quality of humans? We do not believe so. Our dog thinks and expresses thought. It knows the family rituals, habits, and behaves accordingly. For example, in the morning, Jackie lies in her bed until she sees certain signs: someone leaving the apartment to retrieve shoes, someone taking the bag for picking up her "gifts." "

Then she gets up, stretches, wags her tail, and goes to the door, waiting to be let out. She makes a mental calculation: "They are ready to let me out, so I get up."

Another example: if the cat gets into trouble, it looks at us with its ears down, hides under the bed or table. It understands we are scolding it and shows a submissive behavior.

Animals have cognitive activity. For this reason, having a pet for a child is beneficial. We would go further and say that having and caring for plants is also healthy for children.

Nature is abundant, and the more interrelations we offer to children, the more their brains become adept at understanding signals. This enriches their thinking and helps them relate better to all living beings."

3 MAXIMUM SITUATION of THOUGHT Excellence

(The benefits you get if… The situation of pleasure you want to go towards)

The highest aspirations of thought are two:

- **The abstract capacity of Philosophical, Scientific, and Humanistic speculation** that can translate into technology. Thought seeks quality information and methods to apply them: the dream is primarily that thought can foresee the future.
- **Creativity** as the faculty that connects data and produces new results beyond what is already known. (Which are not errors)

Imagine how happy you would be if your child's ideas became new market solutions, innovations that pushed human knowledge forward! Think of that very poor parent whose daughter invented a process to turn shrimp shells, crab shells, and other fish waste into eco-friendly shopping bags. (Think that the father cried when she was born because he had wanted a boy!) Another example of the Digital Family.

What happens to the thoughts of NEETs? They have normal, sometimes superior, intelligence. The problem is that they are pessimistic. They use their creative thinking to predict negative scenarios, feeding fear, mistrust, and aridity. Some statistics from the web confirm this view:

"Of ten NEETs, six have a high school diploma, and four have only completed middle school."

Take ET, who lives in the province of Monza: he dropped out of high school and, at 21, works voluntarily at a private nursery school with no income.

NEETs have an internal flaw: it comes from an objective lack of prospects and a questionable emotional experience. Each failure reinforces their anticipatory negativity, and they become consumed by excuses. They self-exonerate.

Albina: "I interviewed 3,600 recent graduates when we ran post-graduation courses for Adecco (2004-2006) to train coaches. These were young people who had succeeded in school and university but couldn't find work commensurate with their studies. Those who maintained a rational attitude, regardless of the situation, were able to find solutions."

The rational part should not be overshadowed by the emotional one.

Creation and Creativity

Children have a great abundance of creativity. However, it diminishes with age unless we teach them methods to refresh it periodically. It has been proven that creativity is stimulated by the presence of animals and plants. They are very helpful for children in developing their creative, cognitive, emotional, and communicative intelligence harmoniously.

To transform thought into excellent creative activity, there are several steps:

Coaching Steps to Transform a Person with Great Imagination into an Excellent Innovative Creator	
Steps	**Some mini strategies that cultivate ambitions, attitudes, actions**
A Attitude	Express fantasy and imagination with themed games or tests
B Ability	Practice, have tests in different artistic fields to identify passions, continue to invest in courses, ateliers, studies, exhibitions, etc.
C Capacity	Specialize the chosen experience with the languages, rules, roles related to that passion. Study the related technology. Feed on the lives of the greats. Mini-strategies also valid for great manual skills and for the creation of technological innovations.
D Competences	Participation in the chosen sector, exhibitions, fairs, meetings, seminars. Propose your own vision and style, defend new ideas against detractors. Maintain the right confidentiality on research. Defend yourself with patents. Make productive agreements. Start a strong campaign for reputation and fame. Participate in competitions and awards.
E Excellence	Transforming ourselves into the role of inventor, researcher, artist, with the message of the new contribution that you give to humanity
F Accelerating Techniques of the "Flow"	Psycho-physiological accelerators make you enter the "flow" of creation to gain awareness of your great value.

The mini strategies are described with verbs to immediately emphasize the doing and acting required by the coaching training protocol.

Example Twenty-Six: The Story of Mina and Stefania – From NEET to Success

Mina P. is a graduate in economics. She would often share how she preferred working as a cashier rather than staying at home. She felt her brain and thoughts were drying up in front of the television. Previously, she had transitioned from a rigorous study routine, earning her degree with honors while balancing work, to complete inactivity. She was beginning to feel sick. The job as a cashier was humiliating, but better than nothing. She found solace in making statistics while working at the register.

Her friend Stefania, who graduated alongside her, had already become a NEET. Her parents chose to ignore the situation. Surrounded by love (emotional support) but lacking the trust in her rational abilities to support herself, they pushed her toward finding a husband and starting a family. They believed they would handle the marriage and home responsibilities. "Stefania feels like a nobody," Mina told us, "as if she's incapable of providing for herself, incapable of thinking! You get it? Here, women are worth nothing—they think they can't use their brains!" Mina was deeply distressed by this generalization.

Together, we helped Stefania break free from her gilded prison. Today, both women live in Camargue. They are married, but with mutual respect and equality. They have not yet had children. Recently, they told us in Nizza that they are rebuilding their relationships with their families of origin. Though viewed as "settled" by society, they were made to feel guilty for leaving their homeland.

How did we manage to help them? Sad to admit, but against the will of their families.

- We strengthened their rational side by counting on:
    their good grades at university
    their beauty and sincere vanity
    speaking English and French
    reviving their faded dream of working at the seaside
- Carefully calculating their income potential
    knowing how to manage tourist villages they had summer experiences with
    using the gymnastics they had learned in the gym as a profession
    having a car, a graduation gift, which solved the trips to and from the sea from the inland farms of the Camargue to the airports, to Arles and Avignon.

4 MINIMUM SITUATION OF COGITATIVE ACTIVITY

(The price you pay if you don't... The painful situation you want to escape from)

These are the negative conditions that cause damage to thinking and loss of mental clarity. A non-exhaustive list is listed below.

Negative conditions to escape from
Unresolved emotional stress
Ignorance: Thinking is limited because there is a lack of information
Flatness of unexercised fantasy, a function of sterile imagination
Stupidity: The thought is poorly expressed, the mechanism does not work, it skips steps
Superficiality: The damage comes from the lack of serious investigation or inconsistency
Unconsciousness: You are asleep or under the influence of fear
Disease: A Neurological Pathway Doesn't Work
Drugs and alcohol: They alter the state of consciousness
Poor memory: inability to access stores

WHO HASN'T ARGUED OVER SOME MISUNDERSTANDING OR GIVEN UP ON A CONVERSATION WHEN YOU REALIZE THE OTHER PERSON IS MENTALLY LIMITED? NO ONE WOULD WANT THAT TO HAPPEN TO OUR CHILDREN.

It is possible to avoid these mental limitations:

- **Stress**: Combat stress through Transcendental Meditation, exercise, psychological support, and a healthy diet.
- **Ignorance**: Fight ignorance with study and experience. Let's make sure our children value both. For their small achievements, let's applaud and encourage them generously—life already has ways

of punishing. Let's become a little more generous in our praise! Encourage and value their intelligences. They are capable of knowing and understanding much more by the age of 5 than we often believe. Let's speak to them openly and give them trust.

- **Stupidity**: What can be categorized as stupidity? A behavior, an action, a mistaken belief, or a harmful habit? In reality, it's not the individuals who are stupid, but the outcomes of their actions.
- **Superficiality**: This is the major flaw of our current society. People don't approach situations holistically, going into detail afterward. They stop too soon. This is the bad example we set for our children. We are in a hurry, but we must explain to them that we've already done the in-depth work, and now we're taking shortcuts. Children perceive this as us taking the easy way out.
- **Ignorance**: This is typical of adolescents. They act impulsively without considering the consequences. Using the Gabellini model, we reduce the margin of error.

5- RESILIENCE OF THOUGHT

"It is not matter that generates thought, it is thought that generates matter." (Giordano Bruno)

Living beings are programmed to withstand adversity. Resilience acts as an immune system, protecting us from external aggressions in a way similar to how our internal immune system fights infections through white blood cells.

As a metaphor, resilience is like a protective shield around the body—a flexible capsule that adjusts itself, stretches, and tightens, serving as a protective net when needed. This shield remains effective as long as it stays intact and well-maintained.

Resilience behaves differently depending on the internal anchors that we attach to it. Since these anchors are mobile and varied—anchored at different points within our physical, mental, emotional, and relational systems—their strength varies. Using the 10 levels and 18 sensory pathways discussed in this series of books, we can better maintain and nurture this resilience.

A person with a healthy body, functional senses, and high resilience can truly achieve and do anything in life, with full protection. Resilience of thought is a force that makes it explicit, truthful, and clear—acting as a guiding engine. According to the positivist approach, thoughts are valid only if they can be used to produce tangible benefits; otherwise, they remain mere potential energy or theoretical exercise.

Let us not scold us, metaphysical gentlemen! Here, we intentionally aim to use theoretical thought as a practice to derive tangible benefits for our children. The most fragile and sensitive form of resilience is creative thinking. Creative thought is vulnerable to changes in the body's energy.

According to the logical approach, someone trained in Latin or from a classical education already has a structured mind for many forms of translation. A classical education serves as a solid foundation, as demonstrated by our great physicists at CERN, like Fabiola Giannotti, and the achievements of excellence in Germany.

Light, clarity, persuasive power, and the capacity to explain—these dimensions of thought are all advantageous and can be achieved through mental resilience rooted in classical thought. Do you understand the damage inflicted on Thought by eliminating this subject? We are far from excellent; this is one reason we are admired and rewarded abroad!

Those who have cultivated thoughts from an early age possess immeasurable wealth. As Descartes asserted, "Cogito, ergo sum"—to think, for Descartes, was the criterion of truth and proof of human existence.

Resilience of thought must be cultivated. It relates to judgments and the creation of ideas, which are the raw materials from which judgments are formed. Creative thought, however, is sensitive to fatigue, illness, and poor diet.

Ideas are the possible, probable objects of thought, while judgments bring truth to those ideas. So, what happens? How does the mechanism of thought formation unfold? Let's follow it backward from ideas to their origin:

a) The fervor of ideas is possible if:

- The thinking process functions.
- It functions if the brain receives sugar.
- Sugar is delivered if cells accept nutrition.
- Cells work if they are protected by a healthy environment.
- The environment must respect the sensory thresholds of heat, cold, humidity, pressure, and other sensory links discussed earlier.

"Mens sana in corpore sano," as our ancestors said.

If we describe the process backward:

b) The environment must be favorable to the person's life.

- It allows cells to function (including brain and nerve cells).
- Cells support brain metabolism.
- The brain metabolizes sugar.
- Properly nourished, it activates all parts.
- These parts produce organized electromagnetic impulses.
- Electromagnetic impulses generate ideas.
- Ideas lead to judgments.

Thus, the resilience of thought correlates with the resilience of the human body, which thrives in a favorable environment. (We will explore this in detail through sensory pathways in other advanced courses.)

Recovery

How do we recover the resilience of thought? A resilient cognitive activity generates empowering energy that can be shared to help others. Especially for children, we should foster thoughts of this nature. Living with empowering thoughts brings happiness and enthusiasm; only positive thoughts resonate with positive emotions.

What happens when we notice signs of low resilience of thought? We perceive the symptoms:

- Weakness of thought.
- Clouded, opaque thinking.
- Confusion.
- Memory lapses.

The causes? First, we need to understand if the weakness is due to:

- Physical fatigue, lack of oxygen.
- Hunger, thirst, insomnia, or lack of rest.
- Disordered intestines.
- Disorganized memory.
- Weakness in certain organs of the body.
- Poor environmental conditions.

Recovery occurs through environmental control and actions to address these underlying causes.

Control of the Environment

The resilience of thought is particularly important in young children, especially during their first experiences before reaching their first year. Exposure to areas with low oxygen levels and high carbon dioxide concentrations may require special precautions. We should introduce them gradually—since we don't yet know how they will respond to events like concerts, fairs, cinemas, or crowded environments.

If they are in crowded environments, resilience can quickly decrease. Children become less lucid, unconsciously perceive discomfort, and trigger panic episodes, often crying uncontrollably. Mothers often distinguish these episodes from those related to hunger. This discomfort can emerge suddenly even in adults.

For example, being chilled around the abdomen, drinking iced beverages, exiting the sea or pool without drying off properly, or not changing wet clothes can lead to mental fatigue and panic.

At Level 1 of thought, fear arises, accompanied by emotions at Level 3. What happens is a sense of threat, feelings of suffocation, a need to escape, breathing difficulty, and sweating—whether hot or cold. These phenomena last for only a short time, but they can deeply traumatize memory and long-term cognitive abilities.

Low cognitive resilience does not indicate low intelligence. The intelligence quotient (IQ) is a test—an imprecise indicator. We observe that individuals with average IQs can still succeed in life. Cognitive intelligence can be cultivated through exercise and study. It requires effort.

With determination, consistency, willpower, and repetition, we can compensate for mild cognitive weaknesses and mental fatigue.

How to Increase Cognitive Resilience

Here are some techniques to apply. Teach them without emphasizing emotion. Choose them carefully.

List of techniques for recovering cognitive resilience
Stay in clean environments and drink plenty of water to eliminate dry mouth.
Oxygenate the body, eat properly. Sleep
Brainstorming (talking freely about a topic, then summarizing the best thought)
Using Imagination with Color Exercises (Maps)
Using analogical imagination for objects (useful for children who do not yet have abstract thinking)
Using the view (images)
Using meditative reflection (dual process)
Asking Powerful Questions About Solutions (NLP)
Using the new positive thinking (cognitivism)
Shifting attention to something very beautiful (diverting)

How does a cogitative resilience defend itself, what is it attached to?

It is connected to consciousness, to the activity of the anterior part of the brain.

We can move along some lines:

Mini strategies
Develop and alternate various types of thinking, from abstract ideas to concrete concepts, and finally to value judgments, which can be used in communication. Talking with touchable objects
Separating linear, Aristotelian logic from the confusion of emotions
Enriching simple logic with lateral thinking
Creating Thought with Quantum Techniques
Clearing sensory pathways so they send correct input to brains to form correct thoughts

Let's repeat: those who study Latin, logical analysis, cases, syntax, find themselves with a favored brain because they order thoughts sequentially.

They help kids to coherently present a speech in a fluid and coherent way.

Knowing how to speak is a useful oratory skill on the WEB and increasingly necessary in all fields. For years we hated oratory,

thinking it was a futile, pompous way of talking nonsense to deceive! We were wrong!

Albina racconta:

"I loved Socrates so much that I followed his teachings like a Bible! How much knowledge I lost! Today, science proves Plato's way of thinking correct. Clarifying concepts was my highest aspiration. Even today, I continue to schematize, synthesize, and strip away unnecessary details to maintain the resilience of clear, structured, and reliable thinking, as Kant intended.

Why this clarification? Admitting my methodological error allows me to seek new techniques for enhancing thought. Isn't science built on theories that rely on the certainty of concepts? Once scientific research discovers a truth, we expect the ability to replicate the experiment (as demonstrated by Galileo). Even mathematical thought has Socratic concepts—precise language used to express truth.

I structured all my studies based on these principles. To this day, I attempt to interpret events primarily through mathematics and less through creative philosophy.

I didn't appreciate Hegel, but the pursuit of physics aligns with exploration, attempts, errors—concepts emerging from chaos, as quantum logic shows.

Where did I go wrong, and what should I teach young people?

If thought becomes an emergence, a bubbling, provisional truth, how do we manage its imaginative, free, creative, irregular, bold, disobedient, and disorderly aspects?

I recently realized my mistake: I confused the act of thinking with the act of judging. For me, thought was a judgment I issued.

Studying resilience, I understood the shift in meaning. Resilience is tied to the concept, not the judgment, which is a consequence.

It means that if you create incomplete ideas, judgments will be flawed and partial. Low cognitive resilience? Poor ideas, faulty judgments, major misassessments, and disastrous choices!

Let's reverse the sequence: high cognitive resilience? Great ideas, effective judgments, winning evaluations, and successful choices!"

The result affects sensory pathways first and then health.

How can you train kids to avoid this misunderstanding? Have you avoided it? Try to reflect on the difference between your concepts and your judgments.

Thinking activity produces ideas, judging activity subjects them to the criterion of truth.

If you block the process, you lose an important wealth of knowledge.

For example, think about the damage I suffered: I had not hypothesized that those ideas could be valid, they were just too far ahead of their time, so I judged them "not actionable". The methodology for judging the truth may not have been invented yet, despite Karl Popper!

If we want to grow cognitive champions, one secret is to insert all their information into a frame of reference made of physical objects that kids can easily connect. It is a very important loophole, from these grids you can subsequently reconstruct visual maps to help memory. In addition, we can strengthen with the energetic approach.

Thought is energy and as such it can jump the classic cage of space-time and still be new and true. .

We will try this approach with our children. Example: if we want to grow a new idea, we need patience. First step, accept the idea, then frame it (as just said). Then evaluate it and wait again if there are any inconsistencies. Second step, take it back and verbalize it. Those that are not suitable for the moment, we do not throw them away, we put them aside. Then we write them in our diary, where we can fish them out in the future.

6 TIPS, RESULTS AND STRATEGIES ON THOUGHTS

In order to enhance cognitive intelligence, you can use different paths listed below

Mini strategies
Living in environments that always provide new inputs. Gardens, mountains, sea, libraries
Studying philosophical and neuropsychological principles to apply them by experimenting with new models of knowledge, new techniques for training thought such as speed reading or lateral reading which promises a broader vision of the world
Training in both literary and mathematical "virtuous exercises" with meditation
Stimulate memory as a mechanism for accumulating and archiving information
Studying the quantum processes that allow a qualitative leap in the function of "intelligere", that is, in capturing knowledge of the morphological world and developing ESP, the super, super powerful, extrasensory faculty
Exercise all 18 sensory pathways in order to bring out complex thinking that also includes emotional reactions

All these actions must be part of the New Pedagogy to get the best of cognitive intelligence in our children.

As we can see, there are tools that have not yet been activated, which we are convinced will be useful for the economies of tomorrow. Those who learn them today will be a step ahead.

It is like having a more focused mental activity, with a greater ability to understand things in advance.

Once acquired, this intelligence remains, it is an asset, a capital, for life.

Well-cultivated Intelligence represents a guarantee of correct investment in our children. You can have fun creating suitable games for your child with these purposes.

The intelligence quotient

We are not particularly impressed by the standard intelligence index. IQ, intelligence quotient. When taking tests, a good basic culture affects the result, the quality of the answers, unbalances the evaluation in favor of arithmetic calculations and geometric similarities instead of a pure value typical of intelligence.

We have found, for example, that the same tests in India are better passed due to the innate tendency to mathematics.

Parents who want to measure an intelligence index can build it themselves based on their environment. In particular, re-do the questions that aim to observe logical and spatial connections. The children of wealthy people, who live in environments rich in stimuli, will be advantaged, because they can afford the teaching of Advanced Pedagogies. Our dream would be to introduce them in all Italian public schools, which are already among the best in the world in terms of culture and are free.

Try checking the programs of elementary and middle schools in different countries, you will be surprised by their basic cultural poverty compared to us. Be careful if he has a cold the test does not work.

SOME STEPS to stimulate speculative activity

We teach logic to communicate coherently, sequentially (subject, verb, object), revisit Latin, and deepen mathematics to frame problems.

We can construct concepts by combining content and "provisional" truths in three different methods:

- With the analytic method, we generate numerous particular ideas from our imagination and then synthesize them, enunciating a general (provisional) truth.

- With the deductive method, we start with a proven general idea and attempt to derive numerous specific concepts from it (which will be less provisional).
- With the emergent method, from the chaotic set of a broader topic that encompasses one or many ideas, we select those that resonate with others and with ourselves, organizing them within our (provisional) experience.

Truth will be true for now, here, today—provisionally—and may be revised tomorrow based on new research and discoveries. We habituate our children to concepts in flux, subject to improvement! Encouraging an intellectual openness means not fearing social verification. "Panta rei" becomes a true and effective practice: everything changes, everything flows, including truth. We lose certainty in certainty! The Chinese expressed this centuries ago with the I Ching.

By admitting dynamic uncertainty, we are not illogical, only creative. Those who use these protocols will become geniuses.

Did Einstein and his first wife think in certain, classical ways for special relativity? At first, they attempted to follow traditional methods, but then they made the intellectual leap and discovered a new truth.

What exercises to do? They are truly endless. You can have fun inventing games following the above guidelines.

Examples of Cognitive Games
• Case simulation exercises to solve
• Crosswords
• Study examples of heroes
• Thought-provoking readings with questions to answer
• Learn poems by heart
• Let's talk about inspiring content
• Walking in oxygenated environments, mountains, sea
• Running, swimming, climbing, diving, the gym
• Visits to cultural institutions and museums

4 THOUGHT

LEVEL 2 COGNITIVE

Questionnaire to find inspiration about your child's mental capacity

Sample form you need for:

a) **Transforming a person's intellect into a brighter and more creative one**
b) **Sign your ideal contract to train your mind with the coach**

Asking questions to enhance the capacity of the intellect means training logical reasoning in the construction of thoughts with the various methods mentioned in the book, to which we also add the analogical one.

Deductive Inductive Emergent analogical. Remember that thoughts create reality and that memory must store information well.

a) Capital already acquired, riches that come from roots, origins, relationships, epigenetics, positive experiences to be copied and negative ones to be modified

The best abilities of your intellect. What tendencies do you have in your reasoning style? Analytical, synthetic, analogical? How skilled are you at managing multiple styles of reasoning?

How capable is he of using his intelligence to offer original solutions? How expert is he in helping others, competent in making them reason? What excellences has your superior intelligence produced? Write how you can produce positive thoughts useful for life and for a successful business.

List the advantages and benefits

1 _____

2 _____

3 _____

THOUGHT Basic elements. Write or have someone write down his best aptitudes, abilities, tendencies, character, skills, attitudes that make him think according to the Gabellini Model (10 levels). Do the exercises. Do them too.

1 _____

2 _____

3 _____

THOUGHT Technique for copying a mental success. Write how he feels when his judgment is better than the others. Have him reproduce the same conditions of gratification. Self-esteem. Have him repeat it many times until he masters the method. Write what you think and how you feel when you achieve this record.

1 _____

2 _____

3 _____

THOUGHT Technique to change a failure, such as mistakes due to lack of information, haste, nervousness. What mistakes have you made with superficial reasoning? Describe the elements that misled you, how you felt. Help your child to overcome those moments, transforming them into very educational lessons, find their mistakes, do not criticize, make them consider surmountable aspects of knowledge. Children try. Cultivate their coherence, make them do logical analysis. Use a comic style.

1 _____

2 _____

3 _____

b) *Reinforcement training and training needs It is a process*

Help your child identify the growth goal of his thinking. How creative is he? How logical and rational? Observe his verbal and paraverbal expressions and see the concepts he communicates. Make a plan together with the solutions of his language and his clarity skills. Write down where he is today, where you want to continue from. How can you better clarify his logos, his conceptual verbalization, how he makes judgments

1 _____

2 _____

3 _____

Have him compare with his peers and write down his next actions to understand, speak with proper language. (To be reported in his diary). Share his conclusions, talk about daily life

1 _____

2 _____

3 _____

For Continuous Training, check the skills on the market and follow their possible training needs, the various learning methods. (Help, buddying)

What are the sources that can support him? Who can help him? Books, courses, mother, grandparents, uncles, coaches, peers, friends, family collaborators.

c) Goals.

What do you want to improve in his intellectual activity? Logic, creativity, approach to obstacles, rationality? Do you want to learn the law of attraction, quantum thinking? Write 3 aspects of your way of thinking, related advantages and benefits that you get for him, for you and for others.

1 _____

2 _____

3 _____

Witness to progress. Write who measures his transformation with you.

1 _____

2 _____

3 _____

Imagine and make him imagine his goal as achieved and satisfactory.

1 _____

2 _____

3 _____

d) Results Control Objective achieved with witness confirmation.

Goal achieved on........................ Since..............Congratulate and reward yourself at every step.

Update the card with date, signature of buddy, tutor, mentor, coach

Place, date, signatures

1 _____

2 _____

3 _____

7-WHO HAS BEEN SUCCESSFUL IN PRODUCING RICH THOUGHTS

**Example Twenty-Seven: Albert Einstein
and the Birth of Special Relativity**

In Albert Einstein's life (1879–1955), there are four distinct phases:

1. Before discovering the theory of special relativity, he was uncertain and timid. His muse and mathematical helper was his wife, Mileva. He was so dependent on her that the Nobel Prize money, many years later, was given to her for herself and their two children.

2. After the discovery of the formula and acceptance by the scientific world, he became eager to break free, assert himself, and realized he could succeed on his own. His thought had great value as a creator of new connections.

3. Life in Germany, first as an unfaithful husband with his cousin Elsa Einstein (married in 1919 until her death in 1936), then as a husband with her, enduring her tolerance of his extramarital affairs.

4. Life in the United States, struggling cognitively to move forward. He persisted on the same path, trapped by the belief that "God does not play dice." He transformed this "cognitive block" regarding research and calculations into using his influence for world peace and against atomic energy and injustices, becoming an image figure far removed from the role of a working scientist. He expressed great humanistic and universal values and arguably

deserved a Nobel Peace Prize (even though his personal life was highly questionable).

Here, we focus only on his phase as a young man from his work at the patent office to the discovery of relativity. From boredom discussing patents, he moved to theory. For him, only cognitive and mathematical aspects mattered, which he explored not only with his wife but also with his friend Michele Besso.

Here is a summary of the process:

Level 1 – Spiritual

He was completely dedicated to his studies. He wanted to become someone (a struggle for identity and role).

Level 2 – Cognitive

He exerted his creative thinking at work, at home, and with friends. He made connections that were previously unthinkable and unconventional. For him, mathematics was just a tool to express his ideas. Ideas that had been circulating for about thirty years but had never been properly connected. It required changing his perspective and simplifying things. Even when he formulated general relativity, the process remained the same. He had gained confidence in calculation, but then stopped. He brushed against the quantum field as a consequence of his theories but didn't believe in it. He had returned to classical thinking. His peers knew this. The university rector saw him more as a figurehead of thought, the Nobel of Princeton University, raising funds and overlooking his private affairs rather than a great scientist actively discovering new frontiers.

Level 3 – Emotional

He showed little interest in emotions, only in sex. With his wife, he ended up living a physical separation without love.

Level 4 – Physiological

He was a convinced vegetarian but didn't take care of his body.

Level 5 – Financial

As a young man, he didn't care much about money unless necessary. Neither the environment, morality, nor ethical justice mattered to him—these became key topics in the later part of his life. His focus was entirely cognitive.

Level 6 – Logistical

He was a champion, dedicated 100% to seeking tools, competencies related to physics, theoretical scientific development, and calculation. We wouldn't advise such an unbalanced position for our children by principle (75% being versus 25% having and doing together!). Ideally, we'd prefer at least 30% in each area, but geniuses follow different rules. This was his golden phase.

Level 7 – Relational

He frequented a decent circle of friends, always the same. Music was their common bond. He didn't leverage his relationships.

Level 8 – Environmental

As a young man, he showed no interest in the environment.

As an elderly man, he became a great advocate for the earth after discovering the destructive violence of nuclear energy, war, and atomic bombs.

Level 9 – Social Verification

In his youth, he wasn't particularly attached to social verification. His affairs were kept discreet and sober. In later phases of life, especially after his escape to freedom as a potentially persecuted Jew in Germany, he rebalanced—especially with wealth and well-being. Even so, it was his wife and secretary who managed his daily duties.

He never regretted leaving behind Bern and Zurich, which linked him to marital obligations, nor Mileva (1875–1948), who had become neurotic and abandoned her studies, but lived for many years. Nor was he particularly concerned about his relationship with his children: Lieserl was handed over to Mileva's family and rejected, Eduard (schizophrenic?) and his first son, Hans Albert, were his top priorities.

He remained, always, a son with a childlike wonder (music and voice being expressions of physics).

10 Level Analysis Scheme

Levels	Estimated value	Value Invested	Results
Importance in a person's life %	Average Weight	Real Weight	
a) Being	30.00	75%	
1. Spiritual	10	25	He wanted to be "the Physicist"
2. Cognitive	10	40	Max Value.
3. Emotional	10	10	EgoismoSelfishness
b) Having	30,00	10%	
1. Physiologic	10	0	Health
2. Financial	10		Difficulty
3. Logistic	10	5	Messy
c) Doing	40,00	15%	
1. Relational	10	10	Few friends
2. Environmental	10	0	Disinterest
3. Behavioral	10	5	Study only
4. Social Proof	10	0	Non-existent
Total	100%	100%	

N.B. the values on the table are indicative, even if they come from years of studies on Einstein to understand his subtexts, his cognitive, real, emotional processes, from which emerge the official behaviors, the superficial ones, the ones that people see.

What lessons can we learn from Einstein?

From his life: dedication, persistence, perseverance to his Mission and passion, the Physics of "how he saw the world."

The global success, the Nobel Prize, the rediscovery of environmental and human values, his defense of minorities and injustices—how did he achieve all this? We've studied him for years and don't believe his model is replicable.

We can encourage discipline and the study of music as a universal language, just like mathematics (and it's fun too!). A curious observation: when did he visually appear free from his first wife? The day he began growing his hair out in a wild and untamed manner (around 1919) and appeared publicly in that iconic way that became his trademark.

He was at the peak of his self-esteem and didn't care about the judgments of his second wife, who considered herself progressive.

On the contrary, what would we like to avoid? Limiting beliefs. Even Einstein hit a wall. He continued to argue with himself, trying to unify the four fundamental forces into a single law. He became closed off. Even when he discovered entanglement—the phenomenon where an event experienced by one group could instantaneously influence another distant group, without physical proximity—he couldn't accept it. It conflicted too much with classical space-time! He thought there must have been a calculation error; his beliefs made it impossible.

He lacked the courage to shift his perspective again, as he had done with relativity. Perhaps comfort and success make us lazy? Few scientists have received as many honors in life as Einstein. Perhaps when you've already made a monumental discovery, you've given everything, like a squeezed lemon?

An hypothesis.

Abraham Flexner, the first director of Princeton, thought this way. He never truly liked Einstein, even though he enthusiastically spoke of him and invited him to America. He had hired Einstein out of a desire for prestige. A puritan, he despised Einstein's unconventional behavior— from his sockless attire to his vegetarian diet and affairs with women.

Nonetheless, reading all of Einstein's aphorisms is a joy for the spirit, a source of energy for your children. On a rainy day, enjoy transcribing a few of them into your diary alongside him and commenting on them. Let him choose which ones resonate with him.

If you see Einstein as a dream to emulate, hang his photo in your study. It's an interesting subliminal message.

5 CALCULATION

LEVEL 2 COGNITIVE

Revised by Rag. Raoul Pucci

Calculation

Definitions	Goal	Aptitudes, Skills, Capacities, Competencies	Maximum Excellence	Minimum
Calculation	Measuring ourselves and the world	Accuracy Fussiness Objectivity Combination and evaluation skills	Millimetric perfection of evaluations and measurements Recognized as a super-partes expert	Imprecision Superficiality Errors

1 DEFINITION AND PURPOSE OF THE CALCULATION

Calculation is the faculty of the intellect and senses that allows us to measure our relationships with the environment. Its primary purpose is both to defend our safety and to gain advantages.

By evaluating the position of objects relative to us, we unconsciously always calculate both proximity and distance. We answer the question: *What do I need?*

Calculation forms the foundation of social, economic, and technological life. It is the language of commercial exchanges, which underpin the economy, computers, and machinery. In today's world, no event escapes the arithmetic and mathematical analysis of the calculating faculty. Therefore, it is essential to educate children from an early age in calculation and its tool, mathematics. How often do you give or receive information involving numbers?

Every brain, whether animal or human, calculates and measures.

When two people meet, the first thought is a calculation: *Do I need this person? How much do I need them?*—and we calibrate our level of interest based on these answers.

The ability to calculate is used for:

- total understanding of the universe, phenomena, physical, mathematical, chemical languages, then expressed through mathematics
- prediction of the laws that govern the universe and the behavior of matter

LET'S REMEMBER

- **The fifth step to success is clarity of your calculation**

Immediate action, recovery

If you have a cold, your calculations will not work well. Your senses, sight, hearing, smell, the perception of subtle energies, electromagnetic fields will be muffled and you will have false perceptions of speed and objects you encounter, you will calculate badly. You need to reduce your driving speed to avoid risky maneuvers. To react to a sudden obstacle, having slower than normal calculation reflexes, we must drive carefully.

For example, if your children are tired, make too many mistakes in their movements, bump into objects, you need to calm them down and teach them to calculate precisely. By accustoming them to the correctness of information, of measurements, they will cultivate excellence in scientific and work performances even in difficult conditions.

For example, a good architect, trained in calculations, sees the discordance of spatial relationships before others. We have often observed the clerks in supermarkets who sell cured meats. They become skilled in calculating weight, cutting an exact number of slices of ham with respect to the required weight. The advantage is that they serve customers quickly and clear queues easily.

2- THE SKILLS AND ATTITUDES THAT DETERMINE CALCULATION

5 CALCULATION Steps of "know-how"	Signals	Benefits
Attitude	Tendency to measure, compare, count, use numbers to describe objects, prefer spatial games	Natural mathematical approach
Ability	Creation of reference points and high sensory and justice development. Correct and fast intuition of measuring and evaluating facts	Quick understanding of phenomena
Capacity	Development of own calculation methods and cross-referencing of data between different realities	Greater breadth of vision and consequences before others
Competence	Abstraction of physical phenomena at the theoretical level, invention of new uses, paths and results	Application of higher mathematics concepts (functions, derivatives, integrals, matrices, series, diagrams, curves, maps) to philosophical and even practical topics SUCCESS IN TECHNOLOGY

The attitudes of calculation are natural and can be educated and trained. Often, however, these abilities are neglected by educators who instill a fear of mathematics and the digital world. These skills are essential for Scientific Understanding and the correct interpretation of data received by the senses.

Calculation, along with alertness, is the primary tool of the body's defense system and the vital space it occupies.

The distance, pressure, weight, heat, and humidity of an object are measured so that sensory signals inform our brain that the object is harmless. At the slightest doubt, the alert system (from the emotional level) is activated.

The senses send inputs to the brain to calculate the object's dimensions, shape, and position:

- space
- time
- distances
- heights
- depths
- values
- movements
- weights
- volumes

In this way, they identify, calculate, and measure any magnitude that threatens the body. The senses listen to the messages from their receptors—both internal (within the body) and external (on the skin and sensory organs)—and send these messages to the brain via the nervous pathways.

The brain receives, calculates, measures, and sends back orders to muscles to adapt to the environment and perform the necessary movements. Calculation controls the entire process.

We still do not fully understand how the brain measures emotional inputs, pain scales, or value scales. We have scales, but we cannot yet isolate or separate cognitive recognition from emotional perception.

We know pain thresholds are precise, yet we cannot calculate them.

Conversely, we can calculate sound levels in decibels, but the precise personal interpretation and perception of those sounds still elude us.

Children often exhibit these perceptual tendencies, especially in spatial awareness. They may seem clumsy in handling objects due to a lack of experience, hurry, or deliberate distraction, but the system works perfectly.

There are adults who still struggle to judge distances with the naked eye. No one has exercised their ability, including the ear, which contributes to precise measurements through semicircular canals.

MAXIMUM SITUATION OF CALCULATIVE AND MEASURING CAPACITY

Excellence (the benefits you achieve if... the pleasurable situation to aim for)

The aspiration of calculation is to perfectly measure phenomena by communicating through physical, mathematical, chemical, and sound languages. Educating capable and skilled children in calculation clears the path toward science. Their brain frames and integrates information through memory, a sense of time, and space, delivering enriched results. Mathematicians and calculation experts are specialists who perceive the world with an additional dimension—discussed as the meticulousness of Excellence.

For instance, our great painters developed a sense of calculation that allowed them to intuitively calculate natural proportions, resulting in the harmony of their artwork that moves us.

Great athletes, particularly champions of car and motorcycle racing, are highly skilled in spatial-temporal calculation. They become attuned to acceleration—driving at extreme speeds, with distant reference points anticipated and variable speeds—seeing beyond the next curve. This calculation of obstacle surmounting can save their lives.

Calculation and Mathematical Mind

To transform a lazy mind into an excellent mathematical one— capable of making efficient judgments and producing outstanding results—it is necessary to develop calculative, measuring, and evaluative attitudes. Several steps are involved:

Coaching Steps to Transform a Lazy Mind into a Brilliant Mind	
Steps	Some mini strategies that cultivate ambitions, attitudes, actions
A Attitude	Teach how to count, measure, evaluate from an early age, space, distance, weight, movement.
B Ability	Every sense has its own calculative dimension that we transform with the language of mathematics and geometry. But there are many other languages that we are not used to. Opening the lazy mind is dusting off natural aptitudes. Educating to new virtual realities is a new paradigm of calculation.
C Capacity	Mastering mathematical exercises and general rules. Setting the brain to a mathematical approach before making value judgments. Introducing calculus also in humanistic subjects. Those who are good at calculus know how to transform words into numbers, facilitating the progress of knowledge and science.
D Competence	The brilliant mind is one step ahead of the rest. Its most important qualities are its flexibility and its multidimensional function. They are the only ones that can survive in extreme situations, being able to make difficult decisions before others.
E Excellence	Transforming lazy people into brilliant decision makers such as scientists, entrepreneurs, firefighters or security personnel.
F "Flow" Accelerating Techniques	Psycho-physiological accelerators get you into the "flow" of computation, so you can see beyond broader vistas to better alternatives.

4-MINIMUM SITUATION OF CALCULATION AND MEASUREMENT CAPACITY

(THE PRICE YOU PAY IF YOU DON'T... THE PAINFUL SITUATION YOU ESCAPE FROM)

Lack of attention is one of the conditions in which there is damage from bad calculations. Who hasn't happened to pay and receive the wrong change? If you are driving without paying attention, do you calculate distances and accelerations well? If children are inattentive, the ability to calculate is the first to go haywire. Superficiality, in addition to inattention, haste, leads to imprecision, which is harmful to calculation. There is a high price to pay. We have discovered that poor health also modifies the ability to calculate and lowers its resilience.

5 COMPUTING CAPACITY RESILIENCE

The resilience of the computational capacity is the ability to protect yourself from attacks on the "automatic scale of weights and measures" to the measuring system, which orients you in the environment. It is your aiming system, your radar, which protects your mobility in the physical world, you move without thinking too much and do not bump into walls, people. Resilience is the most important faculty for athletes, who achieve excellent performances, exceptional results, precisely by working closely around obstacles.

We perceive signs of low resilience in some behaviors:

a) Movement
   If we often bump into furniture
   If we absolutely don't know how to move in the dark
   If we have trouble riding a bike

b) The value of things
   If we get the change wrong
   If we throw away money
   If we find ourselves in unexpected debt

c) Mathematics
   Poor relationship with the concept of number
   Inability to understand the trend of a function
   Repeated errors in multiplications by ten and two-digit additions/subtractions.

Recovery

The recovery of calculative resilience goes through three phases: Logos, sensory rehabilitation, and exercises.

LOGOS

This phase is about re-calibrating the capacity to accurately evaluate objects. It involves modifying beliefs about the correct relationships of objects, especially if you've experienced shocks or trauma.

SENSORY REHABILITATION

This phase aims to improve movement. If physiological calculation is incorrect, we lose a sense of orientation. It requires checking:

- **Hearing**: the three semicircular canals for balance issues.
- **Vision**: proper diopters for better focus.
- **Touch**: three-dimensional tactile perception.
- **Proprioception**: the balance between the three brains measured in muscles, tendons, and neural pathways.

MATH EXERCISES

These are essential for habituating basic mathematical and geometrical calculations. Consider, for instance, your personal space—how many times have you felt uncomfortable when a stranger encroached too close? If you have low resilience, you may miscalculate your space, allowing unwanted intrusions. This can lead to misunderstandings or conflicts, as others interpret your discomfort as an implicit invitation.

Resilience is better measured under extreme conditions. In the mountains, amidst fog, at night, snow, ice, silence, rain, or when facing the fear of animals—people with strong physical conditioning often fail to overcome these obstacles and panic. In the middle of a seemingly safe forest, they might be unable to descend safely. Even small climbs of less than 25 meters can create panic when visibility is lost due to fog, causing them to lose their grip and become stuck, panicked, or unable to proceed. In these situations, assistance is often necessary, such as guiding or securing them down with ropes, much like delivering a package.

The same happens during dives, even shallow ones at 18 meters. Healthy individuals may panic, flail, refuse safety stops, and rapidly ascend, creating dangerous rescue situations and disrupting the dive for their partners and groups. Thankfully, dive masters often organize dives in areas with hyperbaric chambers for safety. These are individuals who may not have realized that their spatial-temporal sense doesn't accurately calculate distances underwater. In such environments, vision is impaired, and reference points are often lost.

That's why it's crucial to educate children on such experiences from a young age, fostering both mathematical and physiological calculation skills.

6- RESULTS AND STRATEGIES ON COMPUTING ABILITY

LONG LIVE MATHEMATICS

Unfortunately, there are no magic formulas to quickly boost calculative resilience, only attention, study, and consistent practice to strengthen memory.

For instance, a manager must memorize and understand calculations regarding their company's turnover and key division data. During business meetings, they need to handle percentages confidently. To accelerate the development of calculative ability, one can rely on a good coach and improve over time and with patience. To maintain control of a business, increasing calculative resilience is necessary to avoid embarrassing situations!

Geometry, too, is a system of measurement and calculation—the language of the universe, of God. Every moment of our lives is lived based on two unconscious theoretical foundations:

- **Philosophical**: dealing with the purpose of life, the reason for our existence.
- **Mathematical**: interpreting the world and ourselves.

One of the greatest gifts we can give to our children is to educate and instill a love for this language. Italian schools are highly effective in this regard, and we only need to foster greater enthusiasm for the subject. When we transitioned from classical teaching to set theory—thanks to Cantor, Gödel, Frege, Peano (pioneers of this mathematical approach)—teachers may have shaken hands, but not always Italian teachers!

We should be grateful for the contribution mathematics has made to humanity. Instead of sinking into passivity in front of the television, let's engage our children in intelligent mathematical games. These can lay a cornerstone for their development. There are no people "not suited" to mathematics—only parents who are "ignorant of its value" and fail to inspire their children's interest. It's not the teachers' role to foster a love for the subject; they must provide information and instruction. The task of instilling passion rests with the family.

Do you know the price you pay when you show indifference to this subject? Children will grow up believing they are incapable of solving problems and will miss out on countless opportunities because mathematics is foundational to computing, economics, technology, science, and even the arts. The choice is yours!

5 CALCULATION

LEVEL 2 COGNITIVE

Questionnaire to find inspiration on your child's calculation ability. Template you need for:

a) re-develop the mathematical mentality to quickly evaluate and judge phenomena

b) increase the scientific approach, useful to measure oneself and others in an objective way

a) Capital already acquired, riches that come from roots, origins, relationships, epigenetics, positive experiences to be copied and negative ones to be modified

Is your child proud of his achievements in mathematics? How and from whom did he learn mathematics? Find out where, when and if he began to transform his calculation skills into abilities. The skills he has already acquired in mathematical reasoning, logical

List the benefits

1 _____

2 _____

3 _____

CALCULATION Basics. Write or have him write down his best aptitudes, abilities, tendencies, character, skills, attitudes that determine his way of calculating. Try to make him fall in love with science and its heroes like Einstein. Make him play lots of calculation games.

1 _____

2 _____

3 _____

CALCULATION Technique for copying a success. Write how he feels when he completes school problems and gets high grades. Have him reproduce the same conditions of satisfaction, encourage him to help his classmates. Have him repeat these experiences, praise him and use him as an example.

Write down what you thought and felt when you went to school. Can you reproduce the same conditions? Pass them on to his desire to grow and assert himself in class. It will be strengthened.

1 _____

2 _____

3 _____

CALCULATION Technique to change a failure, for example failing homework. What obstacles had you overcome? Describe the elements that had confused you. Help your child to overcome those moments, transforming them into very educational lessons, do the repetitions immediately. Do not scold, make them consider the failure an exercise. Do not waste useless time.

1 _____

2 _____

3 _____

b) Reinforcement training and training needs. It is a process

Help your child identify the goals of his calculus skill. Connect them to physics. Make the plan together with the training solutions. Write down where he is today, where you want to continue. How can you improve his calculus?

1 _____

2 _____

3 _____

Have him compare himself with his peers and write down his next actions to "become good at math (to be reported in his diary) This is a delicate step, listen, observe, do not judge a priori and accept. Let him experiment. Math is inside each of us, we need to rediscover it.

1 _____

2 _____

3 _____

For Continuing Education, check the skills on the market (there are many good university students) to cover his possible training needs (Help, buddying) What are the sources that can support him? Who can help him? Books, courses, mother, grandparents, uncles, coaches, peers, friends, family collaborators.

c) Goals.

What do you want to improve in your measurement and evaluation activity? Theory, field evaluation experiences, new criteria? Write 3 aspects to improve and to start from with relative advantages and benefits that you get for him, for you and for others.

1 _____

2 _____

3 _____

Witness to progress. Write who measures your transformation with you

1 _____

2 _____

3 _____

Imagine and have others imagine your numeracy goal as achieved and satisfying.

1 _____

2 _____

3 _____

d) Results. Control of Results Objective
Achieved with witness confirmation.

Goal achieved on…………………….. From ………….
Congratulations, reward at every step.

Update the card with the date, signature of buddy, tutor, mentor, coach

Place, date and signatures

1 _____

2 _____

3 _____

7-WHO HAS BEEN SUCCESSFUL
(IN CALCULATIONS, IN MATHEMATICS)

Enjoy reading the biographies of these great mathematicians. We highlight a number of important ones. If the passion blossoms in your home, you have won the lottery!

LIST OF IMPORTANT MATHEMATICIANS

Zenone (495 - 435 a.	Newton (1642 - 1727)	Lobatchewsky (1793 - 1856)	Poincarè (1854 - 1912)	Kronecker (1823 - 1891)
Pitagora	Leibniz (1646 - 1716)	Abel (1802 - 1829)	Cantor (1854 -1918).	Riemann (1826 -1866)
Euclide (verso il 295 a. C)	Bernoulli	Jacobi (1802 - 1829)	Andrew Wiles	Kummer (1810 - 1893) e
Eudosso (408 -355 a. C)	Jacques (1654 - 1705) e Jean	Hamilton (1805 - 1865)	Fibonacci	Dedekind (1831
Archimede (287 -212 a. C)	(1667 - 1748)	Galois (1811 - 1832)	Alan Turing	-1916)
R Descartes (1596 - 1650)	Eulero (1707 -1783)	Sylvester (1814 - 1897) e Cayley	Gauss (1777 - 1855)	Boole (1815 - 1864)
Fermat (1601 -1665)	Lagrange (1736 -1813)	(1821 - 1895)	Cauchy (1789 -1857)	Hermite
Pascal (1623 - 1662)	Laplace (1749 -1827)	Monge (1746 - 1818) e Fourier	Poncelet (1788 -1867)	Weiertrass (1815 - 1897)
Sources: Matmedia.it Wikimedia		(1768 - 1830)		Sonia Kowalesky (1850 - 1891)

Example twenty-eight: the story of Évariste Galois (1811-1831), a French boy who discovered his love for mathematics at a very early age.

"Tout voir, tout entendre; ne perdre aucune idée!" A beautiful motto—"to see, hear, understand, and not lose any idea"—still holds true today.

Galois was born into a family of judges, with his mother being a learned magistrate who shaped his humanistic education. His father, the mayor of Bourg-la-Reine, introduced him to republican, revolutionary politics against monarchy and church authority—ideals for which young Galois would pay with his life. He was assassinated at just twenty years old.

A year earlier, his father had hanged himself, humiliated by false letters from a Jesuit priest. They could not isolate him, for his ideas of freedom were too influential.

Évariste was aware of his impending fate. The day before his death, May 29th, he wrote a memorial outlining the algebraic mathematics that paved the way for modern algebra, still in use today. Knowing his time was short, he wrote: "I have no time."

But how and why is Galois considered an "enfant prodige" of algebra? He wasn't born with a natural talent for calculation. As a teenager, he began reading mathematicians like Legendre (Elements of Geometry), Lagrange (Resolution of Equations), Euler, Gauss, Jacobi, absorbing concepts at an astonishing rate. However, his passion for mathematics was truly sparked by Professor Richard, also the mentor of another great mathematician, Charles Hermite. Galois faced many disappointments, as recognized authorities like Cauchy and Poisson did not give him the attention he deserved. His contributions were acknowledged only posthumously.

Mr. Vernier wrote: "It is the passion for mathematics that dominates him. I think it would be better if his parents allowed him to study this exclusively. He's wasting his time here doing nothing, tormenting his teachers and destroying himself with functions."

Galois was fiercely independent and rebellious, educated to think according to logic.

Lessons from this story:

- Reading can ignite passions. Books resonate with one's love and mission (studying, courses, examples). It's a process of rediscovery, absorbing, and emerging. This advice is valuable at any age.
- One teacher can change a life at any stage.
- Logic, a central object of philosophy, enhances reasoning faculties for calculations. A logical approach is a valuable strategy in the Italian high school system, which we should strive to maintain.
- Starting with a humanistic education provides sharper tools for interpreting texts and books, which can foster a passion for science and enhance the ability to understand complex content. Once again, the Italian school system excels here.

10 Level Analysis Scheme

Level	Estimated value	Value Invested	Result
Areas	Peso Medio di vita	Peso Reale	
a) Being	30,00%	40%	
1. Spiritual	10	15	He was looking for esteem
2. Cognitive	10	20	Expert in mathematical analysis
3. Emotional	10	5	Unaffectionate
b) Having	30,00%	35%	
4. Physiologic	10	5	Indifferent
5. Financial	10	5	Poor
6. Logistic	10	25	His research into methods is strong
c) Doing	40,00%	30%	
7. Relational	10	20	Friends of ideals
8. Environmental	10	0	Interested
9. Behavioral	10	0	Improvident
10. Social Proof	10	10	He was in jail and killed by society
Total	100%	100%	

Analysis of his short life

Level 1 - Spiritual

Évariste Galois was deeply motivated to emerge and have his identity recognized. He was fully aware of his mission and driven to make it official, though his life was tragically cut short. Politically, he followed his father's path with considerable success and influence, which ultimately led to his demise.

Level 2 - Cognitive

He became aware of his creative, logical, and sequential reasoning abilities at an early age, applying them with brilliance to mathematics. Galois was a misunderstood genius, particularly excelling in generalization, introducing the concept of "group theory" to solve equations beyond the fourth degree. His key discovery was realizing that after millennia, a concise solution could be achieved: "...as deep as it is delightful is such a problem. Given an irreducible first-degree equation, to decide whether it can be solved through radicals."

Level 3 - Emotional

Galois was not particularly sensitive to emotions. The only attempt at a romantic relationship ended tragically when he fell into the trap of a woman hired by the political police who ultimately killed him.

Level 4 - Physiological

Galois was in excellent health—small and slim but robust.

Level 5 - Financial

He did not concern himself with financial matters, as he was supported by his wealthy family. After his father's death, he briefly attempted a teaching career, but was unsuccessful.

Level 6 - Logistical

Galois was highly active in this area. He read, discussed, studied, and sought methods and solutions like any respected scientist.

Level 7 - Relational

He was a good political motivator, a patriot loved by people, witty, and cheerful. His beliefs were shaped by his father's teachings, which he upheld with passion.

Level 8 - Environmental

Ideologically, Galois was concerned with the well-being of the land—its soil—and was against the power of the clergy, aristocracy, and rising bourgeoisie. He was critical of exploitation through theoretical assertions.

Level 10 - Social Approval

He was not favored by the Restorative Power, nor by the Church, ultimately leading to his suppression. Though described as courageous, he was not; he often drank to gain courage. His rebellious attitudes as a youth—towards teachers and institutions—led to his exclusion from the Polytechnique and later from the École Normale. Yet, he managed relationships, even with those who opposed him.

Some admired and appreciated his ideas, though they were often misunderstood due to his lack of clear expression. More time might have given him greater clarity and acceptance.

Example Twenty-Nine: A Young Man Who Knows How to Calculate – Adam Horwitz

Previously, young people could become stars in cinema, music, or other traditional fields, often relying on physical appearance, family wealth, or the support of talent scouts. Today, those barriers have diminished. If you have the drive to work hard, pursue your goals persistently, treat it like a game, and never give up, success is achievable. Adam's motto is, "Today, now, anything is possible. Start acting and never give up." Adam is well-qualified to give this advice, having failed 30 times but succeeded once, becoming a millionaire at the age of 18. He achieved his dream three years ahead of his own calculations.

Adam created an online course, **Mobile Monopoly**, to teach people how to make money using the secrets of mobile marketing. He has since developed and improved another application, **Yep Text**, a promotional messaging service using geolocation to send targeted messages to people nearby a store.

Adam works and enjoys life just like any other young person his age. "The journey is the most exciting part," he says. Now, he focuses on growing further, calculating new strategies and initiatives to expand his business and revenue. Adam aims to develop high-value services that remain accessible to everyone, generating both financial gain and a social impact through his products.

6 MEMORY

LEVEL 2 COGNITIVE

We are our memory, we are this chimerical museum of inconstant forms, this pile of broken mirrors. (Jorge Luis Borges)

Memory

Definitions	Goal	Aptitudes, Skills, Capacities, Competencies	Maximum Excellence	Minimum
Memory	Archive Remember	Verbal fluency and connections	Pico della Mirandola	Empty confusion

1 Definition and purpose of memory

We use the same word "memory" for 3 different meanings:

- the content, the information stored
- the function, the activity of the memorization action
- the place, the position where the information archive is located.

It is therefore good to ask ourselves the question each time which of the three we are talking about.

To understand the importance of memory, it is sufficient to read the maxims dedicated to it. They are many and enlightening in all eras.

Memory is the treasure and guardian of all things. – Cicero
To lose the past is to lose the future. – Wang Shu

As we can see, memory acts like a purse, suitcase, chest, or wardrobe of our information—our past, our identity, our history. It's a powerful energy-saving mechanism: when ideas or instructions are no longer needed, we store them for future use. Memory plays a crucial role in forming habits that help humans and all living beings adapt to their environment and lead a lighter life. Therefore, it holds great importance for children. We must keep it fresh, organized, and functioning at its peak.

Memory serves two primary functions:

- **Cataloguing** and **storing** information according to personal criteria.
- **Retrieving** these stored memories when needed.

Science has made remarkable advancements in this area—just think of computers. In this context, it's essential to emphasize the importance of maintaining memory efficiency into late adulthood. Unfortunately, we are becoming accustomed to a superficial use of cognitive memory, while we are overwhelmed by emotional and subliminal memory usage. We clutter our memory archives with information from outside our conscious awareness—messages from the environment and excessive promotional media. During sleep, the brain reorganizes these memories, but it doesn't erase them, making our archives heavier. We often neglect the existence of physiological memory. However, every cell has its own memory—historical, genetic, and epigenomic, as well as memories formed throughout life. The same goes for organs and muscles.

LET'S REMEMBER

The sixth step to success is a well-functioning memory

Immediate action, recovery

If you have a memory lapse, it may depend on the perception of a continuous low pain that you have, or from a psychological shock that can temporarily reset the ability to remember. Try to understand what moment you are in. We have discovered that memory is chronosensitive. You do not have the same rate in the twenty-four hours of the day. Everyone must understand their rhythm and use it to their advantage. This discovery is important for kids who study. It is good to eat little and often, because the brain needs sugar, you have to give it every 2 or 3 hours according to the Chrono Map.

Example thirty: the story of Mario, 44 years old and the accident

Mario had a motorcycle accident at eighteen. Then life went on. One morning in August, he felt pain all over his body, especially on the skin that he couldn't even touch.

He called doctors, went to the hospital. Cortisone and antibiotics got him back on his feet. As soon as he stopped them, the pain prevented him from working.

The skin is a huge deposit of information, its surface is about 2 square meters. How do we treat this deposit? Every trauma to the skin, burns, wounds are deposited on it and no one bothers to clean them. Since (except for accidents as adults) we fall and hurt ourselves more when we are young, the skin's memory becomes clogged. Mario partially resolved the situation by cleaning it. Cleaning it with the right methods means freeing up a lot of energy and recovering a lot of mental and functional health.

Example thirty-one: the story of Angelo, 17 years old, and the ritual of purging

Another large repository of memory is the intestine. Its mucosa has a surface area of 300 square meters, the largest in the body.

Angelo was always nervous, to the point of rudeness. Every negative episode installed him in the intestine. Chronic constipation worsened with every exam. The purge had become a ritual.

The person who suffers from constipation, due to the enteric brain, is an impatient, aggressive person. The intestinal blockage acts on the sense of time, of space, on his central memory. He will tend to record more and more negative emotional information. A real self-sabotage.

The probable causes of the effects of this link (blocked digestion, disturbed memory of the cells and intestinal flora, sensory disruption) are due to incorrect behaviors. Below is a list.

By cleaning the memory, the ritual of purging that blocked Angelo at home disappeared.

Even in the lung, memory is installed in about 80 square meters. And then in the fat deposited everywhere.

Let's repeat every muscle, every organ has its memory. With quantum medicine, cellular memory takes on a much more important role.

(We will return to this in detail when we deal with physiological level 4 in the second book).

For example, if the intestine is in disorder, its memory does not work well.

The consequences are threefold:

- **difficulty in memorizing correctly**
- **a reduction in the speed of learning**
- **an automatic increase in nervousness, aggressiveness, and conflict**

Causes of vegetative and digestive dysfunctions that impact memory
the excessive use of astringent foods FOOD
alternating purges, which disrupt memory timing, alter the circadian cycle FOOD
electromagnetic interference ENVIRONMENT
food pollution FOOD and water
stress conflict of thoughts PSYCHE
degenerative diseases BODY
abuse of narcotics or tranquilizers FOOD
too cold ENVIRONMENT
prolonged fasting FOOD

We can prevent our children from falling into this trap with proper nutrition and emotional release.

2-MNEMONIC SKILLS and attitudes

*God gave us memory, so we can have roses even
in December. (James Matthew Barrie)*

6 MEMORY Steps of "know-how"	Signals	Benefits
Attitude	Remembering homework, asking to keep promises, touchiness, aggression, restlessness (emotional memory)	Educated brain as archive and secretary
Ability	Order, data organization, procedure schematization	Competitive strength Retrieving the right information at the right time
Capacity	Fast memorization, content growth, excellent time management, excellent management of sensory memories	Omnivorous knowledge, ease in studying. Seduction by propriety of language
Competence	Breadth of speeches, ease of addressing many topics at the same time. Point of reference for the forgetful or lazy	Intercultural and political mediation, SUCCESS AS MENTOR GUIDES capable of managing universal messages

*Memory has five doors of entry: the five senses; and only
one exit: the imagination. (Malcolm de Chazal)*

Memory skills are natural gifts. They can be developed into skills with education. In fact, we have included mnemonic techniques in the programs of the new pedagogy. (See below)

Memory abilities that handle information are functions of two types:

- from the outside, they make us acquire the data that we will memorize from experience and the environment
- from the inside, they make us recall the memories already archived to consciousness

The former require reading speed, the speed of association between data, in addition to static and dynamic storage

The latter have the advantage of providing Verbal Fluency and a quick communication of the remembered phenomena.

The benefits: good skills make us generate faster and more effective decisions.

Memory is an inner wealth of our Being that can be used to our advantage. It is not synonymous with intelligence, but it makes the jobs we do easier.

There are several methods (not yet in public schools) to enhance these skills, such as speed reading, fast memorization, audiovisual maps, multi-sensory maps that avoid sensory deprivation, proprioceptive tables.

3-MAXIMUM MEMORY SITUATION Excellence

(The benefits you get if... The situation of pleasure to go towards)

"Where interest fails, memory also fails." (Goethe)

The most desirable results, excellence, are:

- in the area of recording, to become like many painters who capture the smallest detail of every sensory, visual, auditory, lexical signal.
- in the area of memory to be like Pico della Mirandola!

The ultimate performance is having control, dynamic management of short-term and long-term memories. The ability to recall memories perfectly, no matter how much time has passed.

To transform an inattentive and forgetful person into one with an excellent memory there are several steps:

Coaching Phases to Transform an Inattentive Person into a Person with an Excellent Memory	
(As an Organized Archive of Memories and as a Management of Logos and Sensorimotor Information)	
Steps	Some mini strategies that cultivate ambitions, attitudes, actions
A Attitude	The first step is to give a peaceful life to our children and ourselves. Memory is sensitive to every change in state. It is the most active and long-lived function because it lasts as long as life itself and always works even when we sleep and put our senses to rest.
B Ability	Exercise attention, degrees, intensity and its directionality. Nourishing the body well, enriching the environment with oxygen and light facilitates memorization. This allows to order the activity of memory and the subsequent retrieval of information.
C Capacity	Mastering memorization methods helps you study better and learn faster. Memory is sensitive to time, heat, humidity, and changes in the 18 sensory pathways. Full memory capacity is achieved only by controlling your chronogram.
D Competence	Becoming an expert in memory means having a vast knowledge of technologies, tools, diets, psychology, as emotions remove and change reality. Expertise requires continuous observation to ensure objectivity and truth. Then judgments will be richer.
E Excellence	Transforming ourselves into a Pico della Mirandola can be an excellent profession as a creator, consultant, stylist and teacher.
F Accelerating techniques of the "flow"	Psycho-physiological accelerators make memories enter the "flow" of emotions, clearing them and giving us clearer visions of the world.

An efficient educational solution is to learn to use multisensory mental, historical and geographical maps. They connect the quantity of data with their immediate understanding, with a time gain in learning of up to 60%! Very useful in studying and planning work.

How useful are they for children? Learning, understanding and remembering at the same time!

We all need memory. To fix memories well, in addition to having the body in order, in a suitable and favorable environment, it is necessary to involve emotional interest. We have discovered that it totally changes the speed of learning.

Example thirty-two: Eugenia's story and falling in love

Eugenia was in England to study English with the Erasmus program.
To our great surprise, she returned to Italy after six months speaking fluent Dutch.
What had happened? She had met love and he was Dutch.
To make herself understood well, the English that they were both still studying was not enough for her!
An astonishing result, because Dutch is very difficult for a Latin speaker.

The lesson is: stimulate the senses and learn with the heart.

4 MINIMUM MEMORY SITUATION

(*THE PRICE YOU PAY IF YOU DON'T. THE PAINFUL SITUATION YOU ESCAPE FROM*)

The minimum is reached when memory deprivation is total! It is caused by accidents or blows to the head that can produce amnesia.
Excluding functional diseases, memory lapse also occurs in conditions of continuous stress.
Anyone who has experienced it knows the effort it takes to remember a fact and not succeed! We should never get to that point.

**Example thirty-three: the story of Sara,
23 years old and temporary amnesia**

Sara was in Paris for a meeting. Curious and in love with the city, she decided to take the metro and go to Montmartre. She had been told that artists stopped at night to paint in front of the Sacré-Coeur on the stairs.

When she arrived, the area was quite deserted. She started talking to two boys and invited them to have a drink. She didn't get there, they robbed her, kicked her down, not even very hard. Some foreign tourists saved her and took her to the emergency room.

The French police did everything they could to make her remember faces; even today she has a total blank. She refuses to remember.

She also had a hypnosis session, with no results. We are waiting. She tells us about her nightmares and we are freeing her.

5 MEMORY RESILIENCE

> *Memory is not what we remember, but what reminds us. Memory
> is a present that never stops passing. (Octavio Paz)*

Memory resilience is an energy-saving and pain-repairing mechanism. Memory has a hectic life: it is never stable. Every night, during sleep, the brain updates the mnemonic state: it reshapes the present by connecting it to the past and leaves out the less important or too painful things. Memory resilience is a tendency to shape the result of the reshuffling with the imagined future. It is the hidden force that consolidates cognitive capacity.

Memory resilience is a capacity that helps protect us from repeating the same mistakes and from reliving pain with less intensity. Remembering and forgetting are two sides of the same coin, and resilience manages this process. High resilience keeps painful memories at bay, while low resilience tends to recall older, more painful experiences, compounding the pain.

The signs indicating poor memory resilience include:

- Distraction during routine tasks (dangerous)
- Forgetting important commitments (leading to punishment and disputes)
- Inability to sequence information over time
- Tendency to respond hastily, particularly to unnecessary disputes
- Sending out messages of fear or danger unconsciously
- Inaccurate speech

The primary causes are psychological, physiological, chemical, and traumatic:

- **Physiological**: Hormonal imbalances and aging
- **Psychological**: Abuse and poor emotional control
- **Chemical**: Pollution and poor nutrition
- **Traumatic**: Interpersonal rejection, lack of dialogue with parents, intellectual delays, attention deficits, burns, falls

RECOVERY

How do we recover memory resilience?

"We are the memory we have and the responsibility we assume. Without memory, we do not exist, and perhaps without responsibility, we do not deserve to exist." (José Saramago)

This concept emphasizes responsibility, which works well for disciplined, shy individuals with a strong sense of duty. However, such rigidity can hinder resilience.

"The world screams and digs its claws into our hearts. This is what we call memory." (Tim O'Brien)

This emphasizes emotional influence on memory resilience. Too many heavy memories slow down the recovery of resilience, especially in the elderly.

Good memory resilience enhances life quality—it makes us calmer, clearer, and more efficient. When emotional memory dominates, mental memory suffers. In our research, we have yet to fully understand why negative memories tend to be more efficient than positive ones.

Trauma, loss, and pain burden emotional memory, impairing mental functions temporarily, reducing focus and self-control. Low memory resilience is linked to decreased attention, which can lead to physical harm, such as accidents. Alcohol and drugs further impair memory resilience, causing hallucinations and nightmares.

Memory resilience also involves the ability to forget quickly— helpful, particularly for children. However, there's a limit: isolating and discarding negative memories too swiftly can disrupt memory organization. To effectively erase deeply negative memories, repetition over time is necessary.

Indeed, if this release occurred instantaneously, the rebound effect would create a tsunami—an enormous burst of energy in a very short period, disrupting connections and leaving the person disoriented because memory influences our frame of reference. If these anchors break, negative perceptions further distort memories.

Children's mental "clean-up" should be done every evening.

EXAMPLE THIRTY-FOUR: THE STORY OF MAURA N., 20, AND LIES

At the age of twenty, Maura began experiencing anorexia, alternating with bulimia.

Reputable psychotherapists couldn't resolve her case. Eventually, she was treated with psychiatric medications that further disrupted her already fragile memory balance. Medical protocols were followed as part of the standard response to her escalating violent reactions.

The grave disadvantage was that Maura's mind confused the reality of life with her imagination. In a session with a specialist, she falsely accused her father of abuse—something that was completely untrue! The rapid triggering of emotions (unexpected) caused chaos in an otherwise loving family. Only three years later was the truth revealed.

This distorted memory stemmed from Maura's unconscious perception that as the firstborn, her father had withheld attention and affection due to the arrival of her sister.

She is now well, but the father, unfortunately, still carries the scars of that false accusation.

We must ask: How reliable is a testimony under emotional duress?

"The memory can change the shape of a room, the color of a car. Memories can be distorted; they are an interpretation of reality, not reality itself; they are irrelevant to the facts." (From the movie **Memento**).

WHAT HAPPENS IN CHILDREN?

Memory formation is much faster in children than in adults. Their experiences require fewer connections to be made.

Memory is tied to the senses, and children's senses are more acute and newly functioning. A rule for storing memories in children is:

To combat disobedience, it's best to repeat instructions three times because children are less drawn to words and more to things—things that we tend to overlook. Their resilience may be lower early in the morning when they are hungry or dealing with other physiological needs.

Avoid giving too many commands in these situations. It's better to delay, respecting the chronological order.

6. TIPS, RESULTS, AND STRATEGIES ON MEMORY

Memory, when used as a personal archive, becomes a zone of comfort. It doesn't require effort; it's merely copied and, at best, reconfigured. People functioning in a "normal" memory state benefit in two ways:

- **Energy Savings**
- **A Filing Cabinet Full of Ready-to-Use Behavioral Patterns**

What happens if the stored behavior becomes outdated or even harmful? Errors are repeated without conscious awareness. Memory becomes a disservice to us.

This is often the case with discouraged individuals or NEETs (Not in Education, Employment, or Training). They lack the motivation or energy to change, and change feels overwhelming.

It's necessary to bring consciousness to the present, engage in a programmed remembering of past positive experiences to increase resilience. Success is often signaled by their first smile.

Then, use reverie—daydreaming or self-reflection—rather than hypnotic tactics to rebuild efficient connections (anchors, hooks, etc.) with them, because NEETs typically won't take the initiative on their own.

It's important to remember that memory:

- **Is light-sensitive**
- **Declines with pollution or poor oxygenation**
- **Slows down during digestion**
- **Strengthens when connected to positive emotions and previously stored objects**

Avoid heavy studying during menstruation, as recall becomes more difficult. Overeating also hampers memory retention.

During exams, avoid overexertion. When children compete in events, their memory of past competitions should be reorganized positively. Since they perform movements automatically, their memory needs to support the "flow" state for optimal performance.

SOME STEPS TO MANAGE MEMORY
Protocol "Quickly forget negative emotions"

"The future at every moment presses the present to be a memory". (Louis Aragon)

"Looking back is a bit like renewing your eyes, healing them. Making them more adequate to their primary function, which is to look forward". (Margaret Fairless Barber)
"The great function of memory is to forget so as not to suffer".

How long (days/months/weeks/years) do you remember having suffered:

- an insult _____
- a humiliation _____
- a treatment in which you were ridiculed _____
- an injustice _____
- a rip-off _____
- a lie _____

How long do you ruminate on having committed:

- a mistake _____
- a minor loss _____
- a misunderstanding _____

If the times are disproportionate to the weight of the emotion - lasting weeks - then we intervene.

Weaken the messages of the experiences and related memories, weaken the resistances. What is blocking us?

- Do not accept the idea of having made a mistake.
- Basking in the spotlight
- Not wanting to change
- Procrastinating out of laziness
- Fearing the consequences

Procedure

- Doing Transcendental Meditation
- The FORGIVENESS technique. Benefits: you gain energy
- The desensitization approach. Benefits: you have more calm and patience
- Reactivate the old sensation in the present, painful. Be careful to do it gently.

Think that it is not current, you no longer need it, that it is wrong and must be changed. Go through it, imagine the cause and then throw it out the window. Try many times.

As soon as you succeed, you notice it, because in addition to feeling freer, you have a change in your state of well-being. A different perception of the Self, you feel lighter.

The unconscious opposes changes, that's why you need calm and repetition.

You can enhance your mnemonic activity through puzzles, mathematical exercises, with calculations.

Memory is also revived with emotional stories from literature, cinema, theater, classical music

If your small child shows irrational fears or cries too much when he falls, proceed with this method.

Give him a single name and write them on a sheet of paper. Make them forgive you, then throw the sheets in the toilet and have the toilet flush. They go away.

6 MEMORY

LEVEL 2 COGNITIVE

Questionnaire to find inspiration on your child's memory activity

Sample you need to:

a) increase your memory skills
b) sign a contract/commitment (even with an invisible coach) for managing experiences

a) Capital already acquired, riches that come from roots, origins, relationships, epigenetics, positive experiences to copy and negative experiences to modify.

How do we know that his working and long-term memory is a trained and reliable tool for him? Write down the best skills to enhance memory, transform it into skills and then into excellence. Remember that memory is a cognitive function that starts from an infinite potential and decreases with age. List at least 3 advantages to enhance it as soon as possible.

1 _____

2 _____

3 _____

MEMORY Basics. Write or have written down his best aptitudes, abilities, tendencies, character, skills, attitudes that make him easily remembered. Look for effective exercises. Take care of the diet that has an influence on it.

1 _____

2 _____

3 _____

MEMORY Technique to copy a success. Write how he feels when he remembers events well. Have him reproduce the same conditions, considering that children add fantasy and color the situations. They are not lies. Exercise their memory in studies.

1 _____

2 _____

3 _____

MEMORY Technique to change a failure, such as the loss of memories.

What obstacles have you overcome? Describe the elements that disoriented you, weakened you, how you felt. Important, traumas must be forgotten. Help your child overcome those moments, transforming them into lessons, try the mental cleansing method every now and then, separating the facts from the emotions and explain it. He will not be afraid of it.

1 _____

2 _____

3 _____

b) Reinforcement training and training needs. It is a process

Help your child manage memories. Make a plan with exercises together. Write down where he is today, from where you want to continue. How can you better exercise his memory? Don't set a bad example. Are alcohol and smoking, excess weight, insomnia eliminated? Start from here.

What can you improve to transform him into a person with excellent memory retention?

1 _____

2 _____

3 _____

Have him compare himself with his peers and write down his next actions for fun with memory games (to be recorded in his diary)

1 _____

2 _____

3 _____

For Continuous Training, check the market for new techniques for fast memorization. What are the sources that can support it? Who can help? Books, courses, mother, grandparents, uncles, coaches, peers, friends, family collaborators.

Check the skills and any training needs to enhance your memorization and your archive. (Help, buddying)

What are the sources that can support you? Who can help you? Books, courses, exercises, mother, grandparents, uncles, coaches, peers, friends, family collaborators.

1 _____

2 _____

3 _____

c) Objectives.

What do you want to improve in his memory? Do you want to use advanced techniques to have high mnemonic performance?

Write 3 aspects to improve in his memory, the related advantages and benefits that you get for yourself and for others.

1 _____

2 _____

3 _____

Witness to progress. Write who measures your transformation with you

1 _____

2 _____

3 _____

Imagine and make him imagine his goal as achieved and satisfactory.

1 _____

2 _____

3 _____

d) Results. Control of Results Objective Reached with confirmation of the witness.

Objective achieved on ....from ....
Congratulate and reward yourself at each step.

Update the card with the date, signature of buddy, tutor, mentor, coach

Place, date and signatures

1 _____

2 _____

3 _____

7 - WHO HAS HAD SUCCESS WITH MEMORY

THE MEMORY CHAMPIONS AND THE MAPS (FROM WEB SOURCE)

Example thirty-five: the memory champions

Matteo Di Cianni from Mondovì (Cuneo) is 28 years old, he is a worker in a meat company. He is the new "king of memory".

He holds 4 Italian records. He can memorize an exact sequence of 55 numbers, one per second, in a step of 100 seconds and not only that, he is able to memorize the sequence of 360 binary numbers out of 1,200 in 5 minutes.

Matteo Salvo, holder of the International Master of Memory London 2013 Guinness World Record.

Lessons and their seeds of wisdom

"I don't have a memory superior to anyone else, we are 'memory athletes' and as with any sport it is necessary to train; three months before the championship, I train for half an hour a day, simulating the tests with numbers and cards".

He has a winning secret: "I have 1,000 pre-set images that I position according to my precise method that I then associate with the numbers to remember".

"You are not born with extraordinary intellectual gifts, the mind must be trained with discipline and passion".

The Memory Man invented "The effective study method, which will make the return to school a pleasant "gym for the mind":

From his courses, books of techniques to "store any type of information and fix it in our memory".

Here is an excerpt:

1. Always have an active posture and attitude: tidy workstation and the right lighting
2. Study to explain and not (just) to learn: film yourself with your cell phone while you speak.
3. Organize and draw key concepts with mind maps: Mind Maps are creative, colorful drawings that translate concepts into images. "They are tree-like structures, drawn using the same logic that the brain uses to function, which makes visual associations and logical leaps, and that is why they facilitate learning."
4. Fearless English with the "Ciceronian loci" technique, which consists of matching the concepts of your speech to familiar places. photos, drawings.
5. Multiplication tables always ... at hand. How to use your fingers to calculate tens and units and obtain multiplications.

LET'S REMEMBER

We have taken and copied the words of these two champions of memory to conclude that the important educational tactics are:

1. To learn and study we need memory. We can develop it like a muscle, by training it.
2. Positive emotion is a memory accelerator. I will change the way we study subjects by inserting love, curiosity, passion.
3. I will use the different maps to memorize the facts in an organized and coherent way.

That memory does not replace the mind, it serves the mind to have more notions. The kids study to understand and know how to redo the processes, acquire a know-how thanks to the memory that helps the two cognitive abilities, speculative and calculation.

We learn that to have a healthy memory we must take care of the body and the senses.

Attention the cognitive level is completed. Attach this module, reconnecting it to the other two, thinking and calculating. You will have the entire map, the answers of the cognitive level in its 3 elements.

COGNITIVE LEVEL 2 SUMMARY

Let's summarize all the advantages of level 2 COGNITIVE
Now you know who you are, what you want, your goals, how to create, reason, calculate, remember: you know how your mind works. You will also need to know how your heart beats and we will see this in the next level 3 – emotional.
I believe in my mind, its qualities _____ _____ My thought creates judges chooses efficiently. Ex. list your successes
My calculation system works well. Ex. list your successes _____ _____
My memory helps me. Ex. list your successes _____ _____
I can excel in _____ I lack training in _____ _____
The 3 cognitive objectives are. _____ _____ 1 _____ 2 _____ 3 _____
Ex. Actions to take. How will you use your mind? How long will it take to improve your skills? Record your thoughts in your journal to share with your peer, coach, or your child. Always remember to write succinctly with a maximum of 9 words.

THEME	STRATEGIES	RESULTS
THOUGHT COMPUTATION MEMORY ACTIONS Within the		

SUMMARY OF COGNITIVE STRATEGIES 4,5,6

Strategy number 4- Wake up your creative and rational thinking

Strategy number 5- Train yourself to calculate, love mathematics

Strategy number 6- Train your memory

The 3 educational tactics in summary

1. Wake up your creative and rational thinking. We are thinking beings. We have a mind that creates solutions and tends to improve the human condition. Let's train our children to be excellent at managing thoughts.

   The richness of ideas, their novelty can make the difference. Let's give our children a lively, cheerful, stimulating environment.

2. To train yourself in calculation, love mathematics and make your children love it. The future world will increasingly have a scientific and therefore mathematical approach. Invent and buy games that stimulate this style.

3. To complete a good cognitive training, exercise and improve your memory. It is a function that can get you out of trouble in many situations. Every now and then remember to do maintenance, the service. Also remember to raise the care of your body and your senses, the soil in which memory is cultivated.

End of Level 2 Cognitive

COACHING THAT IMPROVES
THE COGNITIVE LEVEL

1. CONCEPT MAPS FOR ORGANIZING THOUGHT

Organizing cognitive activity from a young age creates a mindset that lasts a lifetime. A cognitive "imprinting" allows children to reason in different ways, all of which are valid.

- When creating, they use chaos;
- When studying, judging, comparing, they use logical sequences of elements.

Let's remember that the foundation of every analysis is the structure of logical analysis.

To accelerate learning, **mind maps** fix correlations between elements visually on a single diagram, facilitating memory retention.

To reach these structured conceptualizations (which become comprehensible around age 7), we can use mini-strategies that train the child's mind to be orderly.

- Have the child tell their stories, helping them summarize and provide feedback with appreciation.
- Communicate that we understand their expression and message.

The map's structure and colors can be used in two ways:

a) **Creative**, to express imagination;
b) **Geometric**, to draw sequences.

Before about age 6, an effective mapping exercise involves dividing a page into squares to visually represent the sequential parts of a story, like in a filmstrip. Children can draw seasons, months, homes, families, animals, etc., helping them tell coherent stories.

In elementary school, we can begin applying this technique. Benefits include:

- Studying with methodical organization;
- Synthesizing information;
- Speeding up memory retention;
- Recording material for review;
- Ensuring key points are firmly fixed;
- Assigning proper value to parts that compose the overall story and their relative scale.

This structure promotes logical connections and geometric shapes, creating a habit that will serve them well in adulthood when explaining concepts quickly.

2. TECHNIQUES FOR SPEED READING AND FAST MEMORY RETENTION

Speed reading is a useful tool for efficiently consuming information. On one hand, it's effective; on the other, we must teach a love for **content**, not superficiality. Today, videos satisfy many of these needs for fast consumption.

We can introduce speed reading techniques in elementary school, building on the fact that traditional reading is taught in whole words rather than individual letters.

The next step involves reading **groups of words** or **phrases** rather than sentences.

Basic NLP (Neuro-Linguistic Programming):

The part of NLP that restructures, forms, and modifies beliefs will be addressed in more detail in upcoming works.

Part Five
The Emotional Level

Strategy #7- Educate the 18 sensory pathways

Strategy #8- Control feelings

Strategy #9- Obey the warning signals

LEVEL 3 EMOTIONAL

"Feelings weighing you down? Eliminate stress and you will feel light." Albina Gabellini

EMOTIONS

Definitions	Goal	Attitudes Skills Capabilities Skills	Maximum Excellency	Minimum
Sensations	Sensory Channels Open Communication	Sensitivity	Extra Faculty ESP	Lack of sensitivity
Feelings	Understanding affections love Expressing Feelings	Emotional Intelligence	Affective union	Stress Aridity alexithimia
Alert Defense against threats Survival Defense against threats Survival	Defense against threats Survival	Conflict Management	Empathy	Empty Lack of signals

THE EMOTIONS

"Your vision will become clearer only when you look into your heart. He who looks outward dreams. He who looks inward awakens." C. G. Jung

FUNCTIONS AND ANATOMY

Emotions are an expression of the dialogue between the **unconscious** and the **conscious** mind.

They occur when the three brains perceive sensations, receiving nerve inputs sent from sensors distributed throughout the body and processing them.

Cannon-Bard defines the emotional process as "the processing of stimuli by the subcortical centers of the brain (amygdala and posterior nuclei of the thalamus), triggering a neuroendocrine reaction to alert the body."

However, this definition is partial, as it refers to the second part of the process—after the signal reaches the brain and is processed. (The first phase involves the transmission of sensations from the body to the brain).

"In this second phase, emotions trigger various somatic changes such as:
- changes in heart rate
- increased or decreased sweating
- increased or slowed breathing rate
- increased or relaxed muscle tension"

These changes can be measured by electronic equipment, such as **biofeedback devices**. However, this device processes physiological manifestations, not emotions.

In this unconscious process, emotions hold more influence than any other neurological activity of which we are aware, even more than thought itself. They take precedence.

Our **three brains** (see note below) are responsible for more complex functions than emotions, including abstract thought, speculation, creativity, and calculation.

They communicate with each other neurologically and also manage emotions.

When the senses are overstimulated and send conflicting inputs to the brains, what happens? They experience **temporary "tilt"**.

The central brain compares the distorted information received with our memory (hippocampus) and tries to repair the mismatch, adjusting the sensation consciously.

If it fails—if it cannot pair the distorted sensation with the stored images from memory—it sends urgent alarm signals to the other two brains.

We do not easily decode this chatter at a conscious level, and we react with confusion, fear, tremors, sweating, and changes in voice. These effects are physiological and occur before emotions fully manifest.

NERVOUS SYSTEMS

a. Central Nervous System – Brain
b. Peripheral Autonomic System – Organs, Abdomen, Limbs
c. Enteric System – Intestine

THE EMOTIONAL WORLD

It concerns everything related to "feeling," perceptions, the Heart, the space that brings us joy, makes us happy, but sometimes also causes suffering.

If you've gone through a difficult and exhausting period, you know these emotions well – they can be uncomfortable companions. Each of us has experienced feelings of defeat, sadness, fear, and pessimism. By understanding the paths, we can also journey in the opposite direction. Not to eliminate them, but to manage them. Helping people in this reflective process is the role of psychologists, psychiatrists, and doctors.

If the signals are simple, using meditation techniques can help reduce suffering and stress. Therefore, after listening to their sorrows, we can comfort ourselves, as we can help them manage these emotions.

We will nullify their power over us.

The purpose of life is happiness, yet we often practice the sport of lamentation, which evokes negative emotions. Stay away from those who spread these "contagions." There should be no space for them—they are like glue, attaching to everything and everyone, causing sadness and lowering morale like poison.

If we want to recount negative events for educational or cautionary purposes, we can do so. While describing a negative event, involving morbid curiosity, we should already speak of its positive resolution, de-dramatizing it.

Emotional intelligence is the recognition of various perceived feelings: anger, fear, joy, tenderness, which the body unfortunately internalizes in the present.

Be mindful of the evocative words we use!

Emotional narratives are the most effective means of persuasion and seduction.

There are experts in storytelling—poets, writers, artists, screenwriters—who evoke emotions for cathartic purposes.

Words can make us happy or push us into despair. Through words, we can evoke feelings and alter behaviors.

"Aspects of things change according to emotions; magic and beauty are in us." – Khalil Gibran

The Emotional Area is where most NEETs (Not in Employment, Education, or Training) emerge. They memorize their sufferings without resolving them, caused by:

- disputes
- offenses
- humiliations
- accidents
- conflicts
- disappointments
- illnesses
- deficits

If the family is absent and the school remains insensitive to their state, they become demotivated and seek escape, interrupting whatever they are doing.

They feel like unjustly ignored "ghosts." Sometimes, as compensation, when they feel misunderstood by their families, they fall into dangerous hands—friends, drugs. A nightmare.

A human potential that could be salvaged if schools had a listening center focused on cognitive psychology.

And you, father, where are you? It seems you are too absent during adolescence.

So, if you don't take action and don't help your wife, you can stop here.

It would be like a dialogue between the deaf. In fact, the book is a strong call to responsibility to prevent the creation of more NEETs.

There are solutions, and they are diverse:

- Social recovery
- Alternative schools

- Travel
- Sports
- Psychological support
- Volunteering. In Italy, there are five million volunteers.
- Health care
- Support for school reintegration

For some measures, the family can start on its own, while others require support.

It's important to act quickly and create a recovery plan, at least annually.

In any case, the first step is to recognize the gaps or the lack of paternal attention, apologize, and initiate a dialogue with agreements on new rules.

It's a reciprocal commitment, just like in coaching.

Consider that it requires your time—you cannot delegate—and your willingness to engage in discussions, at least on an emotional level.

Emotions have 3 sub-levels:

- Sensations are perceptions of stimuli coming from both the external and internal parts of the body. They are neurophysiological connections; a chill, a shiver, are sensations.
- Feelings are the complete expression of stimuli that the person has recognized, evaluated, and assigned a value to. Love, happiness, gratitude, and fear are feelings.
- Alertness is a physiological state that requires "special attention" to signals that are urgent, important, or dangerous. It activates when signals are perceived as threatening to survival. It is an unconscious emotional mechanism of protection, to be activated rarely as it consumes a lot of energy and easily exhausts the body. It's like driving with the brakes pressed.

STRATEGY #7 - EDUCATE THE 18 SENSES

"Some people don't do well simply because they don't feel well." Jim Rohn

18 Sensory Paths

The sensations, the senses

Definitions	Goal	Attitudes Skills Capabilities Skills	Massimo Excellencies	Minimum
Sensations	Sensory Channel Communication	Sensitivity in the 18 paths	Extra Faculty Exp Mastery Dexterity Expertise (Lvl 6)	Lack of sensitivity

"The world is a synthesis of our sensations, our perceptions and our memories. It is convenient to think that it exists objectively, in itself. But its mere existence would not be enough, however, to explain the fact that it appears to us." Erwin Schrödinger

Sensations in this context we consider only as movements of signals along physical sensory pathways, therefore from the button where they are received, the receptor, to the recognition center, the brain (one of the three).

Follow these steps carefully, because perhaps you will find several explanations of your past sufferings and, by analogy, you will be able to help resolve those of your child. For a more detailed discussion go to the link of the 18 senses on info@gsm-online.it

In short, we have 18 sensory pathways, not 5 as we are used to believing. Only if they are functional, they give us security and efficiency in the way we think and relate.

LET'S REMEMBER

The seventh step of success is the functionality of the senses

Immediate action, recovery

Interruption of sensory pathways. If these are partially obstructed, the signals you receive change, they can even be interrupted and the result is that you receive incorrect or partial information, which causes damage. They propagate from the emotional level to the cognitive system. They become blocks that undermine your certainty and the truth of your final judgments. There is no longer a balanced dialogue between the conscious and the unconscious. Your emotional faculties make your intellectual and physiological faculties suffer. The consequences are that you will act on your behaviors in a disharmonious way and the relationships you carry on could be compromised. Others will not understand you.

To recover from this situation of blockage and related nervousness, you need to isolate yourself for a moment, shift your Attention, free your body, wash your hands, run, take a shower.

Then rest. The senses repair small dysfunctions on their own.

This is obviously an example, the senses do not all close at the same time! Even when a heart attack is reported, consciousness partially blocks them.

Try it, alter your vision. Describe an object that you look at with one eye in the dark to a person who sees it in its entirety.

You will have different judgments. Exaggerate this experiment and you will understand the dissonances.

The person will look at you suspiciously or think you are crazy. This way you risk losing their trust.

Some researchers also attribute to sensory interruptions the effects on the skin (boils), on the lungs (nervous cough), due to the high memory they have incorporated.

In addition to partial information, sensory pathways also influence each other.

Examine your sensations and remember the times when you perceived that a pathway was in difficulty and you did not take it into consideration.

You made a bad impression. For example, yesterday we did an experiment. We observed an object in the dark, our sight did not work at all. We were inattentive. Inside ourselves we made a partial description of the object. It seemed harmless to us. Then we touched it and got burned. It was an ashtray where they had just put out a cigarette.

What happened? Our senses betrayed us. Our eyesight was not in its best condition, it gave us what it could, partially.

The senses are powerful accelerators of messages
Imagine being in a meeting, if you receive urges to evacuate, a stomach ache, do you stay focused? No.

If you are sleepy, do you think that the decisions you make are the best? No.

If someone arrives late, do you get angry? Yes You do not give importance to the fact that perhaps your sense of time is stressed and does not have the correct perception of the work and time of others.

Have fun doing simulations.

Play with the various paths, since it is a new approach, assimilate these concepts little by little.

You will see the improvements: clarity, security, a feeling of freedom and a sense of power. So much advantage at zero cost.

If only you had known these mechanisms before, how much time would you have saved? How much today with this knowledge can you help your children, clients, friends, your partner?

1-DEFINITIONS AND PURPOSE OF SENSORY PATHS

Sensory Paths

1. the sense of self
2. space/time
3. sex
4. pain
5. breathing
6. hunger thirst
7. sleep
8. proprioception
9. excretions
10. weight/pressure
11. humidity
12. temperature
13. touch/possession
14. sight
15. hearing
16. taste
17. smell
18. Subtle energies

The purpose of the senses is communication between brains and the body for their defense: through receptors they receive and forward signals to the brains, keeping our body connected to real events.

2-YOUR SENSORY SKILLS AND ATTITUDES

7 SENSES	Signals	Benefits
Attitude	Sensory aptitudes determine the prevailing attitude of a future personality of a visual, auditory, kinesthetic, proprioceptive, etc. type.	Understanding the premises for developing future champions or excellences or talents
Ability	Ease of performing tasks, preference for methods linked to individual senses, millimetric fussiness in judgments, nervousness, hastiness towards those who do not understand, often sullenness and isolation or inability to communicate with other languages	Depth of themes, specificity, one-way orientations, talent improvement
Capacity	Mastery of the language of its predominant sense, possibility of teaching	Love for excellence, very high general sensitivity to understand where the maximum expression and communication is found
Competence	Theoretical knowledge, great experience, life at the highest levels of its meaning. Authoritativeness and power (often managed by collaborators), extreme positive and negative competitiveness in its field, combative self-referentiality	ARTISTIC SPORTS SUCCESS Development of selected aspects of the personality of specific senses. People see DETAILS that escape those who do not have the predominance of that sense

The senses are responsible for performance. Every athlete, champion, ace, gold medalist knows that the senses play a crucial role in training.

To understand how an exceptional performance is formed, we must follow a long sequence of steps:

- It begins with attitudes. These are qualities, tendencies, and potential of healthy sensory organs. We all have them.

  In fact, they vary from person to person and depend on the characteristics of the sensory organs, such as their shape, position, and size. In this way, some people are more or less gifted.

  (Although the new psycho-pedagogy has demonstrated that consistency in psychophysical characteristics is more important.)
- We can transform attitudes into skills only if we combine several abilities—motor, sensory, and mental—needed to perceive specific situations.

- Abilities become capacities if we follow established patterns and rules that efficiently organize procedures. In this way, we can say we have operational capacity.
- If we add knowledge to capacities, both theory and practice, we achieve competencies.
- Competencies in action produce performance.
    This is the role of the senses, the physical tools of the body. Now we must engage the immaterial ones.

To enhance performance, we need to follow additional protocols:

- Trigger mental activities such as selection, concentration, and focus.
- Focus spiritual forces through imagination.
- Experience or simulate emotional forces.
- Visualize the desired outcome.
- Work with dedication, try alternatives, attempt, and repeat with consistency.

To produce mental improvements, imagination and visualization help us enter the flow.

Entering an emotional state of flow means living within a bubble created artificially to surpass limits and achieve the impossible.

To enhance this process, we must learn a method (unfortunately not taught in schools) such as Proprioception and multisensory mapping. For more information, contact info@gsm-online.it.

LET'S REMEMBER

Opportunity

This model can be learned and you can use this special skill to develop the sports performance of kids and clients. If the senses are at their peak, everything works at its best.

3- MAXIMUM SITUATION OF THE SENSES Excellence

(The benefits you get if... The situation of pleasure to aim for)

*Spirit, idea and love cannot be destroyed. We can erase
the boundaries within which they were enclosed. But they
will always remain with us." Albert Einstein*

The highest aspiration of the senses is to obtain:

- **extrasensory perception**
- **expertise**
- **mastery**
- **skill**

We will cover these skills at level 6, logistics, understood as the discipline that manages time, energy and the set of know-how, knowledge.

We are not perfect yet, research continues but we are on the right path. Imagine the day when we will be able to see, hear, taste, smell, touch, measure reality and its nuances beyond the sense organs. Perceive and consciously dialogue with our body to regulate the rhythms of our life. We will have to go beyond quantum mechanics.

Imagine when we will be able to measure and recognize the subtle energies that pass through us, modifying us without us knowing how. Being able to see the emotions of others with transparency. Peace will be the usual law of that world.

Obtain super performances of the body and manual activities.

Think of artists, musicians, sculptors, dance, a path that requires the following steps:

Coaching Phases to Transform the Body That Achieves Exceptional Performance	
All professional athletes (not amateurs, for pleasure) train for excellence	
Steps	Some strategies that cultivate ambitions, attitudes, actions
A Attitude	The anatomical structure of the body conditions the sport to be practiced. However, exercise and tenacity can develop the tendencies in an exceptional way, while maintaining a basic physiological well-being.
B Ability	Practicing a specific sport requires identifying the relative needs. Practicing it at a competitive level brings stress, it is necessary to verify the elasticity and resistance of the skeletal muscular systems and train the mind to the flows.
C Capacity	Constant practice. The transition from aptitude to ability is easy. The difficult thing is to continue from ability to the excellence of the champion. The ace is number one in the world! Each level grows with repetition and constant training. Determination, sacrifice, passion, mission are mixed together.
D Competence	The capable know the techniques, the competent know the reasons, the excellent win.
E Excellence	The great hero has an extra gear
F Accelerating techniques of the "flow"	Psycho-physiological accelerators, the "flow" need a coach who educates over time. Together they can improve performances to exceptional performances.

4-MINIMUM SITUATION OF THE SENSES

(THE PRICE YOU PAY IF YOU DON'T… THE PAINFUL SITUATION YOU ESCAPE FROM)

The many poor sensory situations in which we can deteriorate sensory pathways are countless. Sensory deprivation is a creeping phenomenon on the rise due to various reasons such as pollution, noise, and junk food, leading to an increase in:

- Insensitivity
- Dullness
- Sensory blockages, including severe ones like blindness, deafness, and reduced sexuality.

Minimizing these abilities reduces knowledge, memory, and overall health. How can we prevent this for our children?

Through self-awareness.

With multisensory exercises.

With proprioceptive boards.

These exercises activate multiple senses simultaneously.

Many are interconnected and enhance each other, such as:

- Vision with hearing.
- Smell with touch.
- Spatial awareness with weight and pressure.
- The sense of self with sexuality.
- Sexuality with smell.

Enhancing sensory activity enriches attention and academic performance. It's a highly effective protocol for inattentive adolescents and is useful in helping recover NEET individuals, as well as enhancing sexual sensitivity in adults for improved couple well-being.

5- RESILIENCE OF SENSATIONS

If the paths are clean, all the sensations are at their maximum, so we perceive the state of health, fullness, power.

The general resilience at its maximum means that in that moment we are very strong and we can dare to carry out operations even at the limit, in exasperated conditions. (For athletes)

If the physical sensations are interrupted, we have a general disability (see table below) as if we were living with a disconnected part of the body.

The person loses the communication channels. High risk. Medical intervention is needed to find the interruption of the path.

The senses and the situation of minimum resilience

SENSORY PATHS	MINIMUM EXPRESSION
1. I the sense of self	1. Alienation
2. Space/time	2. Slowing down, procrastination
3. Sex	3. Lack of affectivity
4. Pain	4. Insensitivity, congenital
5. Breathing	5. Shortness of breath, hypoventilation
6. Hunger thirst	6. Anorexia
7. Sleep	7. Stress, hyposomnia
8. Proprioception	8. Imbalance, falls
9. Excretions	9. Constipation
10. Weight/pressure	10. Risk of breakages
11. Humidity	11. Dehydration
12. Temperature	12. Getting burned
13. Touch/possession	13. Waste, isolation
14. Sight	14. Blindness
15. Hearing	15. Deafness, hearing loss
16. Taste	16. Ageusia
17. Smell	17. Anosmia
18. Subtle energies	18. Hair loss, blindness, anosgamia

Here's the translation:

Recovery

Action is required on each pathway as expressed in the table.
Special attention is needed for drugs.
Drugs alter the senses and then the areas of the brain responsible for well-being.
If you have doubts, several tests can be performed.

Even light drugs exhaust the senses, leading to distress from even minimal use due to the low tolerance threshold.

In this case, detoxification protocols must be followed, along with medical assistance.

Some tests include:

- Eye exam, pupil dilation.
- Hair test, chemical composition (up to 6 months prior).
- Psychological treatments and specialized diets.
- Clearing pathways.
- General detox, a global body cleansing protocol.
- Social-specific programs.
- Proprioceptive plans.
- Multisensory exercises.

These help verify the situation and partially support the senses. However, it is essential to seek appropriate structures immediately.

Create your database, as well as your child's, and update it seriously. See attached table.

Sensory Abilities: Quality and Benefits

SENSORY PATHS	ENHANCEMENT	PERSONAL BENEFITS	RESULTS BUSINESS
1 unit of the self	determination		
2 space/time	Measures reports		
3 sex	sensitivity		
4 pain	moderation		
5 breath	breathing capacity		
6 hungry thirst	satiety		
7 sleep	quiet		
8 proprioception	balance		
9 excretions	waste release		
10 weight/pressure	lightness		
11 humidity	Humidity thresholds strength		
12 temperature	heat sweat salts		
13 tact possession	acceptance contact		
14 sight	acuity		
15 hearing	depth vastness of sounds		
16 taste	differentiation		
17 sense of smell	ancestral memory		
18 subtle energies	perception		

6 – TIPS. RESULTS AND STRATEGIES TO IMPROVE THE SENSES

(Excerpt from the book "18 sensorial paths" by Albina Gabellini et al.)

Compilation of proprioceptive tables.

We attach a form to help you understand how to clean the sensory pathways with the specially constructed tables and the correlation with the parts of the body, of the soma under examination.

Re Stimulating the individual positive or stressful sensations of personal memories accustoms us to raise the thresholds of tolerance and change our soma.

By changing the somatic traces, I change the physical and mental state, well-being returns.

With this beneficial state, I can face any challenge.

Attached model G_3_

G_3_modules _02 Preparation of proprioceptive tables document n.............................proprioceptive tables

1-Sensitivity (name) examined ....PLEASURE PAIN STRESS (there are 36 different situations, two for each positive or negative sense)

2 - Organs, apparatuses, or systems involved in re-stimulation

- Eye
- Ear
- Skin
- Hands
- Feet
- Throat
- Nose
- Stomach
- Genitals
- Stomach
- Muscles
- Liver
- Lungs
- Back

3-MODE (I CAN USE MEMORY OR IMAGINATION)

4-Emotions and Questions (I describe the most pleasant emotions)

5-Description (out loud) of the best memories (describe in detail the pleasant facts, the sensations, the conditions in which they occurred, any people and relationships involved)

Name Surname Date Signature

VERIFY

With biofeedback (special electronic equipment), once the 18/36 sensations have been declared, I can reduce the negative ones and exaggerate the positive ones.

I move away from pain and go towards pleasure. With perseverance, commitment, even phobias can be eliminated.

Resilience increases and health benefits. We are ready to challenge any situation.

7 SENSES

LEVEL 3 EMOTIONAL

Questionnaire to find inspiration on your child's senses and sensory paths.

Template that you need to:

a) *maximize the use of the senses for excellent health and efficiency in every behavior*

b) *establish which commitment to sign. Warning: since these are new protocols all over the world, it is best to practice one path at a time with patience. The results will repay the investment of time greatly also on yourself and your loved ones.*

a) Capital already acquired, riches that come from roots, origins, relationships, epigenetics, positive experiences to be copied and negative ones to be modified

Find similarities between grandparents and your child. You will notice some of them and they will serve as a guide. Study the 18 sensory pathways. Write down which of them are already efficient. What strategies can you adopt for detox cleansing your body? List the advantages and benefits of each.

Internal senses
1 of the unity of the self _____
2 time-space _____
3 sex _____
4 pain _____
5 breath _____
6 hunger and thirst _____
7 sleep wakefulness _____
8 proprioception _____
9 excretions _____
10 weight pressure _____
11 humidity _____
12 temperature _____
18 subtle energies _____
External senses _____
13 touch-possession _____
14 sight _____
15 hearing _____
16 flavors _____
17 smell _____

SENSES Basic Elements. Write or have written down his best aptitudes, abilities, tendencies, character, skills, attitudes that Facilitate his progress.

1 _____

2 _____

3 _____

SENSES Technique to copy a success. Practice one sense at a time and you will be amazed how much more efficient children and young people are than us. Point it out, encourage them to deepen the passages

1 _____

2 _____

3 _____

SENSES Technique to change a failure. It doesn't happen often. Adults have sensory errors. Have you made wrong judgments because of the senses? What bad habits can you change? Write down where you are today, we will continue from there. What can you improve to transform yourself into a super performing person? (Study the proprioceptive tables)

What obstacles have you overcome? Describe the elements that have made your behavior difficult. Importantly, traumas, operations, sacrifices, illnesses, poor nutrition modify sensory pathways. Help your child overcome those moments, teach detox.

1 _____

2 _____

3 _____

b) Reinforcement training and training needs. It is a process

Help your child practice this protocol. What can you improve to transform him into a person with excellent sensitivity?

1 _____

2 _____

3 _____

Have him compare himself with his peers and write down his next actions to test his best skills. (To be recorded in his diary)

1 _____

2 _____

3 _____

For Continuing Education, follow the protocol because there is no other on the market.

1 _____

2 _____

3 _____

c) Goals.

What do you want to improve about his senses? All of them and you will give a gear an extra tool. Write the sense to improve, the relative advantages and benefits that you get from it also for you and for others.

1 _____

2 _____

3 _____

Witness of progress. Write who measures with you of his transformation

1 _____

2 _____

3 _____

Imagine and make him imagine his goal as achieved and satisfactory.

1 _____

2 _____

3 _____

d) Results. Control of Results Objective Achieved with witness confirmation.

Goal achieved on..........................by...............Congratulate and reward yourself at every step.

Update the card with the date, signature of buddy, tutor, mentor, coach

Place, date and signatures

1 _____

2 _____

3 _____

7- THOSE WHO HAVE BEEN SUCCESSFUL
WITH EXCEPTIONAL SENSITIVITY

Who has succeeded? In terms of sensitivity, we would be tempted to say all living beings.

It is enough to observe

a) **The beauty of plants that follow the light. Their embroidery, the delicate designs, the architecture of the branches, of the leaves to receive the sunlight.**
b) **Animals, which have a scale of sensitivity superior to ours. Think of dolphins, sharks!**

Every artist knows and lives the beauty of the senses in a profound way.

Artists have a more pronounced sensitivity than us mere mortals. (We tend to dull them as time goes by).

Let's think of Raphael, Leonardo, Piero della Francesca, Picasso and many others.

Let's think of music, Verdi, Puccini, Mascagni, Bellini, Rossini and all our modern musicians, singers, songwriters, actors.

Let's think of ballet at La Scala in Milan, operettas, concerts, films, what great emotions they communicate to us!

We have frequented the world of creators, stylists, artists for many years.

In fact, they have a sensitivity above average. The only flaw is that they are in continuous energetic imbalance, level 7 suffers, because relationships with them are unstable, at risk.

When you want to talk to them, it is difficult to understand what moment they are in exactly, it is easy to touch their susceptibility and be disoriented, confused.

Another aspect that they all have in common is level 5, relationship with money, they have a vision of non-venal people. Then suddenly they change their minds and become irrational attachments to money. All this happens because their senses conflict. In this case, touch, the sense of possession, sex.

They expose themselves to great social reproof, level 10, which goes into difficulty. They experience contrasts and provoke great hatred. We have studied the thoughts of the people around them: they get tired, they are stressed, depressed. Artists especially exaggerate the situations of cognitive level 2, as if they had their own particular lens with which they look at the world and their judgments were always exasperated and changeable.

Many athletes have some super-trained sensory pathways and super-developed body parts, sight, hearing, weight, space, proprioception.

They are more balanced than painters and musicians, but they still need a strong psychological training and a precise understanding of which training procedures to follow (which must be correct for them and not just for the coach, otherwise the level 2 concepts suffer).

LET'S REMEMBER

IF YOU TRAIN ATHLETIC CHILDREN, STAY AWAY FROM PHARMACIES THAT SELL STEROIDS, ANABOLICS AND ALL THOSE PRODUCTS THAT ACCELERATE THE NATURAL EVOLUTION OF MUSCLE BUILDING.

Example thirty-six: the soprano MARIA CALLAS

Translation:

Let's summarize the senses of an exceptional artistic avatar.

Maria was a great artist, rich in tendencies, abilities, and interpretative skills, with rare and supreme vocal competence that made her excel in her work, to the point of being considered DIVINE.

At the age of 5, she suffered an accident that deprived her of some balance as an adult.

Continuous diets in adulthood, while making her beautiful and desirable in the eyes of others, weakened her in moments when she needed high resilience.

The abandonment in love, family betrayals, abortion, weakness in vocal performance, and three deaths in a short period definitively undermined her survival.

She succumbed at just fifty-four years old.

The feeling of loneliness undermined her physiological resilience and drained all hope.

In addition, medications contributed to depleting her remaining vital energy reserves.

Whether it was suicide or cardiac arrest, from the perspective of our interpretative model, we know that if we eliminate level 1 – the spiritual level – the identity, we remove the perception of our own usefulness.

We erase our mission and motivation.

Suffering excessively at level 3 – emotional level – prevents us from finding the rationality necessary to survive at level 2 – cognitive level – to continue enduring these overwhelming moments of pain.

We lose control to the subconscious and decide to stop fighting.

The subconscious, a perfect mechanism, goes awry, believes it's defending the body, and severs ties with the world.

Maria, in particular, did not care for the senses that ultimately worked against the future of her life:

a) diminishing the sense of self, of human identity, not just professional identity.

b) blocking proprioception (also due to her distorted relationship with senses like hunger, thirst, sleep, wakefulness, excretion, weight, and pressure).

c) distorting her bodily self-perception, making her insecure and dependent on others' approval.

d) blocking subtle energies, particularly those of hormones, which affected her development and survival metabolism.

She positively accelerated external senses like hearing and vision, focusing them on professional success with high performance.

She repeatedly sensed the imbalance, and despite wanting to stop working and become the wife of the wealthy Onassis, he abandoned her, leading to her decline.

The lyric soprano, born from the Greek race, raised in a Greek-American education, married to an Italian, then a Greek – an adored icon even by the stern critics of high society, such as Elsa Maxwell.

She achieved worldwide success, from La Scala to theaters around the world. Who was Maria Callas?

According to Leonard Bernstein, "She was the greatest dramatic singer of our time."

"Anna Maria Cecilia Sophie Kalogeropoulou, born in New York in 1923, died in Paris in 1977, held U.S. nationality, became naturalized Italian until 1966, when she renounced both to obtain Greek citizenship through Onassis."

What can love do?

A myth, a wonderful voice, a unique timbre, a passionate, unforgettable performer.

She was an artist of heightened, exaggerated sensitivity, effectively conveying the drama of her characters.

The bel canto expertise, the technique of the 19th-century opera, and her deep love for the opera she performed resonated (almost like a reflection) with the dramatic events of her real life, characterized by intense emotions.

A unique synthesis between bel canto and dramatic art, from voice to phrasing, from coloratura to acting, posture, makeup, and even hairstyle.

Franco Zeffirelli said, "The emotion of that sound… her voice, which I first heard, reached through the eardrums to the nerves, to the deepest, most secret cells of the mind and heart."

The comments were nothing short of enthusiastic, from supporters to competitors. She was a prima donna who filled the stage.

F. Corelli, a colleague, said, "She was born to sing and to be on stage. Her music and voice entered the heart; she produced melody. Her voice contained life itself."

R. Tebaldi, another colleague, remarked, "The most extraordinary thing was how she could perform coloratura singing with that enormous voice! Fantastic, really."

As for her life, she loved deeply but perhaps was not loved equally.

The few important men in her life – the only one she truly loved was the Greek shipping magnate Aristide Onassis.

She was bitterly betrayed when he married Jacqueline Kennedy, recently widowed, a marriage that came at an immense cost.

He died before Maria did.

LET'S REMEMBER

Let us learn to balance our senses and pick up on the signs of suffering in time for ourselves and others.

Analysis of the senses, which the "Divine" was equipped with, developed to the highest degree

Model nr 25/bis	Positive effects	Negative effects	General behavior
Internal senses			
1 of the unity of the self	Self-esteem singer	Disrespect as a woman	Internal conflicts mood instability
2 time-space	Singing Harmony	Disharmony as a woman	Hasty capricious imposing
3 sex	Strongly pushed	Disappointments and availability	She ended up alone, she cheated outside and inside marriage, she was weak and needy
4 pain	Very sharp	He will take sleeping pills to reduce them	The drugs shortened his life. He was really suffering.
5 breathing	Great great singing		Wonderful skills and abilities
6 hunger and thirst	Exaggerated control	Poor health	Dieta ha dato la bellezza e rovinato la sua salute nel tempo Diet has given her beauty and ruined her health over time
7 sleep wakefulness	Rare	Little control of the circadian cycle	Nightlife style parties then loneliness
8 proprioception		Ruined as a child	Accident Weakness of Health
9 excretions	Rare	Pain	Pain
10 weight pressure		Ruined as a child	Great exercises to stay on stage he got tired easily
11 humidity	Damage to the voice	Ruined as a child	Great concern, anxiety
12 temperature	High resilience	Rare	Resistant to heat less to cold
18 subtle energies	Extremely sensitive with unbalanced hormones	Suffering Obesity	Extreme touchiness Laziness low resilience to changes
External senses			
13 tact possession	Unbalanced	Succubus of the "powerful"	He couldn't live in poverty
14 sight	Alternate	Weakened by diets	She relied on consultants like Biki Like Elsa Maxwell, also a friend
15 hearing	Super sensitive	In the Great music He felt very small differences fear	It was such perfect excellence that it created melody in the song RECOGNIZED GLORY
16 taste	Super sensitive	Great	Precious help in his Art
17 smell	Super sensitive	She selected	Precious help in his Art

8 FEELINGS

LEVEL 3 EMOTIONAL

"Follow your heart, the compass is in your feelings" Umberto Galimberti 2003

Feelings

Definition	Goal	Attitudes Skills Capabilities Skills	Maximum Excellency	Minimum
Feelings	Understanding emotions Expressing them Communicating Acceptance	Emotional Intelligence Empathy	Love Affective union Compassion Tenderness	Stress Aridity Alexithimia Hate

1 Definition and purpose of feelings

There is nothing that cannot be cured with words. (Antiphon) Even feelings.

Feelings are the elaborate expressions of our feelings. Feelings can be:

- **Conscious: we can recognize them, verbalize them and communicate them**
- **Unconscious: we can feel them through paraverbal signals**

For conscious, explicit feelings, we build our own vocabularies, which we use when we try to explain certain behaviors of ours. Love, Passion, Hate, Tenderness, etc.

We also share them ethically, but we do not explain them in the same way. Learning to communicate them, arousing empathy, is a useful work for our children and for our peace.

Neets have difficulty expressing feelings.

Unconscious feelings, on the other hand, are part of the experience of society (every person has them) and serve to reinforce actions, they have a type of universal language, easier to understand, because we deduce them from paraverbal messages.

If we see a face with furrowed eyebrows, we deduce worry, fear.

If we see smiling lips we think that the person is happy.

Living beings experience feelings, in which the instinctive part predominates. We lose mental control and decide on impulse.

With them we often justify illogical or unproductive behaviors, such as:

"I made this crazy purchase for love."

"I made this choice dictated by hate."

You too may have acted under the impulse of feelings.

In this new way of Educating, an important task will be precisely that of showing how to dominate non-productive feelings, so that conflicts are not created, but peaceful relationships from an early age.

Fights come from misunderstandings of feelings and from their poor communication

LET'S REMEMBER

The eighth step to success is managing your feelings.

Immediate action, recovery

How to simplify feelings, at least those most often perceived by children from the face, posture, voice.

Feelings and actions

Positive feelings	Corrective actions	Negative feelings	Corrective actions Interrupt and transform into
Love	Caressing	Hatred	Dark face in serene
Sweetness	Smiling	Fear	Lips closed in an open mouth
Happiness	Singing	Anger	High voice in low voice
Joy	Having light in your eyes	Jealousy	Complain encourage
Gratitude	Thanking	Envy	To despise to appreciate
Jolliness	Laughing	Distrust	Narrow shoulders open shoulders

LET'S REMEMBER

Listening to your heart is not easy. Discovering who you are is not easy. It takes a lot of hard work and courage to know who you are and what you want. (Sue Bender)

How do you explain to kids in simple ways their feelings and the most effective actions to manage them?

Question How do we understand other people's feelings?
Answer: Cognitive psychology, listening, observing, accepting, paying attention

Question How do we share our feelings?

Answer: Transactional analysis, speaking honestly, asking for help, offering respect

Question How do we manage the exchange of feelings?

Answer: Communication, leaving room for others' responses, silence, then alternating responses.

2-YOUR FEELING SKILLS AND ATTITUDES, EMOTIONAL SKILLS

8 Feelings Steps of "know-how"	Signals	Benefits
Attitude	Tendency to console others, to listen to them, to observe the emotions of others from their face, voice and posture. Emotional intelligence is an innate aptitude that, however, diminishes with suffering. It must be re-educated.	Communication of affection, joy, disappointment. Externalization of discomfort
Ability	Finding solutions to suffering, effective communication	Less argumentativeness, more serenity. Reduction of fear and stress
Capacity	Emotional intelligence reactivated	Effectiveness in the resolution of disputes, excellent mediation, sales
Competence	Complete mastery of the psycho-emotional theme, teaching	MANAGEMENT SUCCESS commercial, entrepreneurial, productive, marketing

The ability to manage feelings should be a natural gift, except in cases where a painful imprinting or specific conditioning is received as a child. The rare cases come from unloving, cruel parents or educators or officials of reception facilities of people who in turn have been abused.

The sentimental attitudes exercised become the ability to understand one's own and other people's feelings. The steps require a basic psychological culture.

Mothers, grandmothers, have these caregiving skills in their DNA, enriched with parental love. Animals have them too. Just watch a cat with her kittens.

Males, with difficulty, can learn.

Emotional Intelligence is the sum of psychological and relational competence and knowledge.

Daniel Goleman, an authoritative scholar, states:

"Emotional Intelligence is based on three fundamental abilities: self-awareness, self-control and empathy"

To develop these skills we must:

- Pay attention to our internal states and question ourselves about their nature and origin
- Accept emotions as a fundamental part of us
- Learn to recognize and block the automatic thoughts that often accompany emotions
- Contextualize events as temporary and dependent on specific causes
- Listen to others, suspending judgment and interpretation of messages.
- Try to understand what the other person really wants to communicate
- Learn to pay attention to non-verbal language

3-MAXIMUM SITUATION of feelings Excellence of Emotional Intelligence (The benefits you get if. Pleasure Situations to Go Towards) (Source Seligman)

We tend to understand life events spontaneously, it is the cultural superstructures that confuse us. The older we get, the more complicated we become.

There are two methods to enhance skills:

- Study psychology. Theory. Define concepts well, remembering that sentimental education is different from sexual education, with which it is often confused.

- Have many experiences, share them, decode them with others. Different points of view of the same experience multiply knowledge and save time.

In short, we strengthen emotional intelligence by asking for help and explanations. People are willing to explain if they notice a genuine interest.

The highest aspiration of feelings is the union of hearts, which communicate without using the mediation of language. Supreme love changes the mind, changes concepts.

The happy couple shares this unifying force with complicity. It is a single unit perceived as a unit to be defended against everyone, even against the family of origin and society, if they try to separate it.

In the context of a complete love relationship, the senses are expressed to their maximum strength and modify the body chemically, with hormones, oxytocin.

We exist, the other, within the couple.

This type of super-love builds a favorable environment for children.

In families, where there is true love, all issues are resolved.

LET'S REMEMBER

Love is not free, it must be trained, maintained, it is necessary to invest and commit. Let us love each other sincerely and we will have happy children.

If there is no longer love between a couple, it is better to live together in separate areas in the interest of the children. Do not hide

the truth, speak to them honestly from the heart, confirming that the love towards them will remain the same.

We witness many situations of extended families and the children become too spoiled, for too many gifts given out of guilt. Better to have an extra hour of presence and less waste.

Coaching Steps to Efficiently Manage a Feeling	
Steps	Some mini strategies that cultivate ambitions, attitudes, actions
A Attitude	Recognizing the feeling in the soul and the two protagonists of the relationship is the first step. We all have feelings (except illnesses) naturally.
B Ability	Educating emotional intelligence is the second step. Listening, interpreting emotions is a system that must be learned. It is learned quickly to avoid pain. Emotional skills facilitate learning.
C Capacity	Mastering feelings gives the possibility to improve relationships from the initial level, falling in love. The ability is learned with study, experience and the pain experienced, in which to go through. Transmitting this path to others, teaching, showing the solutions allows to increase the "know-how".
D Competence	Becoming an expert in managing feelings means having a vast culture in technologies, psychology, tools. Having a lot of experience allows you to take on many roles both as a protagonist and as a consultant.
E Excellence	Excellent management of feelings is achieved with harmony between the spiritual, cognitive and affective levels. The result is controlled at the physical, physiological, relational and social levels.
F Accelerating techniques of the "flow"	Psycho-physiological "flow" accelerators help to quickly reach balance between the levels mentioned above.

4- MINIMUM SITUATION OF FEELINGS

(THE PRICE YOU PAY IF YOU DON'T... PAINFUL SITUATIONS TO ESCAPE FROM...) THERE ARE MANY SITUATIONS THAT GENERATE EMOTIONAL DEFICITS, HERE ARE SOME:

Situations that generate emotional deficits
•   Alexithymia (disease that does not recognize feelings).
•   Stress and Diseases That Absorb Too Much Energy
•   Spiritual aridity that despises feelings
•   Deceptions that generate anger
•   Falsehood, Infidelity, which generate pain and resentment
•   Humiliations that generate revenge
•   Selfishness that calls for more selfishness

Children can recognize the nonverbal cues underlying the attitudes mentioned above: due to the mirror neuron mechanism, they will imitate them.

It is crucial to minimize simulation; hypocrisy is quickly exposed, leading to a loss of trust.

The lowest point of feelings occurs when, unfortunately, one encounters a person who lies, whether as a profession or out of habit.

The signals become confusing, making it difficult for the receiver to interpret them.

A seasoned liar can even beat a lie detector. They understand the biophysical reactions the machine is designed to detect and modify them (according to our experience).

As a result:

"Those who look outside, dream. Those who look inside, awaken." (Carl Gustav Jung).

If we only look outward, we end up seeing what pleases us, what we want to happen. We tell ourselves stories. We delude ourselves.

Instead, we should delve into the details of feelings, even though the process is painful. Teaching children the correct process immunizes them and makes them stronger.

Play with your child and define emotions. He will have a clearer understanding.

FEELINGS classified by levels

Positive Feelings	Positive Feelings	Negative Feelings	Negative Feelings
1 Affection	1 Honor	1 Indignation	1 Sadness
1 Love	2 Wonder	2 Indifference	1 Frustration
1 Enthusiasm	2 Carefree	5 Misandry	1 Meloncholy
1 Pride	7 Pardon	5 Misogyny	2 Distrust
2 Faith	7 Admiration	5 Mourning	2 Despair
2 Trust	7 Friendship	7 Nostalgia	2 Guilt
2 Estimation	8 Solidarity	9 Misanthropy	4 Anguish
7 Compassion	8 Philanthropy	9 Revenge	7 Envy
7 Mercy	9 Repentance	9 Vendetta	7 Hatred
7 Gratitude	10 Devotion	9 Abandonment	7 Anger
7 Gratification	10 Complicity	9 Regret	7 Jealousy

5-RESILIENCE OF FEELINGS

Positive feelings, feeling loved, loving, can enhance general physical resilience and increase mental faculties. Let's cultivate them, it costs nothing and they yield a lot.

Try to focus on gratitude, tenderness and you will see how fit you will feel.

The resilience of feelings in children changes depending on the perception that they have had of the parental care received in childhood.

It used to seem that mirroring was determined up to about 3 years of age.

Today we know that not being cared for until about 10 years of age, gives a sense of lasting deprivation, and can produce Neets.

The feeling of abandonment appears as a cause that determines bad behavior in "bullies", children from about 7 to 18 years of age, who use violence against the weakest. Think about it carefully.

Recovery

The signs of low emotional resilience are:

- **Illnesses**
- **Psychosomatic reactions**
- **Emotional deficiency, dryness**
- **Depression**, particularly in teenagers who feel victimized
- **Withdrawal**
- **Low self-esteem**: We attribute value to ourselves based on the people who love and seek us out. For instance, if a boyfriend leaves us, we may form the belief that we are worthless.

SOLUTIONS TO THESE CHALLENGES ARE OF THREE TYPES:

Personal interventions, social support, and specialist assistance

- **Illnesses**: Requires a doctor immediately
- **Psychosomatic reactions**: Requires a doctor immediately
- **Emotional deficiency**: New emotional education to be practiced in groups
- **Depression**: Medical and psychological intervention
- **Withdrawal**: Requires family or social support
- **Low self-esteem**: Requires family or social support
- **Repression of feelings**: Logos dialogue and family support

Maintaining low emotional resilience is self-sabotage. If a person with low resilience also adopts a belief like, *"No one loves me, I don't feel emotions, not even friendship. I feel lonely, abandoned, forgotten,"* they set the stage for a lack of love for life, leading to extreme consequences.

If we feel isolated (loneliness), we suffer; if we feel forgotten by everyone, we question the purpose of our own existence. (This phenomenon often occurs in the elderly and, in the last decade, has started affecting young people as well.)

When you meet elderly people, remember to greet them, smile, help them with groceries, and offer compliments. They will no longer feel useless. A simple gesture could save their life.

6-TIPS, RESULTS AND STRATEGIES OF FEELINGS

Feelings matter to us because we consider them the foundation for building and maintaining relationships:

- **In social life**, with friends, family, couples, parents, and relatives.
- **In business**, with clients, colleagues, suppliers, bosses, and employees.

Art is the ultimate expression of life. Any form of artistic expression can help manage and control emotions effectively. Artistic expressions have a cathartic function.

For this reason, children should be educated to appreciate artistic emotions, starting with the foremost one: **the sense of Beauty**.

Beauty is a hallmark of the human soul, a *logos*—an Italian language concept.
We feel the call of beauty much more intensely than other ethnic groups.
Aesthetic sensibility in a philosophical sense is part of our DNA.

TYPES OF EMOTIONAL RELATIONSHIPS BY INTENSITY

Level 7 Relationships Feelings in relation to others
• respect
• sympathy
• friendship
• empathy (it is an alert skill)
• compassion
• tenderness
• affection
• falling in love
• love
• passion
• complicit love

Each of these feelings can be cultivated with simple repeated actions, affirmations, written messages, small gestures.

Each of the 11 themes is important, because the human soul needs emotional confirmation, especially children.

Small frequent steps build solid relationships of trust and loyalty over time.

LET'S REMEMBER

Let's Practice Daily on These 11 Themes
For each individual experience, record the benefits.

EXAMPLE THIRTY-SEVEN: TRANSITIONING FROM ONE COMPANY TO A GROUP OF TEN

In 1990, we transitioned from working with a single company to managing a group of ten.

Initially, we maintained a distant but respectful relationship with individual clients, and everything worked wonderfully. However, when we expanded to a group of ten companies, the challenges multiplied. The commercial commitments became demanding, and the cultural differences were significant. We went through dozens of salespeople each year.

Then we introduced the **"first-name basis policy"** and a **friendly service approach**. We applied lessons from coaching, and it worked. Friendliness turned into friendship, and revenue grew significantly.

We built relationships with 2,400 clients, knowing each one personally. Over time, with this heightened emotional engagement, we developed good friendships. With 360 of them, we even established personal relationships and shared in their family challenges. When we sold the business, they followed us faithfully in new ventures.

These strategies were naturally suited to us, being from Romagna. Anyone who has visited Romagna as a guest can attest to the difference— the spontaneous quality of hospitality, the heartfelt sentiment infused into every *piadina* (and that's not just rhetoric)!

FEELINGS, ATTITUDES, AND WINNING STRATEGIES

Feelings and attitudes	Profitable strategies and actions
Level 1 Tenderness	open yourself to affection
Level 1 Love	offer yourself with happiness in giving
Level 1 Super Love	to unite two souls with complicity
Level 1 Respect	to recognize the other and their values
Level 2 Empathy	to respect the emotions of others
Level 2 Affection	to have the well-being of the other at heart
Level 4 Falling in Love	to intensely desire the presence
Level 5 Gratification Success	to be happy with beneficial gains
Level 5 Friendship	to share interests
Level 7 Compassion	to accept the needs of others regardless
Level 6 Passion	to dedicate yourself without calculation
Level 8 Generosity	to clarify, help the justifications of others
Level 9 Sympathy	to share values, principles, references

These 13 mini strategies are effective, useful for everyone. Practiced together they have a multiplier effect, as already explained.

They have been tested in thousands of cases with success.

The limitation lies only and exclusively in bad faith, against which it is not possible to find an antidote, but only to move away.

Feelings are the active part of emotions.

The word "feelings" has two interpretations:

- **Recognition of sensory perceptions:** A conscious awareness of various sensory pathways. This is a physiological event, a process of the physical body.
- **Psychological aspects with spiritual value:** An "affective" event that connects us to other people or things.

In this context, we are discussing the second type. When we set a goal, we must measure it, set a deadline, and have the freedom to control it.

Feelings are the one exception that requires special management, beyond standard rules. Each person needs to define their own approach. There is no authoritative manual certifying what a person "feels."

The unconscious phenomena hidden from our awareness, combined with the variability of the field, are beyond statistical control. Each of us expresses what we feel when we choose to.

When it comes to bringing feelings to the surface—always diverse and impossible to categorize—we can only offer advice that stems from genuine personal experience, while applying the necessary precautions.

8 FEELINGS

LEVEL 3 EMOTIONAL

Questionnaire to find inspiration on empathy and understanding other people's emotions (language and emotional intelligence). Sample that you need for:

a) improvement and transformation of the child in understanding and transmitting feelings

b) signing a contract/commitment to reduce suffering, stress, lack of affection, hyperactivity.

a) Capital already acquired, riches that come from roots, origins, relationships, epigenetics, positive experiences to be copied and negative ones to be modified

Exercise for you. Epigenetics also has its effects on feelings. Observe your grandparents, your uncles. Find the similarities. Do you know your submerged feelings? Can they act on you? Are you free to manage them as you want? Discover your unconscious feelings. How can they help your success? Remember your aptitudes, to what degree you have transformed them into skills. Find the advantages.

Your Emotional Intelligence can accelerate enthusiasm, concentration, shift attention where your program requires it. Have you tried to move your feelings? Can you trust them? List the advantages.

1 _____

2 _____

3 _____

FEELINGS Basics. Write down your best skills, character tendencies, and attitudes that can control them. What skills have you developed? What competences? Do you aim for emotional excellence?

1 _____

2 _____

3 _____

FEELINGS Technique to copy a success. Practice one feeling at a time and you will be amazed how much the children will improve in learning. Point it out, encourage them to make their feelings more explicit, to talk about them and describe those of others to increase empathy. Have you had positive experiences using feelings as a lever? Children are masters of it! Write down what you did and how you felt when they worked. Reproduce the same conditions. Paste them into your memory of today. You will feel better.

1 _____

2 _____

3 _____

FEELINGS Technique to change a failure. Have you experienced painful feelings, bereavements, abandonments? How did you improve or overcome them? What lessons?

Quickly study some NLP techniques and review the theory

1 _____

2 _____

3 _____

b) Reinforcement training and training needs. It is a process

Raising your child with conscience and emotional intelligence will create a peaceful future for you.

Write down where you are today, from which to move forward. How can you become a free person, able to rejoice instead of suffer? What is the path for your child?

1 _____

2 _____

3 _____

Make him compare with his peers and write down his next actions to have virtuous behaviors. (To be reported in his diary) This is the most delicate step, listen, observe, do not judge a priori and accept. Make him experiment. Guide him, give him strength, courage. Get him used to externalizing his feelings, especially the harmful ones.

1 _____

2 _____

3 _____

For Continuous Training, check the skills on the market check the skills and any training needs to enhance the management of affectivity, emotional health? (Help, buddying)

What are the sources that can support you? Who can help you? Books, courses, mother, grandparents, uncles, coaches, peers, friends, family collaborators. Remember the best example comes from the family (and from children)

1 _____

2 _____

3 _____

c) Goals.

What do you want to improve in managing your and his feelings? How to find unconscious phenomena, bad habits to transform yourself into an independent person who also loves himself? How many skills do you want to transform into abilities and Skills? Do you want to aim for excellence?

Write 3 aspects of sensations, love, free, pure, controllable affections, and the related advantages and benefits that you get for yourself and for others, improving them. Make the program for your child

1 _____

2 _____

3 _____

Witness of progress. Write who measures your and his transformation with you

1 _____

2 _____

3 _____

Imagine your/his goal as achieved and satisfying.

1 _____

2 _____

3 _____

d) Results. Control of Results Objective Achieved with witness confirmation.

Goal achieved on........................from..............Congratulate and reward yourself at every step.

Update the card with the date, signature of buddy, tutor, mentor, coach

Place, date and signatures

1 _____

2 _____

3 _____

7- WHO HAS BEEN SUCCESSFUL IN FEELINGS

A beautiful love story?

The history of feelings of love is full of tragic lives, such as Romeo and Juliet, Orpheus and Eurydice, Jack and Rose from the Titanic. Love has enriched many novels of the nineteenth century, Anna Karenina, Madame Bovary. There are also those with a happy ending such as Cupid and Psyche in which love triumphs, as in all romance novels.

Example Thirty-Eight: The Story of M.M., Where Friendship Triumphed and Saved a Life

M.M. is a brilliant young bank manager, charming in appearance and character. Life seems easy and positive for him: beautiful women, luxurious cars, lively social circles.

One day, a car accident abruptly halts his vibrant life, confining him to bed for several months. Driving recklessly that night was Gianni, a friend. An unexpected obstacle in the dark causes Gianni to brake sharply and crash into a pole. M.M. is thrown from the car, while the driver emerges unscathed. M.M. recovers but distances himself from his friends, especially Gianni, the reckless one.

He focuses on his career, advancing steadily as time passes. But M.M. is changed—harsher, more selfish, stricter. He harbors deep hatred for Gianni.

Fifteen years later, M.M. begins to experience frequent pain. His work suffers, and he starts spiraling into depression. He resigns and spends his days visiting hospitals and doctors. His illness becomes his defining state, his favorite topic, and an obsession. Poorly managed insurance fails to cover his mounting costs. M.M. begins contemplating suicide.

His finances collapse, forcing him to give up his cars and homes. He can no longer keep up with his loans. Meanwhile, Gianni has become a successful entrepreneur and steps in to help.

Today, M.M. works with Gianni. Together, they've built a profitable business that has erased his debts. M.M. is now married with a child.

Friendship triumphed over resentment and hatred. It seems miraculous, but it's a true story.

Behavior analysis according to the 10 levels

MM From glory to fall, from hell to redemption thanks to a friend totally forgiven			
Before the accident	Definitions	Before Actions	After Actions
Level 1 Spiritual	Winning person	Disinterest in difficulties	Loser Depression
Identity	Ambitious	Selfish fulfilled	Loss of self-esteem
Mission	He didn't have it clear	Loss of purpose	No purpose
Motivation	High standard of living	Random focus, low energy	Total closure demotivation
Level 2 Cognitive	Brilliant person	Storyteller	Silent distrustful
Thought	Intelligent	Good speech convincing	Unable to create alternatives
Calculation	Very skilled	Only capital and wealth	Unable to calculate
Memory	Superficial	Tendency to forget, simplify laziness	Only negative memories Anger
Level 3 Emotions	Self-centered	Indifference to others	Hatred
Senses	Not well cared for	Going towards pleasure	Closed completely
Feelings	Not very developed	Lightness to not make an effort	Closed
Alert	Not very trained	Exposed to risks	Self-produced stress
Conclusion	Personality Happy Not very conscious	Rich Head in the air Youthful selfishness Confidence in the future	Scared, destroyed, resentful character
Level 4 body	Healthy	Healthy	Seriously ill
Level 5 finance	Lots of money	Not generous	
Level 6 logistic	Repetitive	Good know-how	No skills
Level 7 relations	Lots of friends	Lots of parties	Total closure
Level 8 environment	Indifference	Not respected	Awareness
Level 9 behavior	Optimistic cheerful risky	Friendly As long as left alone	Non-virtuous actions Vindicative
Level 10 social proof	Envied	Emulated	Hatred and lack of compassion

MM finally, his redemption phase, after the help of his former friend and their collaboration with two integrated skills.

Level 7 Loving friendship has worked wonders. Just one action from one person can save another's life.

7. The relationship between friends has prevailed on all levels, bringing with it level 1 self-esteem, level 9 creating self-aware behavior, freeing it in level 3 and opening to love for life with wife and children.

His transformation is not over, his mission is still pending.

Conclusions

After the ex-friend's proposal How he transformed Level 1 sub2	Character Self-aware Busy With family To fix	Redeemed paid debts New serenity achieved	Character More mature Empathetic Serious reliable

LET'S REMEMBER

Friendship is a great saving value, help. Make friends everywhere. Sow friendship, you will reap the fruits over time. Help your child make friends everywhere. Well-managed social media is an effective tool for creating relationships. Then kids have all the time to invite friends and transform the virtual relationship into a proximity one. (Always remember the value of this concept, proximity facilitates conflict resolution)

Example thirty-nine: the story of Elisa and an old friendship

Elisa is an Italian manager who travels all over the world. When she returns to Italy, she always has some guests at her home. In this way, a global friendship network has been created. The years pass. Her children grow up. The eldest goes to live in Australia. He finds himself in great difficulty, due to a sort of scam to which he is subjected. His parents leave Italy, scared, distressed.

In the meantime, the one who saves him is an old colleague of Jenny's whom she hasn't seen for twenty years.

Example forty: the story of a love for a dog and of the dog for its owner.

Tubo is a large sheepdog.

Pietro, fifty years old, finds him injured on the road. He takes care of him, saves him. They live in symbiosis for about ten years. Pietro is alone, his creative work does not make him rich. One sad day in November he has to go to the hospital for a check-up, a dear friend accompanies him and then goes away with Tubo to the countryside. The city where they live, Pesaro, is not very big.

One morning Tubo shows up in front of the hospital. He is cold, shivering but does not move. Moved by compassion, we start a race to bring him water, food, a blanket, under the tree in front of the entrance.

Days pass. The owner dies, his funeral takes place on the opposite side of the entrance to San Salvatore, but Tubo stays there.

One day a boy named Giuseppe who knew Tubo decides to let him get into the car and patiently takes him to the cemetery in front of the grave. Tubo understands.

He wants to stay there. The boy manages with great difficulty to bring him home.

Tubo, as soon as the door opens in the morning, runs to the cemetery. It is a long distance from the sea to the cemetery. Tubo knows the way. At first, it was necessary to go and get him. For many years he has become accustomed to making his visits alone and in the evening, when they send him out of the cemetery, he returns to the new house. Now Tubo has reached his beloved master.

LET'S REMEMBER

Keep friendships alive if you can and leave a good memory be loyal and above all generous.

Love animals. Create relationships with them. Give your children animals, you make them responsible and they will be loved. (Pet therapy)

9 ALERT

EMOTIONAL LEVEL 3

"I'm going out. I'm going to get a breath of anxiety" (Anonymous)
Reply "If you control the alert, you'll get some fresh air"! A. Gabellini

Alert

Definitions	Goal	Attitudes Skills Abilities Competencies	Maximum	Minimum
Alert	Defense Against Threats	False Alarm Management Balance	Safety Empathy Survival	Anxiety Emptiness Panic Ignorance of signals Disorientation

1-DEFINITION AND PURPOSE OF ALERTNESS

The alert system is an additional protection that nature has endowed us with, beyond the individual signals we receive from our senses. It is a non-rational, pre-conscious system. Its main purpose is to warn the body of an impending threat or imminent danger, taking precedence and priority over other signals or stimuli. Animals have a more developed alert system than ours. It seems that, having developed the habit of covering ourselves, the sensitivity of the soma, which signals alertness, has been reduced.

Alertness goes against the normal cognitive and emotional operations of a person, diminishing our energy. It also seems that static charges affect alertness.

Recently, through stressing and provoking alertness exercises, we realized that it also has a very important function at Level 8, the social level.

Acting as a quick signaler, bypassing the filter of consciousness, alertness can detect and highlight a relational danger with our peers, and if we listen to it, it prompts us to resolve the conflict in advance. For example, by lowering our voice, redirecting a conversation, staying silent, or leaving the situation.

The body has a marvelous defense system. While we are working, running, or playing, our nervous system is designed to alert us as soon as "strange" signals enter the sensory proximity of the body.

With external senses, spatial-temporal threats are perceived inconsistently, as each external sense has its own alert system (sight, hearing, touch, smell, taste). As a result, we react in ways that follow different rhythms and rules.

Sometimes, we might become alert due to a false indicator, a signal that is too loud, a burst of energy, or a sudden flash of light.

On the other hand, internal senses (self-awareness, time/space perception, sexual impulses, pain, breathlessness/increased heartbeat, hunger/thirst, yawning, need for evacuation, etc.) are more coherent because they work together, recognizing the intensity of internal stimuli, which are much slower and more controllable than external ones.

While we work, these signals can interrupt or distract us, potentially causing feelings of embarrassment.

The purpose of alertness is to safeguard our life and to:

- Take precedence over all other physiological signals.
- Find the energy to face exceptional events, even drawing from vital reserves if necessary.

Modern Changes in the Alert Mechanism

In modern times, the alert mechanism is changing, lowering its threshold of perceptibility. Unconscious alert signals may activate without us recognizing an immediate danger, functioning only as a "simulation." Young people might seem more restless and agitated. Electricity and all electrical devices also appear to be a contributing factor.

Indoor Factors

Inside homes, we may unconsciously feel agitated by appliances, wiring, and electromagnetic pollution. Symptoms include itching, thirst, and dry skin.

Outdoor Factors

Outside, excessive noise, traffic, unbreathable air, and unpleasant odors induce a continuous state of alertness, leading to negative stress, palpitations, anxiety, panic, and a sense of dirtiness toward one's body, with greasy hair and skin.

Psychological Impact

We feel that our sweat must go away, that it smells, even though sweat is a natural manifestation of good body thermoregulation. We want to wash away our body's natural odor using detergents and perfumes, as if this could reduce the oppressive sense of fear tied to alertness.

Managing Alertness

To regain focus and keep our attention where we want it, it is important to maintain clean environments and, subsequently, personal cleanliness. Soap is not necessary—only water. Showers, baths, and sponge baths are natural remedies for reducing stress from false alerts, and they are effective.

LET'S REMEMBER

The sense of alertness is the final step of verification towards success.

To succeed, the inner judge must be silent. Without anxiety, you will receive the "green light" signal for your project, which will be destined to win, because your inner judge will give you permission.

Immediate action, recovery

An uncompensated alert leads to panic of thought that becomes an emotional challenge.

Once this process has started, subsequent experiences no longer require all the conditions, just one is enough to reactivate the fear, so that the emotional memory finds the images and anticipates the crisis.

This iterative behavior reduces the prospects of personal development in life and business, because fear anticipates the feeling of panic and makes it happen. It prohibits success, even if it does not affect survival.

We tend to stay in the comfort zone, fear blocks new experiences.

If you observe drops in freshness of thought for yourself or your children, implement all the measures we have talked about, before it becomes a pathology. Going out, taking a shower, touching the plants. Rocking children, using mantras about safety, are winning actions.

We do not believe much in "anxiety disorders" as a disease. It is just a defect in the sense of time, which, if cured, the emotional and behavioral effects go away on their own, if the alert is in order.

2-SKILLS, *THE ATTITUDES THAT SUPPORT ALERT*

9 ALERT Steps of "know-how"	Signals	Benefits
Attitude	Dissatisfaction, discomfort, restlessness, nervousness	Re-education to dangers
Ability	Recognition of unconscious signals, palpitations, sweating, sudden as predictive activities	Balance harmony greater mastery of the body
Capacity	Better management of time and effort, control of circadian cycles and biorhythms, of the BTM (the best moment), adjustment of flow phases	Advanced methods for athletes in association with Transcendental Meditation and flow
Competence		SUCCESS AS A COACH TRAINER JUDGE CONSULTANT OR DIVISION LEADER

As we grow, gaining experience, we automatically transform alert sensitivity attitudes into skills. Over time, we memorize these experiences and adapt virtuous behaviors.

We transform skills as children into the ability to perceive emergencies. The 18th sense, the ability to perceive subtle energies, is connected to alertness.

How they influence us, we still do not know perfectly today, even if quantum research is providing us with many answers both from the world of subtle energies and from those of very low frequencies, linked to cellular functioning.

The terminals, the earphones, the warning system is exploding, putting the health of children at risk?

We do not know the extent of it, let's wait for the results of the biometric research in progress, before unleashing useless worries.

We already have experience in this field. In 1987 we studied and produced the anti-glare protective screens for computer monitors.

Together with the University of Florence, Department of Workplace Safety and Health, we performed a series of tests on the effects of radiation emitted by large video terminals. We designed them, built screens of different sizes to apply in front of the videos, shielding them with these crystals treated with metal coating.

We took the idea from Polaroid, which made them in low-performance plastic, and transformed them into highly protective crystals.

We studied in depth the sense of sight, neurological connections and the effects on the human body of the various frequencies emitted by the terminals.

The most important manufacturers accepted them IBM, Honeywell, Control Data, Univac. Over time, videos lost their harmfulness, overtaken by flat screen technology. (We have specific expertise on the subject to continue research).

How to enhance the alert path

In order to enhance the alert abilities or better balance them, we need to act in reverse, weakening the conditions and agents that send the danger messages.

If we aspire to obtain superior performance, excellence in various disciplines, it is important to do it as soon as possible.

The transitions from alert to danger
At the beginning the Inputs are sent under consciousness At the end the outputs make the person act consciously
•   the reception of inputs are the sensations
•   the recognition of their value are the feelings
•   the memory map is their functional anatomical archive
•   the communication path is the recording in the 3 brains
•   Outputs are the commands from the brain sent to the body parts
•   Chemical-hormonal reactions are the output orders for the release of neurotransmitters and hormones
•   the changes in the soma, the skin, the physical body are the reactions to input and output
•   the movements of the muscles, the circulatory system, the respiratory system are the orders carried out
•   Rebound and biofeedback are the reactions that tell what is happening, measuring the various interactions

What skills are capable of intercepting these passages (with minimal expenditure of time-energy) to maintain a correct Alert?

The "correct" Alert means that it is neither imaginary nor late, it is ready when needed.

Answer

It is positive emotional memory that helps us build good alert capabilities.

After having respected the protocol of the senses, which is common to all emotions, for an optimal alert, we need a triad.

The triad - relax, sleep, rest - knowing how to relax, rest and sleep well (for example avoiding horror films in the evening).

It fights the opposite triad - anxiety, fear, anger - which could send the alert haywire, which would then send us threatening messages without a real cause, and we would suffer from de-stress.

3-MAXIMUM ALERT SITUATION, Your Excellency

(The benefits you get if. The pleasurable situations to go towards)

The highest aspiration of the alert is twofold.

a) **the perfect functioning as a danger spotter**
b) **the anticipated pacifying function of conflicts.**

Cleaning the mechanism is mandatory.

It is connected to the balance of the senses and calm of thought.

If these signals have been triggered inappropriately, we do not create empathy.

Calmness, serenity can produce a situation of excellence in behavior that will be without potential conflicts. (Effect also on level 7 - relational).

Optimal alertness is obtained by giving the right cognitive weight to events and maintaining its resilience elastic.

We have had cases in which the panic attack has disappeared, along with its abnormal alertness in entrepreneurs too attached to profits. How? By restructuring their emotional relationships with financial and economic values.

Coaching Phases to Transform a Person Who Perceives the Messages of His Alert	
Steps	Some mini strategies that cultivate ambitions, attitudes, actions
A Attitude	The first step is to recover this sense. Distinguish it from anxiety.
B Ability	Exercise stress control. Listen to internal messages about the body's safety status. Check them one by one. Understand unnecessary and harmful deviations.
C Capacity	The ability is to intelligently use alertness to predict future behaviors and avoid stress. This ability saves us a lot of time for the recovery of the balance of the senses and emotional reflex.
D Competence	Becoming an expert in alertness is a relatively new profession, as sense has only recently gained importance.
E Excellence	We have noticed that it is able to contain stress even in extreme situations, modulating its intensity, for example with Transcendental Meditation.
F Accelerating techniques of the "flow"	There are no accelerators for alert.

4-MINIMUM ALERT SITUATION

(THE PRICE YOU PAY IF YOU DON'T... PAINFUL SITUATIONS TO ESCAPE FROM)

There are many situations where negative signals are deficient or exaggerated:

a. Stress already present that alters the perception of the event
b. Super stimulating environments
c. Extremely crowded environments (stadiums, concerts) in which the Oxygen Lack Alert is triggered.

We have discovered very low alert situations in people with dulled senses.

Example forty-one: the story of engineer P.A., 33, and Jenny, 16

PA is a very successful IBM executive. She risked her life because she never alerted herself, due to the loss of sensation of touch and skin. When a fire broke out at a customer's office, she did not feel the heat and did not run away. She was saved by the caretaker who pulled her away.

On the other hand, a college girl, Jenny G, suffered from stress dermatitis and frankly was a bit ugly to look at. When she realized that she had to work on the emotional memory of the alert and calm her agitated state of false alarm, in three months her scars disappeared. She was beautiful again. She got engaged soon after.

5-RESILIENCE OF ALERT SYSTEMS

The Emotion of Alertness and Its Dual Relationship with Resilience

- **Conflict Management Resilience**: When tied to conflict management, alertness enables a broad tolerance range, which can be cultivated through Transcendental Meditation (TM).
- **Physical Resilience**: Conversely, in relation to the body's physical resilience, alertness wastes energy by fabricating non-existent threats, imaginary enemies, and perceived offenses. *Caution!* Always verify with a buddy!

The alert system, which lowers physical resilience, might fail to warn you about being in a dangerous environment, leading to unnecessary energy depletion, as in the case of Engineer P.A.

RECOVERY

Signs of Distorted Alertness Resilience:

- Sensory degeneration
- Claustrophobia
- Anxiety states
- Imaginary panic
- Stress

These effects are harmful to mental and physiological health and to the senses overall. Since alertness is linked to the skin and muscles, it is one of the most ancient human mechanisms and has played a crucial role in survival. However, today, many of these signals are redundant, overloading the mind's safety system and wearing down sensory pathways. This system requires constant maintenance, especially in children.

Measures to Address Alertness Issues:

- **Sensory Degeneration**: Regular maintenance and cleansing of the nervous system.
- **Claustrophobia**: Consultation with a medical professional.
- **Anxiety States**: Use meditative techniques or seek medical assistance.
- **Imaginary Panic**: Seek medical assistance.
- **Stress**: Logos therapy and Transcendental Meditation (TM).

6-TIPS, RESULTS AND STRATEGIES TO MANAGE THE ALERT

Some practices
If you suffer from anxiety, deactivate your alert system.

Detox, cleansing, the sea, the mountains, sports, fitness, swimming, outdoor activities, and fun are non-specific, yet effective solutions.

A personalized protocol involves examining individual Emotions as they arise, controlling the painful connections they trigger. Once identified, these connections are deconstructed and cut.

These protocols are particularly necessary for children who have experienced violence, including bullying. They have also proven successful with NEETs (Not in Education, Employment, or Training).

Strengthening or deactivating your alert system can help accelerate personal growth and bring more tranquility. On the other hand, many parents stress the alert system without understanding its mechanisms, overly controlling their children through hyper-protective anxiety, unnecessarily instilling fear in them.

This overly protective approach weakens resilience. Alertness is tied to the belief in "defining and recognizing obstacles and difficulties before they arise."

Society often refers to this as a "problem." Just this simple word can lead us down a winding path. Alertness is a powerful emotional activator. When we think of the word "problem," the alert signal activates, bringing with it danger, effort, and negativity—exactly what we want to avoid.

Coaching Phases. The secret to removing the word "Problem" from our beliefs, which is a word that can disturb the alert.

Simply translating:

Merelyevokingorpronouncingtheword"problem"strengthensit.Why? Out of habit, we've learned to associate it with emotional weight—fear, discomfort, annoyance, effort, danger—so by saying "problem," we evoke those threatening emotions. We load it with negative anticipatory feelings.

Neurophysiological discoveries have proven the material impact of words (in the sense that they leave a mark on the brain, like grooves on an old record) on the nervous system.

This is the circuit made up of 4 phases, a back-and-forth dance of messages that drains our energy for no real purpose. Try to follow it, and you'll see how much you lose.

First phase - Input

- The word "problem" is sent to the brain through the ear, eye, or internal senses that remind us of it.

- It's compared with the memory already registered in the alert zone—associated with danger.
- The alert system, with its priority circuit, observes what happens.
- If nothing urgent occurs, the alert sends information to the conscious, frontal part of the brain, including sensory characteristics like tone of voice, facial expressions, or the fear triggered by a past memory.
- The conscious part gives it attention and energy, making it seem real.
- The hippocampus and amygdala circuit then registers it in memory with its time-space labels, priority, importance, and value.

Result of the input

Now, in the present moment, I know I have a "pending problem" to address—even if I've only misinterpreted its meaning. It's a debt I've created myself, draining energy that could have been better spent elsewhere, since energy is limited.

Second phase

- The brain, once aware of the negative-emotion-evoking word, sends back the enriched information to the nervous system.
- The message travels back through the sensory pathways (rebound).
- The word "resonates" throughout the peripheral nervous system, particularly the enteric system in the gut.
- It activates various physiological systems, like muscles and limbs.
- Finally, the physiological response settles down.

Third phase

- On a quantum, sub-nuclear level, cells are informed.
- Each cell processes the information and responds accordingly.

- Behavioral consequences vary—sweating, rapid heart rate, coughing, sighing, anxiety, shouting, urinating, diarrhea, vomiting, hair loss, etc.
- Fortunately, the conscious frontal part follows up by re-evaluating:
- The word is processed by our 10 levels (cognitive, spiritual, emotional) in conflict, disrupting each other.
- After this internal dialogue, the brain assesses importance and calms the situation.

Fourth phase

Surprises come from other brains!

- The body reacts through the gut, a physiological level that handles memories and associations and sends them back to the brain (rebound) for comparison with memory and lived experience.
- Finally, it reaches the conscious part, processed through the principle of interest—financial, egoistic, defensive, relational filters from the 10 levels of the Gabellini model—and the brain delivers its verdict in the form of a command.

It's worth trying to remove the word "problem" from our vocabulary, even if we've been taught to use it for safety. Let's educate ourselves and others to focus on well-being and avoid negativity.

Advantage

By following this approach, we clear the mind of harmful beliefs, reducing the alert system.

9 ALERT

LEVEL 3 EMOTIONAL

Questionnaire to find inspiration on your child's sense of alertness. Sample that you need to:

a) reduce fear and anxiety
b) Enrich your child with a very powerful defense tool (it is not necessary to write a commitment because it is an unknown sense, but mandatory for survival.)

a) Capital already acquired, riches that come from roots, origins, relationships, epigenetics, positive experiences to be copied and negative ones to be modified

Educate yours first to train your child. Alertness is an emotional phenomenon whose job is to warn the body to protect it meticulously. Its signals take precedence over cognitive ones. Observe your grandparents, uncles, how they behave. Find similarities.

How do you know that your Alertness ability works? Are you calm or agitated? How much can it affect you? Write down your best skills to keep a cool head or escape when necessary. List their advantages

1 _____

2 _____

3 _____

ALERT Basics. Your safety. Were you free to handle the warning signals as you wanted? Did you have healthy eustress? What character skills make you master of the situation under threat? What about your children?

1 _____

2 _____

3 _____

ALERT Technique to copy a success. Write what you did and how you felt when you recognized a just danger and saved yourself. Reproduce the same conditions. Paste them on your situation today. It will strengthen you. Do them with your child.

1 _____

2 _____

3 _____

ALERT Technique to change a failure Have you experienced your fears resulting from wrong alerts that made you waste time, concentration and distracted you from your goal? Identify them well, the mechanism is very useful for your children.

No one teaches it. You will save them a lot of useless suffering. How to change for the better.

1 _____

2 _____

3 _____

b) Reinforcement training and training needs is a process

Help your child identify their alert level. Experiment together. Avoid making them anxious. Write down where you are today, where you want to continue. How can you clarify your alert better?

1 _____

2 _____

3 _____

Have him compare himself with his peers and write down his next actions to know how to defend himself quickly. (To be reported in his diary) This is a delicate step, you must learn and teach!

1 _____

2 _____

3 _____

For Continuing Education, what are the sources that can support you? Who can help you? Books, courses, mother, grandparents, uncles, coaches, peers, friends, family collaborators.

1 _____

2 _____

3 _____

c) Goals

What do you want to improve about your alertness? Write down your next actions to strengthen or weaken fears as substitutes for alertness. Use Transcendental Meditation techniques, NLP to change beliefs and wrong habits, stress, imaginary fear, and the anxiety that comes from it. Start from here to transform yourself into a balanced and serene person, conditions necessary for the proper functioning of Action. Write down 3 aspects of positive alertness, related advantages and benefits that you get for yourself and for others.

1 _____

2 _____

3 _____

Witness your progress. Write down who measures your transformation with you.

1 _____

2 _____

3 _____

Imagine and have others imagine your goal as achieved and satisfying.

1 _____

2 _____

3 _____

d) Results Check Results, Objective Achieved with confirmation of the witness.

Objective achieved on .... From ....
Congratulate, reward yourself at each step.

Update the card with the date, signature of buddy, tutor, mentor, coach

Place, date and signatures

1 _____

2 _____

3 _____

Attach this form, reconnecting it to the other two, senses and feelings.

You will have the whole map, the answers of the emotional level in its 3 elements.

Fill out this form for your child if he is young.

Summary

7-WHO WAS SUCCESSFUL IN THE ALERT

Example forty-two: the time when the two dogs saved the family from death.

The sense of alertness exists in animals as well. In a small village in Northern Italy, a landslide occurred following the collapse of a dam. All the technicians knew the dam would fail.

No one prevented it. It was the chronicle of a disaster foretold.

We wouldn't even want to utter that name. Many lives were lost.

Before the landslide, the two dogs had become restless. They barked incessantly.

Their elderly owners went out into the garden, thinking it was burglars. They turned on all the lights and began inspecting the flower beds, the barn. Suddenly, darkness, wind, and a torrent of water arrived.

The small house was soon engulfed by mud.

The two elderly people found themselves just five meters away from the front line, protected by trees, and saved by their dogs. Was it a sign of forewarning?

Certainly, the alert system in the emotional system of animals worked.

Let's summarize all the advantages of the EMOTIONAL level 3
Now we know who you are, what you want, how you think, how you feel. We know everything about your being, how good, capable, gifted you are. You can start off GREAT.
I can use these sensory pathways of mine to
I can use my relationship statuses to
I can check my alert system for
I can excel in

I miss the training in

_____

_____

_____

The 3 emotional goals are.

_____

_____

_____

The emotions that I can transfer into my products and services

_____

_____

_____

In order to

_____

_____

_____

_____

Ex. Actions to take. How will you use your emotions, your sensory abilities, your inner judge? How long will it take for them to improve further? Record your reflections in your diary to share them with your peer, coach, or your child.

Always remember to write succinctly with a maximum of 9 words

THEME	STRATEGIES	RESULTS
FEELINGS		
SENSATIONS		
ALERT Conflicts		
ACTIONS By		

SUMMARY OF EMOTIONAL STRATEGIES 7, 8, 9.

Strategy #7- Educate the 18 sensory pathways

Strategy #8- Control feelings

Strategy #9- Obey and control alert signals

The 3 educational tactics in summary

1 Educate the 18 sensory pathways

2 Control feelings

3 Obey and control the alert signals

We have understood that to improve and obtain excellent performances the 18 sensory pathways must be healthy and clean. We know some practices related to the external senses, the known ones, we must also take care of the internal ones related to digestion, sleep, proprioception, subtle energies.

If you want to become good at manual or expressive activities, the senses of space, time, humidity, pressure, weight, temperature must be kept active. See table below.

Internal senses	Goal	Utility, impact
1 of the unity of the self	Defense of the self	realized personality
2 time-space	measure, calculation	body development, sports, art
3 sex	defense of the species	attraction between genders, health
4 pain	survival	overcome fatigue, sport, work
5 breathing	survival	Sports, health, performance art
6 hunger and thirst	life maintenance	Aesthetics, energy, performance
7 sleep and wakefulness	working brain	Performance, creation, innovation
8 proprioception	body balance	Sport, health, serenity, harmony
9 excretions	digestion	enteric brain, metabolism
10 weight-pressure	measure, values	Sports, health, ratings, art
11 humidity	environmental measures	Sports, art, life safety, sleep
12 temperature	survival	Sports, health and 3 brains
18 subtle energies	environmental measures	Life, sport, brain, mood and peace
External senses	Goal	Applications and impact
13 touch, possession	Body defense	Property, sports, art, development
14 sight	Social functions	Brain, sports, art, health
15 hearing	Social functions	Communication, music and art
16 taste	Body defense	Health, gratification, beauty
17 smell	Survival	Relationships, Defense, Sports, Art and Health

END OF EMOTIONAL LEVEL 3

COACHING THAT IMPROVES THE EMOTIONAL LEVEL

To manage emotions, the subjects to be added in schools are:

- Cognitive psychology, of which use at least personality tests to understand character and mission.
- Cognitive-behavioral psychology. There are many protocols. Choose those that enable you to make the correct anchors to

improve habits and learn new ones. Anchors strengthen the ability to maintain motivation alive, level 1, even without a tutor, coach, or parents. This psychology is found in other levels 3/4/7/9 as it is the most common in addressing behavioral disorders. Having discovered the interrelation between various levels (2, 3, 9) as thoughts, emotions, reactions, and behaviors, if we change the cognitive structures of recurring ideas, we can improve ourselves, replacing them with more effective beliefs and healing. Every school has its techniques, some common with NLP (neuro-linguistic programming), others related to doctors who use physical movements of the senses, such as eye movements (e.g., EMDR by Dr. Shapiro), blinking (Dr. Nader Butto), Bates method, grounding, tapping, theta healing, etc. They work.

Example Forty-Three: The exemplary story of Erick, 16, and his phobias.

Erick is a 16-year-old boy who was afraid of spiders. They lived in a villa and often saw them in the garden. His parents joked about it to demystify it, until the day he was dumped by his girlfriend. That trauma strengthened the phobia. He started seeing spiders everywhere. Visits to doctors, medications, treatments, and disappointments followed, along with the fear of going to a psychiatrist (he was ashamed!). The boy withdrew, avoiding friends who could have helped him. His school performance also suffered. His parents ended up feeling worse than he did.

However, with cognitive-behavioral psychology sessions combined with feedback, the phobias disappeared within two months. The boy regained his normal weight, his parents got back their smiling son, and they achieved excellent school results.

LET'S REMEMBER

We can train a single sense with millimeter precision to enhance performance in multiple phases.

First, we follow the development of senses at various stages, transitioning from attitude to skill to capability.

Second, we use performance and competence as tools to enhance activities, arts, or sports towards achieving excellence in results.

Coaching helps people with operational difficulties, not terminal illnesses.

If we observe strange behaviors, physiological signs, and mental signs of diseases, we should not be afraid to consult experts—doctors, professionals, psychologists, and psychiatrists. This saves time, money, and ensures health, serenity, and quick recovery.

Feedback Equipment

These are electronic systems that help identify a person's identity through their emotional state (similar to a polygraph measuring truth, used alongside proprioceptive tables).

Through certain parameters such as anxiety—an acknowledged indicator of spiritual-level crises—differences in reactions are considered. Anxiety arises when we are in conflict with our mission.

The importance of biofeedback lies in its dual function of signaling and correction, using applied psychophysiology along with behaviorist theory.

The feedback equipment should measure heart rate, skin conductivity, sweat, myoresistance, which can indicate anxiety, stress, fear in response to a challenge.

In polygraphs, which measure truth in what's said, blood pressure, heart rate, and respiration increase when lying.

To improve and achieve optimal performance, use biofeedback, exercising, and monitoring "vital functions"—heart rate, blood pressure, muscle tension, breathing, and brain function. Biofeedback is used in sports to identify athletes' performance characteristics and correct any dysfunctions to optimize performance.

Source: Wikimedia.

Summary

The parameters to consider in biofeedback are:

- Muscle tension (stress)
- Skin electrical conductivity (analyzes sympathetic nervous system reactions)
- Peripheral temperature (nervousness)
- Thoracic and abdominal breathing (fear, anxiety, shortness of breath)
- Brainwaves (neurofeedback) alpha, beta, theta, gamma
- Heart rate and its variability

With knowledge of these parameters, strength and weaknesses can be identified, and coaches can adjust behaviors, training flexibility or resilience, changing mental attitudes, muscle errors, posture, and proprioceptive balance. These machines provide feedback, then guide toward the correct reactions, reducing errors.

The benefits are significant. Competitive athletes use them to enter a flow state and increase high performance every day.

Can equipment improve mental state at any age? Yes.

These techniques are excellent to use even with our elderly loved ones. If you notice memory loss, difficulties in finding words, sadness, lack of motivation, or crying, you can administer tests and educate them. The results are remarkable— grandparents with available energy for grandchildren are a true blessing. This type of mental exercise helps prevent cognitive decline and depletion.

Part Six –
The Projects

STRATEGY NUMBER 10 - BECOME A COACH CAPABLE OF HELPING 5 TYPES OF USERS

PROJECT NO. 1: ADOLESCENT ENTREPRENEURS AND DIGITAL FAMILY

PROJECT NO. 2: BEAUTY ITALY

PROJECT NO. 3: DIGITAL NATIVES

PROJECT NO. 4: A SCHOOL FOR PUBLIC ADMINISTRATION

STRATEGY #10 - BECOME A COACH WHO CAN HELP 5 TYPES OF USERS

The management and coaching methods change according to the age of the users.

Learn the different models, so you can adapt them to the needs of your interlocutors.

In the meantime, you can improve yourself by using the modules above with your children.

Type 1 THE CHILDHOOD COACH

The objectives of the program are linked to the development of the child's personality and his harmonious coexistence in family, school, society.

We dream that the child can become a happy adult. With the Gabellini Method you can achieve this result.

I will list some benefits for you.

Benefits of Childhood Coaching
• realize his personality in all its facets
• grow physically
• play, keeping the child's curious spirit
• play sports, improving performance
• knowing how to manage the first emotions
• understand the reality that surrounds him
• relate to technology (digital native)
• receive the cognitive tools to judge experiences
• develop the senses and cognition
• knowing how to relate
• respect the environment
• knowing how to defend yourself and predict risks
• to love and be loved

Coaching 4.0 is aimed at parents and educators who like to introduce new strategies and more effective tools. If you are in a particular moment, you are too busy, even if you could not delegate the parental figure, you can practice coaching and find help in the Mastermind of Oriented Coach Parents, on the Facebook blog. You can share opinions with other parents and receive advice.

Coaching will provide nursery and primary school teachers with a new pedagogy, which includes indicative skills listed in the table below.

Additional teaching subjects	Advantages
• Cognitive Behavioral Teaching	Efficient and Proven Method
• Meditation and mental training	Reduce hyperactivity
• Interpersonal psychology	Understanding behaviors
• Conflict management	Guarantee of broad social peace
• Home economics and nutrition	Better health°°
• Basic computer science coding	Living with technology
• Mathematics, the foundation of every science	A new mental approach
• Learning different languages from kindergarten	Intercultural communication
• Time planning	Maximum efficiency
• Finance concepts	Getting used to saving
• Reintroduction of civil and sporting values	Defense of democracy
• Respect for the environment	Safety and quality of life
• State administration	Defend the "common thing"

°° **Themes to be reintroduced because the "singles" are increasingly numerous and we must reduce consumerism, waste and junk food.**

Type 2 COACHING FOR ADOLESCENCE

Adolescence is a world in progress that accompanies the child's passage from childhood to maturity. He detaches himself from the family and becomes part of the external society.

Today it is a territory not yet fully explored. In this field the municipality of Reggio Emilia is a leader.

The main objective is to raise happy and successful children in an environment where you no longer allow them to copy their parents' behavior as in the past.

Just think of multiculturalism. It is an increasingly competitive and complex situation where new habits and customs break traditional balances and generate insecurity.

We cannot count on epigenetic experiences, children must build them.

Adolescents should transform some abilities into skills as specified below.

Additional teaching subjects

- **techniques for the state of flow**
- **advanced tools for studying, reading, fast memorization**
- **sexology**
- **career guidance**
- **development of creativity experienced in groups (such as the ateliers of Reggio Emilia)**
- **internships at companies to bring them closer to work.**
- **experiences abroad**
- **logistical independence**
- **Financial autonomy**
- **IT**

Teachers should use the new teaching, building, where possible, the related tools, tables, drawings, videos, boxes like the Montessori method. Who teaches them these new skills? With what quality standards? Today teachers study, update themselves, but, they use old learning methods, they forget half of the knowledge after a few months. Instead, with the Gabellini method, they remember eighty percent! This is why this is a growing market. See how many doors are opening for you?

TYPE 3 COACHING FOR THE SENIOR

Today's adult is a conscious child, who loves his parents and feels the duty to take care of them when they are old. For the first time in the history of humanity, children are the ones who have to teach their parents technology to keep them active in society. If we train them to manage the PC, the cell phone, we will all be more serene. °° Often it is the grandchildren who take on this beautiful task towards their grandparents because they have particular emotional relationships with them.

Being a family coach also means understanding the dynamics of various people. But there is more!

Think about how much the average life span has lengthened. People who retire today are still in full mental vigor. Think of the thousands of managers who have been invited to leave companies with a financial parachute, interesting but short. Where can they reintegrate? How to do it? How to renew their skills with the world of the Internet to then launch themselves into the consulting market?

How much capital do they have in know-how and how much Valuable Advice can they still give to young people?

With the skills they have they can become rich coaches.

°° **It is a circular phenomenon, which we will return to later in the Project, where the whole family can collaborate, and obtain the guarantee of producing an income and, once started, automatic.**

We anticipate here a passage from the "Digital Family" project, a new entrepreneurial family model (which is replicable):

a) the younger generation can upload the experiences of their grandparents online
b) the grandparents contribute their knowledge and skills
c) the fathers (us) will verbalize, organize resources, and handle marketing

To realize this great opportunity, your contribution is needed. Think about how much you can offer.

There is a new demand emerging in the Education and Coaching market:

- On one side, managers or former professionals (often younger, unfortunately) seeking reintegration into the workforce. They can be educated on methods, and then they will pass on their knowledge and expertise to the family, which will create a website.

- On the other side, young people searching for quick solutions to enter an overcrowded market and learn methods to stand out.
- In between are adults seeking additional sources of income while waiting to be repositioned.

To meet this demand, guides, mentors, coaches, experts, and specialists—**including YOU**—will be needed!

What has changed compared to before? New users no longer prefer theory; they no longer settle for simply buying information but demand immediate practical application—"How to do it," "How to create an info-product," and "How to sell online." These needs lead directly to Coaching.

TYPE 4 COACHING FOR COMPANIES

OPPORTUNITY FOR MANY OF US: FROM MANAGER TO BUSINESS COACH.

If you are a manager, an expert, you already have the content to teach, indeed you know more than the coach in your specific field. You, like your colleagues, need to learn a Method. Learn to hold sessions, training and restructure behavioral skills, as indicated below.

Your manager will transform your skills
1. you will no longer command as the head of a structure, but as an influencer leader
2. you will acquire a different emotional language
3. you will reconfirm your confidence, self-awareness, self-esteem
4. you will increase Resilience
5. you will find balance, recovering energy to help others
6. you will learn effective communication methods and means
7. you will practice effective teaching, regardless of whether at home or in the office
8. you will use the online business model
9. you will create your own social and membership communities
10. you will optimize techniques to renew relationships
11. you will learn modern strategies

We have only mentioned some skills to be fixed, the protocol is more complete.

The 3 Lessons

It's important to reaffirm:

a) that parenting can become a sellable skill
b) that children can play an active role in the new information economy, where physical labor (like in the past) is no longer required, helping to avoid raising NEET children
c) that there are alternatives, there are second chances at any age

As mentioned earlier, experiences are ready to transform into probabilities and then certainties, thanks to coaching. You will narrate them and apply them.

If you're not an expert in the results achieved? Become a research coach. There is vast literature in English where experts teach, even starting from no knowledge, how to become a research coach.

Interviews with experts are conducted, leading to reports, articles, books to publish (on blogs, websites, masterminds, and groups with various opinions).

Type 5 COACHING FOR ADULTS - LIFE COACH

In the adult age range, we are all included. We all have lives. We share the same need to support our families, raise children, seek recognition, and achieve a successful career. The relationship with the people we love and interact with is part of LIFE COACHING.

But the great opportunity is tied to our personality.

In a 4.0 world, by selling our identity, credibility, and reputation as individuals with good standing, we have the obligation to understand "ourselves" before relating to others. We must manage the 4.0 world we've already defined as fast-paced and accelerated.

The Germans made an agreement with the Japanese, already calling it 5.0.

Thus, we need coaching to move quickly.

Once confident in our ability (not just competency) in relationships, there are many paths to finding employment, either within companies or as entrepreneurs.

All these systems help you optimally manage time, money, and relationships, ensuring that you become, not only a parent-focused individual, but also a "credible, authoritative, and expert" coach.

Thinking and visualizing a second chance helps you recover during difficult moments. Each time you find a path or a good practice, you make a deal. You can monetize them and use them when needed as a Life Coach.

Life doesn't move in a continuous and predictable manner, but in abrupt, discontinuous jumps. When a negative event occurs, you don't have time to fully study it.

To be the master of these unforeseen surprises, you need a standard Method that respects your style and provides the know-how to respond efficiently to your own needs and those of your children.

This is where the true value of personal growth and the coaching myth lies: having a secret that optimizes your behavior at every moment. Your actions will determine events in advance and in your favor. Of course, it requires courage, health, and the right mindset—nothing is handed to us by society.

Everything must be earned, but if there are honest, intelligent, and effective shortcuts, it's our duty to take them and be more available for even greater goals.

Coaching, in the end, is precisely this: training to use the most intelligent paths ready when needed. And they are needed at every moment of life.

PROJECT #1: TEEN ENTREPRENEURS AND DIGITAL FAMILY

The idea isn't original to us. We studied American and Indian models of young adolescents who challenged conventions and

became successful entrepreneurs at a young age. Comparing their lives to European conditions, we concluded that it's possible here as well.

In summary, who can we educate, and on what?

The ideal candidate is an adolescent with these characteristics:

LEVEL 1: SPIRITUAL

- Big dreams
- Strong identity: a sense of self, a desire for realization, a drive to stand out, and a bit of "recklessness."
- Strong mission: a push to do good for others, compassionate generosity.
- Strong motivation: the need to prove oneself, or scarcity in the family.

LEVEL 2: COGNITIVE

- Great calculation and logical reasoning skills
- Strong thinking: creativity, imagination, ideals.
- Strong calculation: mathematical skills, a love for measurements, coding ability.
- Strong memory: visual, spatial, and emotional memory.

LEVEL 3: EMOTIONAL

- Great joy and optimism
- The 18 sensory pathways: strong sense of time/space, self-awareness, extroversion, optimism, and health.
- Emotions: a desire for revenge in love, trust in friends, confidence in the market, and courage to try.
- Strong alertness: a sense of challenge, danger, or great wisdom (if influenced by grandparents).

These traits can be nurtured and developed.

FAVORABLE CONDITIONS FOR DEVELOPING IDEAS:

- Parents must value their child's originality, respect their freedom, encourage them, and love them both at home and defend them in the outside world.
- Their behavior may sometimes be disobedient, disorganized, and irregular, requiring patience and pride in their achievements regardless.
- The ideal setup includes the presence of elderly figures (grandparents, friends, teachers) who dedicate time at home or school as mentors.
- Community involvement, whether religious, social, or participation in peer groups (e.g., sports) helps cultivate these traits.
- Even solitary adolescents with strong digital and web skills, determined to redeem themselves through this knowledge (nerds), can succeed in entrepreneurship.

IDEAL BUSINESS MODEL:

Sale of Information Products

a) Grandparents are experts in a field, providing advice and content based on their career or experience. They need only to digitize this knowledge.
b) Parents provide minimal financial support, along with tools like PCs, software, and apps.
c) The adolescent operates online and handles marketing.
d) The adolescent can collaborate with other young people on initiatives.

Sale of Physical Products

e) If physical products are to be sold alongside the digital ones, parents can arrange with local producers. No investment in offices or warehouses is needed, as Amazon will handle distribution.

ADVANTAGES

- Young people take these initiatives as play and enjoy the process.
- Families receive an additional source of income. As they say, one thing leads to another.

BENEFITS

- Reduction of the 2,500,000 unemployed youth.
- Support for families, grandparents, children, and the poor.
- The model will be explored further in the third volume, focusing on ACTION.

EXAMPLE FORTY-FOUR: STORIES OF YOUNG PEOPLE WITH BILLIONS OF DOLLARS

a) **Entrepreneurs Who Began Alone**

- **Mark Zuckerberg** – 31, Facebook Founder
- **Dustin Moskovitz** – 31, Asana Founder
- **Eduardo Saverin** – 33, Co-founder of Facebook
- **Elisabeth Holmes** – 31, Health Tech Innovator, Theranos
- **Nathan Blecharczyk, Brian Chesky, and Joe Gebbia** – Airbnb Founders

b) **Entrepreneurs Who Started with Grandparents' Help**

- **Tom Persson** – Co-founder with his grandfather of H&M clothing

c) **Heirs**

- **Hudyan Yang** – 31, Real Estate Heir
- **Scott Duncan** – 31, Oil Industry Heir

These are practical examples. While some achieved revenue smaller than English-speaking markets, they all show great promise and potential.

JACOPO MELE

"At 16, Jacopo was already a successful web developer. He later focused on music videos. Today, he works as a digital life coach, offering consulting to celebrities and businesses."

ANDREA STROPPA

"Hacker from Torpignattara, at 18, founded Uribu, a platform for citizen complaints, and was featured on the front page of The New York Times as a 'cybersecurity expert.'" – Source Wired

MOZIAH BRIDGES, 13 – BUSINESS PRODIGY

MADDIE ZIEGLER, 13 – AMERICAN DANCER, ACTRESS, AND MODEL

ASHIMA SHIRAISHI, 14 – AMERICAN CLIMBER

FLYNN MCGARRY, 16 – THE NEW YORK TIMES CALLS HIM THE CHEF OF THE FUTURE

MARTIN ODEGAARD, 16 – PRODIGY SOCCER PLAYER, REAL MADRID MIDFIELDER, EARNING €105,000 A WEEK

MALALA YOUSAFZAI, 18 – PAKISTANI ACTIVIST, NOBEL PEACE PRIZE WINNER

BETHANY MOTA, 19 – AMERICAN VIDEO BLOGGER EARNING $40,000 MONTHLY VIA SOCIAL MEDIA, WITH 5.2M INSTAGRAM FOLLOWERS

NICK D'ALOISIO, 17 – SOLD HIS APP SUMMLY, WHICH DELIVERS NEWS, TO YAHOO! FOR $30 MILLION

There are many more examples online. Explore them and share with your family.

ITALIAN SUCCESS STORIES

Search for successful teenagers online and inform yourself. Your family and children can do it too!

Example:

- **Adriana Santonocito and Enrica Arena** – Invented a yarn made from orange peels. Secure future! Visit Confindustria's website to find best practices from young entrepreneurs.

Detailed proposals of certain initiatives will be found in the third volume.

The beauty of working on the web is its ease of entry. The online business development model used by "American Marketers" is fundamentally the same. (We've been following 28 marketers daily and confirm this basic model is widely used.)

Without this information, you could spend a fortune on marketing. In the third volume, we'll explain it all for free, preventing you from making costly mistakes.

Operations to increase revenue, profits, positioning, and reputation are always the same (though you can refine them with advertising techniques or branding), comprising only seven steps:

1. Provide high-value services and offer small, synthesized content for free. (The secret behind photos will be revealed in the second volume.)
2. Offer a clear presentation of the services provided (communication and messaging).

3. Build a growing email list by giving away free gifts (this database is a monetizable asset).
4. Maintain updated blogs with useful content (user loyalty).
5. Improve and expand services (building the future, upgrading).
6. Create alliances, participate in groups discussing similar topics.
7. Seek official recognitions and use these references to build your portfolio, like a model book. Hold events for customers with contests and prizes, rewarding their participation. These official recognitions work in their favor for free, building their image, and they will be eternally grateful. (This is also a valuable, spendable asset.)

Project No.2: Beauty Italy

A Project to Create Job Opportunities for Young People

"I would insert the word Beauty into our Constitution, which is the essence of Italy, from its villages to the sea, to Enogastronomy, culture, and traditions that express our people." – Dr. Pietro Grasso, President of the Senate

Build a business on "Being Italian" with your child.

We have truly traveled the world, and only abroad do we fully understand what our Italian identity means. Generosity, availability, a smile, affection, good taste, good manners, culture, intelligence, and the desire to maintain relationships with kind people who visit us. A foreigner, even a friend, who receives exceptional service from you may take it for granted. We, however, remain eternally moved and grateful. That makes all the difference! These feelings are the foundation on which to build lasting friendships. Try connecting with an average American and you'll understand our value.

We are and can be recognized as unique in the world, differentiating ourselves from everyone else. Let's create the dream of Italy and showcase our Unique Beauty.

Let's plant Metaphors of Beauty = Italy through the web!

We can do this at negligible cost on social media for the coming years.

Offer visitors proof by providing high-quality products, starting with organic and locally sourced foods.

Here's an example: In Italy, there are thousands of types of bread.

Try the bread from Milan, Piandimeleto, Carpegna, Puglia, Umbria, or Tuscany.

You'll taste the difference! Even if made the same way, the air trapped inside and the water differ (teach your child to have a refined palate, discerning lightness, crunchiness, and quality).

Details of the Bellezza Italia project will be developed in the third volume. Here, we provide a summary. We will work to create unique professional roles in the world. Don't worry – despite differences, languages are not a barrier.

We'll discuss attraction, seduction, love, gratitude, lasting memories, historical, scenic, artistic, cultural, educational, behavioral, multisensory, relational, sentimental support. An offering that touches all 10 levels of the Gabellini Model.

PREMISE

The aim of this proposal is to open the door to an Italian Way for the jobs of our children. No other nation has a material and cultural history as rich as Italy. These assets should be accounted for in the state budget. Our children are truly the richest in the world. We can reclaim this great Beauty and make it productive. Some of our children will dedicate themselves to art, humanities, while others will take on more technical roles, focusing on preserving cultural heritage. A significant portion will contribute to service industries, including:

- Commercial activities and marketing
- Hospitality and museum services
- Development of individual municipalities, as Italy is an open-air museum
- Building global online relationships via the web
- Supporting agriculture and entertainment services

- International transport services
- Coordinating embassies, consulates, and cultural centers
- Securing sites and the entire peninsula

There are many other economic potential areas we could list. Here, the important message is to convey and share its validity.

We have all the educational tools to teach our children:

- Finding employment that aligns with their studies and passions within the Bellezza Italia project.
- Rediscovering, cataloging, and managing Italy's vast material and cultural capital if drawn to heritage.
- Developing professional skills to safeguard artistic works if drawn to history.
- Organizing, modernizing, and making geographical areas economically viable if drawn to technology.
- Communicating in many languages, in addition to Italian, about Italian Beauty if drawn to dialogue.
- Encouraging the return of our brains from abroad if convinced of new opportunities and attracting new generations of foreigners to our universities.

We have solid Certainties to build upon and share.

The positive aspects of the name Italy (beyond the excellence in industry)
Italy has world-class excellence in physics, medicine, astronomy, art
Italy is the nation in the world that has generated the most works of art
Italy is an open-air museum and underground has another museum to discover
Italy has panoramic beauties unique in the world
Italy has some historic villages that are unique in the world
Italy has a Roman tradition unique in the world
Italy is a great place to study: high quality, lower costs
Italy has a reputation for world-class food
Italy has a first position in fashion in the world
Italy is the master of taste, elegance, style
Italy is the most important historical country of lyric poetry
Italy has sea, mountains, hills, concentrations unique in the world in a small space
Italy has the right climate for everyone
Italy has amazing spas
Italy is generous, cheerful, noisy, friendly
Italy is the center of Christianity
Italy has the best longevity. There must be a reason!
Italy has some of the best schools in the world (according to OECD)
Rome and the Vatican are in Italy

Do you have any other good news to add to the ones listed above about Italy?

Write to: info@gsm-online.it

Authoritative sources

DR. ANTONIO PAOLUCCI, BORN IN RIMINI ON SEPTEMBER 29, 1939

The proposal we have put forth is based on the ideas of Dr. Antonio Paolucci, our fellow countryman. A great admirer of Italian Beauty in all its forms.

Concrete data and facts: 6 million visitors annually at the Vatican Museums – a record for Italy – a well-deserved achievement of Antonio Paolucci, a global excellence.

We, the proponents of Beauty, aim to turn this into a business for our children.

To describe the value of this great authoritative figure, we reference texts published by **Corriere della Sera** and **Wikipedia**.

Dr. Paolucci will leave the Vatican Museums, which he has directed since 2004, with 6 million visitors annually. A preventive conservator, respectful of the ordinary maintenance of artworks, Dr. Paolucci is an Italian art historian and the former director of the Vatican Museums. He has also served as Minister of Cultural Heritage and Environmental Affairs and Superintendent of the Florence Museum Complex. See Wikipedia.

"It is preventive conservation, the secret weapon of great museums, that allows, with limited investment, the creation of a virtuous circle for the protection of collections and historic environments," his words.

"It was Antonio Paolucci who initiated this culture of daily heritage care at the Vatican Museums, elevating it to an institutional level," writes **Corriere della Sera**.

"The establishment of a Conservator's Office was my dream," Paolucci confessed at the presentation of the manual *'How to Preserve a Great Museum: The Experience of the Vatican Museums'* by Vittoria Cimino (Musei Vaticani-Allemandi Editions).

PUBLIC ADDRESS BY DR. PAOLUCCI

Dear Guests,

A warm welcome from the Director of the Vatican Museums. You are entering one of the most important places in the history of human civilization. Here, in the museums built and enriched by the Roman Popes over five centuries, you can feel the vast echo of great history and, almost, the breath of the Sacred. As you enter the Vatican Museums, you will encounter the glory of Art and Culture, placed in service of Faith. You will be welcomed by the greatest artists of all time: Raphael in the Rooms, Michelangelo in the Sistine Chapel, Giotto, Leonardo, Caravaggio in the Pinacoteca, Van Gogh, Matisse, Moore in the Contemporary Art section.

You will meet, in the Laocoon and Apollo of the Belvedere, the greatest masterpieces of Classical Antiquity. The centuries and millennia will come to you in the Etruscan and Egyptian Museums, alongside the cultures of non-European civilizations in the Ethnological Museum. It will take much time to see everything, to understand, and to remember the historic collections of the Popes. I wish you to return again, and each time will be a precious, unforgettable enrichment. But for the first-time visitor, even in just one hour, what can and should be understood as they traverse the Vatican Museums is their multifaceted, layered, and universal character.

If, upon leaving the Museums under the shadow of St. Peter's Dome, you understand the historical interest and the attention of the Church of Rome toward Art in every time and form, to all that has emerged from the hands of "homo faber" – the only figure capable of comparing with God as Creator – then your visit will not have been in vain. You will have grasped the essence: that the Vatican Museums are the identity-laden site of the Catholic Church. With their pluralistic and universal character, they represent its history and signify its destiny.

Welcome, dear guests, and may your visit be fruitful and unforgettable! I wish each of you a journey through the Vatican Museums that is both intellectual and spiritual, along the path that Pope Benedict XVI calls the "via pulchritudinis," the way of Beauty.

We have nothing much to add to Dr. Paolucci's reflections, except applause, honored by so much love for Italian art.

Some initiatives reported by Corriere della Sera

Milan, November 15, 2016 – Extract from the newspaper:

"In 2018, Milan will have a new museum dedicated to Etruscan culture and art. The museum, hosting the Cottier-Angeli collection from Switzerland, purchased by the Rovati family, will be located at Corso Venezia 52. The Bocconi-Rizzoli-Carraro Palace will be completely renovated under the design of architect Mario Cucinella, featuring an underground pavilion that will house the most comprehensive collection of Etruscan vases from the archaic period, with over 700 bucchero and impasto vases dating from the 9th to the 6th century BC. The Luigi Rovati Foundation will manage this new museum, creating a new cultural hub in the city, alongside the PAC, the Planetarium, and the Natural History Museum."

Praise to the family, the ministry, and the mayor! We must move forward!

The FAI - Fondo Ambiente Italiano

An excellence restoring Italian heritage

Support this foundation, which revives castles, cleans up neglected areas, and brings new life to Italy's many neglected treasures. Their mission aligns with our vision: young people revitalizing every corner of Italy and transforming them into sources of income.

Let us remember that laws are being passed in favor of oil multinationals, which could further damage our hydrogeological stability and strip citizens of the power to make decisions regarding necessary interventions. Stay informed and react regarding what Environmental Impact Assessments (EIA) and subsequent regulations entail. Listen to environmental organizations.

IF ONLY WE CARED MORE AND TRULY ABOUT THE FUTURE OF OUR CHILDREN!

PROJECT #3: DIGITAL NATIVES

OUR CHILDREN CAN DO RESEARCH IN ITALY.

They are already digital natives, recalling little of the analog, mechanical world. A digital education from a young age is essential.

We already train them to think sequentially—we must harness this ability, the gift left by the Latin mindset.

We have the knowledge, infrastructure, technologies, and raw material: their brains. Let's make learning fun while fostering creativity!

If only we would channel their natural abilities, talents, and guide them towards specific goals that we, as more experienced individuals, understand.

If only we would fund those who show potential, not those driven by political affiliations.

If only scientists could find a place for themselves in Italy. "If only."

The "if only" depends on us! Let's reflect and take action in this direction.

We don't need to spend exorbitant sums:

a) ateliers, laboratories, mentorship, industry exposure from a young age, and territorial protection are not costly.

b) Computing, so-called coding, and the system that digitizes information—what's its purpose? If you can express an idea digitally, it becomes universally transferable, always identical, free from external interpretation, and accessible to all via a universal language: digital, electronic, machine-readable.

What do those in positions of power do instead? Very little.

PROJECT NO. 4: A SCHOOL FOR PUBLIC ADMINISTRATION

We need to recover wealth everywhere. We need competent figures.

Do you want public affairs, which belong to your children, to be managed properly?

Let's create a specialized school to train competent individuals capable of:

- Mastering public finance science and administrative law.
- Performing calculations and managing both budgetary control and planning.
- Understanding which laws are necessary to improve the situation.
- Acquiring knowledge of banking and financial techniques.
- Evaluating projects and public tenders.
- Managing investments, costs, and public revenues with prudence, honesty, and wisdom.
- Understanding the public estate: its composition, usage, and alienation.

The benefits are numerous:

- Reduction of waste
- Freedom from corruption
- Better democracy
- Improved justice
- Increased respect for our nation on the global stage
- We will revisit this project in Volume 3.

Part Seven
Conclusions

WE HAVE EMBARKED ON A JOURNEY OF 10 STEPS, IN WHICH WE HAVE GAINED AWARENESS OF BEING AND PERSONALITY. THIS MINDSET MUST BE PASSED ON TO OUR CHILDREN, AND WE WILL BE THEIR COACHES.

We will train them to be present to themselves and attentive to others. We will strengthen them with powerful pedagogy, creating robust psychology capable of enduring any storm, confident that the sun will always rise.

What future will we leave to our children? What scenarios lie ahead? We have identified trends—we are optimistic, not catastrophists.

We will be able to halt the crime of harming the environment. We will find ways to feed 9 billion people globally. Health will improve.

But how will we address the lack of job opportunities?

How will we reduce the number of NEETs?

How can we be more conscious, oriented, and effective parents?

How can we reclaim the conditions that created the NEETs?

The first 10 strategies related to Being can help us shift perspectives, gain awareness, improve, and become capable, competent, and authoritative Coaches—especially for our children.

Using the Gabellini method, we will create excellent adults.

THE 10 STRATEGIES

We have shared a journey of many steps. We have completed the first stage, focused on the themes of Being. We have learned an original approach.

We have come to understand strategically what must be done to grow balanced, capable, and happy personalities who can face future challenges with full autonomy.

In particular, we have focused on three key points that contribute to avoiding NEETs—young people who, by isolating themselves from society, would burden the economy and our collective consciousness. Instead, they will form complete and competent personalities made up of:

- **Identity**: Who we are, what roles we play, and what great, beautiful, and unique individuals we will become.
- **Mission**: What we are called to do on Earth.
- **Motivation**: How to stay focused on our dreams.

Additionally, we have listened to the voices of NEETs, whose experiences have been overlooked, often confused with depression or borderline behaviors.

We have followed the path of resilience—the strength that moves mountains!

Finally, we have laid the groundwork for a major Italian Project, to which each of us can contribute through the free "Oriented Parents Mastermind" group, helping Italian youth utilize their national wealth—beauty, history, art, fashion, food, lifestyle—and transform it into a source of income.

Learning must become a way of life, as Pablo Picasso said:

"I always try to do what I'm not able to do, in order to learn how to do it." (Pablo Picasso)

The 10 strategies of being	
Strategy number 1	Define your identity
Strategy number 2	Find the mission
Strategy number 3	Always motivate yourself, your children
Strategy number 4	Awaken your creative and rational thinking.
Strategy number 5	Trained in calculation, love mathematics
Strategy number 6	Train your memory
Strategy number 7	*Educate the eighteen sensory pathways*
Strategy number 8	Listen and control your feelings
Strategy number 9	Obey and check the alert signals
Strategy number 10	Apply the Method and become a coach
The projects: build with your son the web business, the Bellezza Italia business, the research business, the control of our assets	

To follow the entire process, you can extract the forms, fill them out and update them easily.

Have a good trip!

Attachments:

1. THE TRANSCENDENTAL MEDITATION: A NATURAL AND EFFECTIVE TECHNIQUE FOR THE NEW CHALLENGES OF OUR TIMES

A New Tool to Face New Challenges

The historical moment we are living in is particularly stimulating and full of potential, but it presents new challenges to all of us, particularly to the youth, their families, and future generations.

Technological development, accelerating at an unprecedented pace, offers countless opportunities to improve our lives, but also generates instability and uncertainty. Even advanced knowledge becomes quickly obsolete, necessitating continuous updating.

To meet these challenges, young people need to develop greater flexibility and adaptability compared to previous generations. They must enhance their creativity, intelligence, confidence, and self-assurance to find new solutions that allow them to organize their lives and work efficiently, maintaining stability and well-being without succumbing to the stress resulting from rapid change.

Today's school system does not offer a precise and effective tool or path to help young people develop their potential. To address these new challenges and needs, innovative strategies and effective tools are required. The Transcendental Meditation technique has proven, in practice, to fully respond to these new demands, allowing practitioners to naturally and continuously develop their full physical and mental potential.

Transcendental Meditation is a simple and natural personal development and stress prevention technique, whose benefits are well-documented by science. There are more than 700 sociological, medical, and scientific publications attesting to its effectiveness.

Introduced in the West by Maharishi Mahesh Yogi over 60 years ago, Transcendental Meditation is practiced by approximately 6 million people worldwide. It is used in schools, companies, as a rehabilitation program, and recommended by doctors to promote health and prevent disorders like insomnia, anxiety, stress, and cardiovascular issues.

Transcendental Meditation is a universal technique that allows individuals to simply be themselves. It is not a religion or philosophy, nor does it require changes to habits or lifestyle adjustments. As we will see, it promotes full brain function, the physiological basis for success in learning, stress prevention, full mental development, healthy lifestyle choices, and positive behaviors. We will also discuss how it is practiced and learned. Additionally, we will talk about the "School Without Stress" program, already adopted by hundreds of schools worldwide, which includes two 10- or 15-minute breaks, one at the start and one at the end of the school day, during which students and teachers can meditate together. The experiences developed globally demonstrate that this program improves student outcomes and teachers' effectiveness, reduces stress, anxiety, learning problems, poor academic results, bullying, and school dropout rates.

The Natural Antidote to Stress

Stress is considered an epidemic of the modern era. Most medical visits (ranging from 75% to 90%) are linked to illnesses and disorders related to stress. Chronic or acute stress damages health on all levels, causing psychological discomfort, resistance to change, and impairing quality of life.

Stress does not spare adolescents and young people. More than ever, they are subjected to frequent and continuous stimuli that, if not managed, contribute to stress. They live in a rapidly changing world with few stable reference points and uncertain future prospects. They are stressed by their daily schedules, academic demands, and the expectations placed upon them by peers and adults.

It is concerning that they suffer from disorders previously associated with old age (like hypertension and sleep disorders) and that they experience unprecedented levels of stress and related psychological disorders.

A study by Jean Twenge from San Diego State University found that adolescents and young adults today are 5 to 8 times more likely to show symptoms of depression and anxiety than those who lived during the Great Depression, World War II, or the Cold War. A recent survey by the American Psychological Association found that adolescents are showing stress levels typically seen in adults, largely related to chronic sleep deprivation and increased academic pressure.

Technology also plays a primary role in creating stress for today's teens, who are "connected 24/7." Excessive screen time is a significant risk factor for physical and psychological problems. Scientists have long suggested that young people spend less time on computers and tablets and connect more with themselves.

Teachers, too, seek an antidote to help calm the restless minds of youth. Excessive stress can hinder normal maturation processes and is a primary cause of many youth-related issues: learning disorders, poor attention, poor academic results, insecurity, anxiety, depression, substance abuse, violent behaviors, bullying, and school dropout. Rest is the most natural antidote to stress, and the deeper the rest, the more effective. Studies show that Transcendental Meditation induces such deep rest that the body can naturally release fatigue, stress, and accumulated tensions that nightly sleep cannot fully disperse.

Transcendental Meditation also changes how the nervous system responds to stress. According to Hans Selye, who first scientifically defined stress, "the effects of Transcendental Meditation on metabolism, skin resistance, blood lactate, brain waves, and the cardiovascular system are precisely opposite to those identified by medicine as characteristic of the stress response."

Transcendental Meditation: What It Is (and Isn't) and How to Learn It

We all, young and old, need a clear mind and good health, to feel good about ourselves and interact with others in satisfying ways. We all seek success in our studies and work and wish to achieve our aspirations.

Science agrees that the full and harmonious functioning of the brain is key to achieving all these goals. The practice of Transcendental Meditation stimulates total and coherent brain functioning, naturally allowing the expansion of mental potential, improvement of health, vitality, interpersonal relationships, academic performance, and work effectiveness. What is Transcendental Meditation?

It is a technique that is entirely natural.

- It is easy to learn, enjoyable to practice, suitable for everyone, regardless of age, starting from 4 years old.
- It has been scientifically validated by over 700 studies published in international journals.
- It is practiced twice a day for 20 minutes, seated comfortably with eyes closed.
- The benefits continue to grow over time.
- It is different from any other type of meditation, and the studies documenting its benefits do not apply to other meditation techniques.

What Transcendental Meditation is not:

- It is not a concentration technique, mind control, or suggestion.
- It is not a philosophy or religion.
- It does not require changes to habits or lifestyle.

What happens during meditation

Normally, our minds are continuously occupied with thoughts. When they stop being active, they fall asleep, and we lose awareness of ourselves. During Transcendental Meditation, however, the conscious mind calms down but remains awake, experiencing increasingly deep and subtle levels of thought development until it transcends—going beyond all activity—and experiences the inner Self, the limitless reservoir of energy, intelligence, creativity, and well-being that resides in the quietest level of our awareness, at the source of thought. At the same time, the body enters a state of rest that can be deeper than sleep and dissolves even the deepest stress that nighttime rest cannot eliminate. When we emerge from meditation, the mind is calm and alert, and the body is more rested and vital.

The Meditation That Regenerates the Brain

The described experience of transcendence is considered a fourth state of consciousness, distinct from waking, dreaming, and sleeping states we experience daily.

Neuroscientists have identified a "default mode network" (DMN) as a natural brain state to which the brain returns to regenerate. This "default state" is essential for good mental health and creativity, as well as for self-awareness.

A study by American University of Philadelphia published in *Cognitive Processing* found that DMN is activated much more intensely during Transcendental Meditation than during sleep or relaxation.

During Transcendental Meditation, brain wave coherence and synchronization from different cortical areas increase, accumulated stress is removed, the nervous system is revitalized, and psycho-physical functioning is normalized. A fully developed and integrated nervous system corresponds to overall individual improvement, better physical and mental health, increased efficiency in every field, and a positive impact on behavior and influence on the environment.

Regular practice of Transcendental Meditation improves sleep quality and increases energy, reduces psychosomatic disorders, anxiety, depression, hypertension, and cardiovascular issues. It reduces physical wear associated with aging and increases resilience, enhances intelligence and creativity, self-sufficiency, psychological stability, and self-esteem, boosts attention and memory, and strengthens decision-making abilities. All of these factors positively influence work and academic performance, improve interpersonal relationships, and foster a positive impact on the surrounding environment.

Practicing Transcendental Meditation is, metaphorically speaking, like watering the roots of a plant to nourish the entire plant without needing to water every leaf individually. With a single natural action, the entire plant is nourished and enriched.

The alert yet restful experience provided by Transcendental Meditation delivers these benefits. There is no need to have faith in the technique or in Maharishi, nor emotional adherence or intellectual acceptance of the theoretical principles underlying it. Simply practicing it yields results, as supported by over 700 studies conducted by 250 universities and research centers in 33 countries.

The Origins of the Technique

Transcendental Meditation is a universal technique that is not in conflict with any religion. It is practiced with equal satisfaction by people of different faiths, including Catholics, Protestants, Jews, Muslims, Buddhists, Hindus, and secular individuals.

It derives from the Vedic tradition of India, a complete and natural body of knowledge that describes the functioning of nature, human potential, and the technologies for its development.

How to Learn and Practice: "20 Minutes, Twice a Day"

Maharishi developed a standardized teaching program for Transcendental Meditation, applied globally. The technique cannot be learned through books, videos, or friends who practice it. It must be taught by a certified instructor from the Maharishi Transcendental Meditation Association, which, along with the Maharishi Foundation, represents the organization created by Maharishi to spread the technique worldwide.

The learning process begins with a presentation of the technique, its function, benefits, origins, and practice. This is followed by a personal consultation with the meditation teacher.

The actual learning course takes place over four consecutive days: the technique is taught on the first day, followed by three follow-up sessions to review and understand experiences, as well as additional instructions. At this point, practitioners are capable of meditating independently for 20 minutes in the morning and 20 minutes in the evening.

This method of learning Transcendental Meditation ensures the technique's correct transmission, adherence to the tradition, and guarantees long-term benefits.

2 - TRANSCENDENTAL MEDITATION FOR DEVELOPING FULL MENTAL POTENTIAL

Our mind is like an ocean. Even when the surface is turbulent, the deeper we go, the more calmness we find, and when we reach the depths, we find complete stillness. Our mind operates similarly. It's always agitated on the surface—at the level of the conscious mind, where we are aware of our surroundings, and where thoughts constantly race and pull our attention in various directions. However, as we go deeper into the part of the mind that is usually beyond our awareness, we experience a sense of peace and fulfillment, which becomes complete bliss when the mind transcends even this deep level of activity and experiences its source— the silent, self-sufficient field of being. The limitless reserve of energy, intelligence, and well-being that exists at the source of thought is our most valuable asset, and failing to fully access it represents a significant loss to our life. It is always there, even when we feel anxious, frustrated, or overwhelmed by problems; just as the depths of the ocean remain calm, even when the surface is agitated by waves and storms. However, we must regularly awaken the awareness of our inner Self—this limitless reservoir of energy, intelligence, creativity, and well-being—which resides at the quietest level of our consciousness, at the source of thought. Daily practice of Transcendental Meditation allows us to enjoy its benefits in everyday life. During Transcendental Meditation, the mind naturally gravitates toward its source, drawn by a desire to experience that deep fulfillment.

As Maharishi Mahesh Yogi describes this process: "When the mind moves toward bliss, each step it takes experiences increasing fascination. It's like moving toward light: the intensity of the light keeps growing. When the mind experiences increasingly greater happiness, it ceases to wander; it remains focused in one direction, stable, resolved. This is the state of the mind moving toward bliss, and when it reaches the direct experience of bliss, it loses contact with the external and remains satisfied in the state of transcendental bliss consciousness." By alternating meditation with daily activity, the nervous system stabilizes the capacity to maintain the experience of inner peace and balance, even when exposed to the more dynamic aspects of everyday life.

The development of the human hardware enables young people to express their latent potential. To improve the quality of society, eliminate obstacles to economic growth, and ensure advancements in science, healthier medicine, and sustainable agriculture that does not harm the environment, we need people who exhibit a new sensitivity—those who are more aware and creative than they are today. Psychological studies have shown that whatever an individual is able to express of themselves is only a small part of their full potential—only 5 to 10 percent of their true potential. The most important parts of a person's mind do not find expression in their behavior or life activities because the conscious mind reflects only a small part of the total mind. If the conscious mind of an individual represents only one-tenth of the total mind, then whatever they do or think is only one-tenth of their true potential. In order for our children and young people to fully utilize their qualities, the full potential of their minds should become conscious—not just 10 percent, but 100 percent. In this way, their thought power would be ten times stronger, and they would be ten times more aware, sensitive, creative, and happy. Their thinking would be much deeper and more complete than it is now, and love and respect for others and their surroundings would multiply tenfold. To achieve this, it is necessary to refine and complete the functioning of their brains. Programs used in education are like the "software" of a computer: they give instructions to the "human computer," teaching the knowledge needed to organize one's future and contribute to societal development. However, they offer little to improve the quality of one's being. As in enhancing a computer's performance, not merely adding new software, but improving the "hardware"—the brain—allows young people to spontaneously express their rich potential. Scientific research shows that high psychological maturity is a characteristic of those who are best able to realize and fulfill themselves in life. Psychological maturity, in turn, depends on integrated brain functioning, particularly in the frontal area. This is the area that guides life: evaluating situations, planning, deciding, controlling impulses, being responsible for ethical sense, short-term memory, and how we perceive ourselves. Chronic or acute stress damages this area, limiting judgment capacity and triggering impulsive behavior, anger, violence, anxiety, and, in extreme cases, depression and substance abuse. The experience gained from practicing Transcendental Meditation systematically and continuously increases brain integration, supporting ongoing psychological maturity at every stage of life. In this way, adolescents and young people grow into mature, balanced adults with clear minds, capable of making decisions, aware of what they need, and able to realize their goals. They can contribute positively to collective growth. They will be people who create their future rather than just experience it; who lead events rather than remain at the mercy of circumstances.

What is brain integration and why is it important? At birth, infants do not have fully developed and integrated brains ready to process the world around them. They are born with 100 billion neurons that are sparsely connected. As these neurons are stimulated by continual sensory input, their integration increases, and new abilities emerge. Adolescent brain maturation is very slow. For instance, the connection between the frontal lobes and other brain areas begins to develop around age 12 or 13 and can continue into the 30s. During this period, the brain is capable of excellent performance, as evidenced by many young artists, musicians, mathematicians, and scientists. However, because the brain is still developing, it is more vulnerable to chemical effects, such as drugs, alcohol, and stress hormones. Adolescents can be more susceptible to stress than adults, and chronic stress affects developing brains more deeply, often with lasting consequences. For these reasons, it is important that young people begin using a technique like Transcendental Meditation as early as possible to foster and enhance brain integration. Different areas of the brain specialize in specific functions, such as seeing, hearing, thinking, experiencing anger or happiness, deciding, planning, and acting. In a healthy brain, all these areas are integrated and work together. Integration is important because our environment is constantly changing, and we need a brain that evaluates where we are, decides where we want to go, and determines the steps to get there. The frontal lobes, also called the associative cortex, are crucial for evaluating all information. These lobes do not receive information directly from the outside but integrate what the senses have introduced through hearing, vision, touch, and other senses. The frontal lobes act like a conductor integrating different sections of the orchestra into a complete piece of music. Transcendental Meditation promotes and enhances brain integration and the functioning of the frontal lobes, allowing everyone—especially young people—to fully utilize their mental potential.

What happens to the brain under stress. Stressful experiences, such as a dysfunctional family environment, living in constant fear of violence and crime, or substance use, impede the development of the frontal lobes. Alcohol, in particular, destroys brain cells and disrupts connections with the frontal lobes, causing irreversible damage—especially in young people. The underdevelopment of the frontal lobes leads to living almost "reactively," without the ability to assess situations, make thoughtful decisions, or regulate impulsive behaviors. This contributes to increased anxiety, lack of control, and a higher likelihood of engaging in risky or destructive behavior. Transcendental Meditation provides a systematic approach to strengthening and integrating the brain, allowing individuals to experience greater clarity, self-control, and mental well-being.

3 - ATTENTION DEFICIT/HYPERACTIVITY DISORDER (ADHD)

Learning Disorders, ADHD, Autism: Overcoming Them with Transcendental Meditation

It is well known that stress exacerbates symptoms of disorders such as ADHD (Attention Deficit/Hyperactivity Disorder), Asperger's Syndrome, autism, and mood and learning disorders. New experiences and scientific studies show that Transcendental Meditation, by reducing stress levels and activating an individual's full mental potential, can be a valuable tool in addressing these disorders.

ADHD, in particular, is the most common psychosocial disorder during school age. It affects 3% to 5% of children, and a significant percentage (30% to 50%) carry these symptoms into adulthood. ADHD impairs executive brain functions, creating difficulties with attention control and behavior. Those who suffer from it tend to be impulsive, hyperactive, unable to maintain attention, have slower-than-average brain development, and reduced capacity to cope with stress. Stress interferes with learning capacity, and we all find it difficult to complete tasks when under stress. It is reasonable to think that a technique like Transcendental Meditation, which reduces stress, could alleviate ADHD symptoms.

According to the U.S. Centers for Disease Control and Prevention (CDC1), although stimulant medications are an effective immediate treatment, there are concerns about possible side effects and the long-term impact on health from stimulant use. Furthermore, ADHD medications are effective for some children but marginal or ineffective for others.

Unfortunately, there is no clinical test for ADHD. Diagnosis relies on subjective information gathered from parents, teachers, and the child itself, rather than objective diagnostic methods. This makes obtaining a definitive diagnosis difficult. Children change rapidly, and signs of impulsivity, hyperactivity, and inattentiveness are common and may reflect normal immaturity rather than ADHD symptoms. Misdiagnosis and unnecessary pharmacological treatment can occur as a result.

In contrast, Transcendental Meditation offers a non-pharmacological, safe, and effective alternative for treating this syndrome. Electrophysiological studies indicate that TM reorganizes brain functions, revitalizing various areas of the brain and integrating them. This leads to a more complete brain function and increased resilience to stress.

1. Centers for Disease Control and Prevention (CDC): A U.S. government agency responsible for public health and safety.

What Causes ADHD?

The brain consists of billions of cells that continuously communicate with each other through signals that use synapses to pass from one neuron to another. The messengers that carry these signals are called neurotransmitters (such as dopamine, norepinephrine, and serotonin)—chemical substances produced by brain cells that regulate, among other things, hyperactivity, impulsivity, attention deficits, emotions, and depression. An imbalance in these chemicals can cause disruptions in brain function, which are often considered symptoms of ADHD.

Medications for ADHD target these brain chemicals. Common active ingredients in ADHD medications, such as Ritalin, Adderall, and Concerta, are amphetamines. Amphetamines artificially increase the levels of certain neurotransmitters in the brain, accelerating brain function, at least while the medication is in action. The mechanism described reveals that, in fact, medications do not cure ADHD but merely control it temporarily, often creating undesirable side effects. The medications flood the brain with neurotransmitters, potentially convincing the brain that it no longer needs to produce them. Over time, this can lead to the suppression of the natural growth and development of brain cells that create neuronal networks. Specifically, a young brain may never fully develop and mature spontaneously.

There have been some very promising results using Transcendental Meditation (TM) with children suffering from ADHD and related disorders, such as Asperger's syndrome and mood disorders. Unlike medications, TM does not focus on alleviating symptoms but addresses the root causes of the condition. This means it can produce lasting improvements, rather than temporary relief.

Dr. Sarina Grosswald, a cognitive learning expert, is the lead author of a pioneering randomized study on the effects of TM on students with ADHD and other learning disorders. The students were from Kingsbury Day School, a school in Washington, D.C., for children with learning disorders.

The study found significant results for a group of children diagnosed with ADHD who practiced TM twice a day for ten minutes each session at school. The children sat comfortably, eyes closed, and meditated alongside teachers who had also learned TM. The group practicing TM was compared to a control group, following established scientific research methods.

Children under stress often suffer silently. They may not tell anyone that they feel stressed, and adults rarely ask. Stress can be observed in their behavior, however. A child may become withdrawn, difficult, or unable to control their anger. In the study conducted by Dr. Grosswald, children aged 11 to 14 all reported knowing the meaning of the word stress and said they often felt stressed.

Teachers reported that, from the outset, TM practice made the children appear less stressed and more open to learning compared to before. Many children showed stress reductions of 50% or more. They described themselves as more relaxed, less stressed, and, most importantly, happier. Within a few months of learning TM, the school observed a significant reduction in instances of anger, conflicts, and aggression. The children reported being better able to focus and more independent in completing their homework.

Executive functions in the TM group also showed significant improvements. Standardized methods for assessing executive functions were used in the evaluation. These children showed improved organizational and planning abilities, problem-solving, task execution, attention, and memory.

The positive results of TM are due to the unique experience of restful alertness during meditation, which creates increasing connections in the brain's frontal areas—the areas responsible for controlling impulsive actions, discernment, and social relationships. This means more parts of the brain work together. The integrated functioning resulting from regular TM practice strengthens brain circuits, activating a virtuous process that improves communication between different brain regions, thus enhancing overall coherence.

1. Kingsbury Day School – A school that has integrated Transcendental Meditation into its program for students with learning disorders.

For children with ADHD, meditation is not difficult.

The practice of Transcendental Meditation does not require effort or concentration. It is so simple that even those with ADHD can practice it. The very act of being able to sit quietly for ten minutes is already a significant change for these children. While practicing the technique, they do not strive to remain quiet—they naturally become calmer.

Scientific research on children with ADHD shows that just a few minutes of practicing Transcendental Meditation twice a day:

- Reduces stress, anxiety, and anger
- Increases attention
- Enhances impulse control
- Improves problem-solving abilities
- Boosts organizational skills
- Enhances academic performance

"Transcendental Meditation works—it is improving the lives of children: it enhances their sense of self, makes them stronger and more attentive. I see every day how much of a difference it makes. I believe, thanks to this technique, their future will be much brighter," said Linda Handy, Academic Director of Kingsbury Day School1.

1. Kingsbury Day School – A school that has integrated Transcendental Meditation into its program for students.

4 - THE "STRESS-FREE SCHOOL" PROGRAM

An Education System Designed to Unleash the Full Potential of Students

The quality of education determines the quality and well-being of a society. The current alarming state of life around the world clearly demonstrates that existing educational systems are incomplete because they fail to provide a comprehensive understanding of the student's creative potential or the means to develop it.

Research shows that the initial cognitive and emotional development of students largely determines their academic success. However, programs designed to enhance these aspects of students' lives have not consistently demonstrated success.

Another troubling factor is the inability of educational institutions and systems to cultivate in students the values and qualities that support societal integrity and progress, such as self-sufficiency, health, justice, compassion, and open-mindedness.

It is clear that, without a deeper understanding of human potential, societal progress will always be hindered by what John Goodlad1 refers to as "the educational gap: the distance between the noblest visions of what humans could become and their current level of functioning."

For these lofty ideals to become reality, education cannot rely solely on teachers, curricula, or parents. Students themselves must develop their vast untapped potential.

In his address at the annual American Association for Higher Education conference in 1993, Maharishi Mahesh Yogi identified the problem and offered the solution:

"It is clear that education has been grappling with problems for decades, even centuries. It has been unsatisfactory... What is missing should be obvious to all. If we examine the process by which knowledge is acquired, we see that knowledge has two aspects: the object of knowledge (the subjects studied) and the subject of knowledge, the knower (the student). What the current education system provides is knowledge of the object; what is missing is knowledge of the subject, knowledge of the knower."

For Maharishi, the term "knowledge of the knower" refers to the direct subjective experience of the entire field of one's own consciousness, from the surface level of thinking awareness (the ordinary wakeful state we use) to the deepest inner silence at the source of thoughts, where the full potential of the mind resides.

Educational systems have thus far provided no effective procedures or training paths for systematically allowing students to access the entire field of the mind and knowledge. For this reason, the deepest reserves of creative intelligence within each student remain unused in daily life, and individuals can only express a small fraction of their mental potential, as confirmed by modern psychology.

Just as a tree becomes dry when disconnected from its roots, an individual's life becomes frustration, struggle, and suffering when the connection between their outer life and inner reality is lost, and harmony between these two levels is no longer consciously recognized.

If the knower does not know itself in its entirety, the entire structure of knowledge lacks a foundation, and such knowledge, without foundation, can only be unsatisfying. We see, in fact, that dissatisfaction is widespread, despite the benefits of technological progress. Illness, poverty, political and social instability exist everywhere, in both wealthy and developing nations.

According to the philosophy of information2, knowledge has organizational power. Limited knowledge is harmful, while the more complete the knowledge, the greater the ability to apply it successfully and without creating imbalances. It is clear that a comprehensive knowledge base is missing, which would enable individuals to become more fulfilled, happy, vital, and creative.

Most problems are created by humans due to their limitations and weaknesses: they stem from a lack of awareness, creativity, and the inability to make sound decisions and achieve aspirations. The inability to access full mental potential lays the groundwork for any type of problem. Issues such as crime and drug use result from this limitation— the inability to feel fulfilled and meet personal goals. Similarly, many health problems are caused by behaviors that promote disease.

The solution to this situation lies in a comprehensive education system that integrates the Transcendental Meditation technique into the school curriculum to fully develop the student's unlimited creative potential.

Notes:

1. John Goodlad – A prominent educator known for his work on educational reform.
2. Philosophy of information – Refers to the idea that complete knowledge has the power to organize and create positive outcomes, while incomplete knowledge leads to imbalance.

THE ENGLISH SCHOOL SYSTEM AND THE "STRESS-FREE SCHOOL" PROGRAM

The English school system has adopted the "Stress-Free School" program, also known as the "Quiet Time in Class" initiative, in many institutions.

The Maharishi School 1, a private school in Lancashire County, Northern England, received "Free School" status from the Department of Education in 2001 due to its students' outstanding academic results.

Free Schools2 are part of a government initiative in the U.K. that allows economically disadvantaged students to access high-quality academic institutions. They are funded by the government but, compared to public schools, have greater freedom in key decisions like lesson schedules, curricula, and budgets.

For the quality of results achieved, the Maharishi School was rated "excellent," the highest grade in the Ofsted3 rating system, an independent organization tasked by the British Parliament to evaluate English school standards. According to Ofsted's report: "...students are calm, confident, and friendly. They are enthusiastic about their studies, eager to acquire new skills, and enjoy learning."4

In secondary school diploma exams, Maharishi School students consistently score at the top, not only in Lancashire County but across the entire nation. These results have remained consistent since the school opened 25 years ago.

The fundamental principle of Maharishi School's education is the daily experience of restful alertness, easily achieved through Transcendental Meditation. This meditation combines deep physiological rest with inner alertness, creating a neuro-physiological balance that supports positive learning processes, enhances intelligence and creativity, fosters academic success, and establishes the physical and mental conditions for lifelong achievement.

EFFICIENCY AND SATISFACTION OF SCHOOL STAFF

Teaching is one of the most stressful professions. Teachers are required to maintain focused attention amidst many distractions while quickly adapting to changing circumstances. When these demands exceed individual capacities, a process of burnout begins, reducing teachers' adaptability and communication skills, leading to fatigue, anxiety, dissatisfaction, and a desire to leave the profession—creating a vicious cycle that fosters harmful compulsive habits and, ultimately, burnout.5

Hundreds of schools, organizations, and companies have adopted Transcendental Meditation as a corporate training program. The technique is considered highly effective for developing human resources and increasing organizational productivity. Studies in workplace environments, including schools, show that individuals practicing meditation experience significant reductions in workplace anxiety and worry, lower smoking and alcohol consumption, and improved sleep compared to non-practitioners. The studies also indicate increased job satisfaction, better health, improved interpersonal relationships, greater efficiency, and productivity.

The flexibility, resilience, and creativity gained through the practice of Transcendental Meditation help prevent apathy and fatigue in the profession, allowing the development of new and more effective teaching strategies. The greater job satisfaction among teachers and school staff, along with reduced absenteeism due to illness, strongly justifies the integration of Transcendental Meditation into any teacher and administrative development program.

A study found that teachers at the "Maharishi School of the Age of Enlightenment" in Iowa, all of whom practiced Transcendental Meditation, reported lower levels of emotional exhaustion and depersonalization, along with a higher sense of personal accomplishment compared to the norm (Maslach Burnout Inventory)[6].

Notes:

1. Maharishi School – A private school promoting Transcendental Meditation.
2. Free Schools – Government-funded independent schools offering more freedom in governance.
3. Ofsted – Office for Standards in Education, Children's Services, and Skills.
4. Ofsted Report: Ofsted's evaluation criteria that highlight students' calmness, confidence, and enthusiasm for learning.
5. Burnout – A state of emotional, physical, and mental exhaustion caused by prolonged and excessive stress.
6. Maslach Burnout Inventory – A psychological tool used to measure burnout.

Testimonies from Religious Figures

Father Dubi, Parish of San Vittore, Calumet City

"I can only recommend Transcendental Meditation to everyone, especially those responsible for the spiritual growth of the congregation and students. I have used meditation as a tool that has helped me in my vocation as a man of faith and prayer. It has helped me experience the core of my religious belief on a deeper level."

Father Thomas R. Miller, Rector of St. Gabriel and All Angels Church, Fairfield, Iowa

"Transcendental Meditation is not an alternative to faith. The practice itself strengthens faith in God. To those who wonder if it's a religion, my answer is no. There is nothing to fear and everything to gain from meditation practice for Christians who wish to deepen and enrich their prayer life and faith."

Father Gabriel Mejia's Experience in Rehabilitating 'Throwaway' Adolescents

Father Gabriel Mejia is a Catholic missionary of the Claretians who lives in Colombia. He is the founder and director of the Hogares Claret Foundation. Today, the Foundation has nearly 600 employees and 47 specialized centers for drug recovery and the rehabilitation of abandoned children, guerrilla fighters, and refugees. It has cared for 50,000 people.

In Colombia, street children are called "throwaways." Father Gabriel Mejia launched the "Save the Throwaways" campaign through the Hogares Claret Therapeutic Communities. Thanks to his experience with these children, Father Mejia learned that the strong desire to escape street life must come from them.

When he first encountered Transcendental Meditation in the late 1980s, he realized he had found the answer to the intense stress that plagues these children. He understood that the technique could help them reconnect with themselves and awaken their desire for change.

The results were outstanding: 5,000 of his residents learned Transcendental Meditation, which Father Mejia now considers one of the fundamental pillars of his work. His efforts have proven to be the most comprehensive and effective in addressing social issues and substance abuse problems. This initiative is supported by the Latin American Federation of Therapeutic Communities (FLACT) and the Clarettian University Foundation (FUCLA).

THE MAHARISHI FOUNDATION AND THE "STRESS-FREE SCHOOL" PROGRAM

The Maharishi Foundation, in collaboration with the David Lynch Foundation, promotes the "Stress-Free School" program aimed at introducing Transcendental Meditation into schools.

David Lynch has dedicated his efforts to raising awareness among institutions, parents, teachers, and policymakers about the importance of meditation practice, as well as collecting funds to provide it to vulnerable groups such as war veterans, homeless individuals, prisoners, and substance abusers.

This approach has proven to positively impact students' education and well-being, as well as support people in social hardship.

These initiatives have already enabled the introduction of meditation in schools across the United States, Latin America, the Middle East, and Africa.

This safe and reliable program is a crucial tool for addressing school-related issues. Scientific research demonstrates that students who meditate perform better academically, are more creative and intelligent, experience reduced anxiety and depression, have no need to resort to alcohol or drugs, and face fewer suspensions and expulsions.

In Italy, in 2016, the Maharishi Foundation was established, in partnership with the David Lynch Foundation, aiming to replicate the same actions and initiatives promoted globally, starting in Milan and then expanding nationwide.

The Maharishi Foundation contributes by spreading knowledge and the practice of Transcendental Meditation, helping reduce stress and promoting the full psycho-physical and social development of individuals, ultimately aiming for improved quality of life and reduced social conflict, laying the groundwork for a knowledge-based consciousness and stable world peace.

Specifically, the Maharishi Foundation:

- Actively promotes Transcendental Meditation within institutions, policymakers, local stakeholders, and citizens.
- Creates conditions for the spread of Transcendental Meditation among people of all genders, ages, social backgrounds, religious beliefs, including disadvantaged groups and those in socially marginalized or isolated settings, utilizing resources from private donors and public institutions.

The Maharishi Foundation plans to collaborate immediately with institutions and educational, research, and university entities to support and promote the "Stress-Free School" program, believing that young people represent the most important and strategic investment for a society aiming for a better future of peace and prosperity.

COACHING FOR ENTREPRENEURSHIP

What do we need to start a business? Download the Manual (Free Bonus)

While developing the overarching "Italian Beauty" plan, we can begin parallel, smaller, personal projects aligned with this vision.

Let's educate our children to become independent entrepreneurs of initiatives, with repeatable, non-overlapping models.

Together, we can create a "Unified Productive Reality at a National Level of Beauty," where local initiatives, individual municipalities, and citizens align like puzzle pieces, harmonizing with a reinforcing leverage effect.

We can implement layered measures, waiting for more comprehensive ones that take longer to complete.

MARKETING

On one side, our youth engage with their peers, the children of wealthy individuals from emerging countries, who, as they grow, dream of visiting us. A journey to Italy will become a distinctive, luxurious act that makes a difference in their lives. We've experienced this firsthand. Working in multinational companies, we had colleagues from around the world who expressed a desire to visit Italy, many of whom have done so. These friends can become customers and, as tourists, contribute to our income. We won't need to seek employment abroad anymore.

Additionally, with our innate generosity, we can allocate part of our earnings to help children in poorer countries, fostering love, gratitude, and PEACE!

Based on our experience, a plan can follow two strategic paths:

a) a general framework from which to derive detailed small projects
b) many smaller plans that are coordinated and integrated into a larger one

We will pursue the second path, which aligns more naturally with the purpose of this book and can be accomplished without direct governmental intervention (though it would be welcome). We shouldn't waste too much time!

WHAT DO WE NEED TO START A BUSINESS?

- Capitalizing on Italy's assets
- Providing training
- Securing resources
- Launching

How to start a business (startup)? Three years ago, we prepared a manual on entrepreneurship that can now serve as a valuable guide. You can read this book and find all the answers. Request it at <u>info@gsm-online.it</u>

Bonus Included

"The greatest waste in the world is the difference between what we are and what we could become." (Ben Herbster)

Did you enjoy this book? Leave a positive comment on Amazon. Thank you!

The other two volumes covering topics that complete the development process and a splendid future are coming soon. Leave us your best email below, and we will keep you informed:

<u>info@gsm-online.it</u>
Thank you.
Happy reading!

Acknowledgments

First of all, we thank the many young people who write to us and share their stories from their point of view. Thank you to all of you, our numerous readers, who have read us. You are the best source for improving our protocols. We also thank the many parents who do their best to help their children on their journey and share their difficulties with us.

We thank our family, especially our niece, who, in addition to the greatest love, along with her friends, helps us understand.

Resources

You can also follow the Courses from which these books are extracted. Read the continuation of the first book.

This book is divided into three parts (following the same sequence as our courses):

1. How to create winning personalities and not future Neets (Being) – strategic pedagogy
2. How to produce wealth with children and build new family relationships (Having) – operational pedagogy
3. How to develop capital, businesses, super-abilities from champions (Doing) – frontier pedagogy
   Contact us: info@gsm-online.it +39 3391602075 Facebook Group Genitori Coach Orientati

Legal Notes

The operational strategies and recommendations in this document are the result of years of theoretical and experimental study. The models and standard programs mentioned represent our Best Practices so far regarding brain and sensory functioning. They are provided for illustrative purposes and represent a statistical median.

As each person is unique and irreplaceable, each event can trigger their specific reactions, so following the advice does not guarantee the same result.

The authors reserve the right to update or modify the content of this book freely, based on new discoveries or changed conditions.

www.bettercoaching.it

Please note that the advice provided, examples, and behavioral guidelines are general in nature and apply "with minimal deviation from the normal behavior of the average person." If there is any doubt about a child's "precautionary health" – whether physiological, mental, or emotional – the Coach cannot and should not replace the specialist doctor, who is the only one institutionally authorized to carry out investigations and recommend official therapies in the field of pathology (Diagnostic and Statistical Manual of Mental Disorders, DSM). This document has only informational purposes, and the author assumes no responsibility for the improper use of this information.

The author and the co-authors

About the author Albina Gabellini

OVER 80 YEARS OLD, MOTHER OF 2 CHILDREN, GRANDMOTHER OF 1, AUNT OF 6 NEPHEWS AND NIECES

DIPLOMA OF QUALIFICATION FOR TEACHING, PESARO, MINISTRY OF PUBLIC ADMINISTRATION 1960 FOR TEACHING IN PRESCHOOLS, NURSERY, AND ELEMENTARY SCHOOLS.

ATHLETIC DIPLOMA OF FIRST GRADE, PESARO, MINISTRY OF PUBLIC ADMINISTRATION No. 165272 / 1960 FOR TEACHING GYMNASTICS IN PRESCHOOLS, NURSERY, AND ELEMENTARY SCHOOLS.

SCIENTIFIC HIGH SCHOOL DIPLOMA, PESARO, MINISTRY OF PUBLIC ADMINISTRATION 1961.

DEGREE IN ECONOMICS AND COMMERCE, ANCONA (FORMERLY CARLO BO - URBINO), 1967, POLYTECHNIC OF THE MARCHE. CERTIFICATE IN PROGRAMMING IN RPG, IBM 360, MILAN, 1968, AND SUBSEQUENT LANGUAGES UNTIL 1981.

SPECIALIZATION IN MARKETING, COMPUTER SCIENCE, AND TELECOMMUNICATIONS FROM 1969 TO 2004.

E-LEARNING, PLATO, CONTROL DATA CORPORATION, MINNEAPOLIS— THE FIRST DISTANCE LEARNING SYSTEM IN THE WORLD FROM 1976 TO 1981.

TECHNOTEC, THE FIRST NETWORK/INTERNET/GOOGLE/LEXITEL IN THE WORLD CREATED BY CONTROL DATA CORPORATION, TESTED IN BRUSSELS/PARIS IN 1975, AND INSTALLED AT ALL CDC SITES WORLDWIDE, A NETWORK OF SUPERCOMPUTERS PROVIDING TIME-SHARING FOR LARGE ENTERPRISES FOR INTERNATIONAL INFORMATION EXCHANGE, TECHNOLOGIES, JOINT VENTURES, AND PATENTS. IN ITALY, IT WAS RECOGNIZED FOR THE RESTRUCTURING AGREEMENT GEPI, MINISTRY OF STATE HOLDINGS / IRI, WITH ITALIAN GROUPS SUCH AS ENI, PIRELLI, FIAT, OTOMELARA, ETC.

1975 COURSES IN STRATEGIES IN THE US AND UK (INCLUDING INSEAD, FONTAINEBLEAU, FRANCE, 1985).

CREDIT MEDIATOR, EX-BANK OF ITALY NO. 96359/2007.

CIVIL AND COMMERCIAL MEDIATOR, GIURIFORM, INTERNATIONAL CHAMBER OF CONCILIATION & ARBITRATION, MINISTRY OF JUSTICE ACCREDITED BODY NO. 174, 2011.

POSTGRADUATE TRAINER FOR FINANCIAL ADVISORS IN ECONOMETRICS TO OBTAIN CONSOB CERTIFICATION AND MARKET MANAGEMENT, 1998/2005.

Coach – Life & Business – based on cognitive psychology, focusing on supporting (social and free) banking/financial managers from 1981 to the present.

Author [et al.] of the book "Cognitive Coaching: The Complete Code of Business Coaching for Physical and Financial Well-Being of the New Management: Harmony between the Humanities, Economics, Medicine, Fitness" / Albina Gabellini, ISBN 8870907392, Biblioteca Braidense, Milan.

Practiced free climbing/alpinism and diving in various countries.

Passionate about comparative cultures (Christianity, Islam, Buddhism, and African animism) with frequent visits to their places of origin, particularly Egypt, India, Bhutan, Cameroon.

Conducts field research on "Resilience," believing that the Resilient Method of her New Cognitive Pedagogy, modeled after the functioning of the brain and senses, governed by cognitive psychology, can help children overcome life's difficulties autonomously from an early age. Strengthened, the dream is for them to grow in peace with themselves and others, contributing to reducing aggression, conflicts, and violence worldwide.

About the co-author Lorella Pucci

LORELLA IS A MOTHER OF A DAUGHTER, AUNT, AND GREAT AUNT TO NIECES AND HAS MANY COUSINS.

SHE EARNED A HIGH SCHOOL DIPLOMA IN LINGUISTICS FROM THE MANZONI INSTITUTE IN MILAN, GRADUATED IN ARCHITECTURE FROM THE POLYTECHNIC OF MILAN, AND HAS WORKED AS A FREELANCE ARCHITECT SPECIALIZING IN RENOVATIONS AND INTERIOR DESIGN.

SHE HAS TRAVELED EXTENSIVELY, VISITING AFRICA, EUROPE, THE UNITED STATES, HAWAII, NEW ZEALAND, AUSTRALIA, AND RETURNING VIA SINGAPORE AND INDIA.

THESE CULTURES, ALONG WITH ITALY, WHICH HOLDS THE TITLE OF BEAUTY, HAVE BEEN A SOURCE OF INSPIRATION FOR HER. SHE HAS STUDIED FENG SHUI, APPLYING ITS PRINCIPLES IN HER WORK.

SHE HAS WORKED IN ITALY FOR THE CARLO BESTA NEUROLOGICAL INSTITUTE, THE BASSINI HOSPITAL, AND PIRELLI.

CURRENTLY, SHE OPERATES IN SWITZERLAND.

About the co-author Daniele Giannini

DANIELE IS BORN BY THE SEASIDE IN RIMINI (ITALY), MARRIED WITH 3 CHILDREN, 2 GRANDCHILDREN, UNCLE OF 6 AND "ACQUIRED UNCLE" OF A TONS OF BOYS AND GIRLS.

BACHELOR'S DEGREE IN COMPUTER SCIENCE, UNIVERSITY OF MILAN IN 1989, GRADUATED WITH HIGHEST HONORS, STARTED JUST AFTER THE GRADUATION HIS CAREER DEDICATING EFFORTS AND GETTING IMPORTANT RESULTS IN THREE DIFFERENT AREAS: TRAINING, ORGANIZATION, SOLUTION DESIGNING AND DEVELOPMENT. MANY IMPORTANT COMPANIES HAD HIS JOBS, BOTH PUBLIC AND PRIVATE, AND ALWAYS MAINTAINED A CONSULTANT POSITION ABLE TO GIVE THE BEST TO HIS CUSTOMERS AND PARTNERS.

EXPERT IN TRAVELING, HE KNOWS 4 LANGUAGES (ENGLISH: EXCELLENT (SPOKEN, WRITTEN, COMPREHENSION), FRENCH: GOOD (SPOKEN, WRITTEN, COMPREHENSION). GERMAN: BASIC (SPOKEN, WRITTEN, COMPREHENSION) AND BRAZILIAN PORTUGUESE: ELEMENTARY (SPOKEN, COMPREHENSION)), HAS DEEP EXPERTISE IN SPORT TEAMS MANAGEMENT, PHOTOGRAPHY, BALLROOM DANCING, FLORICULTURE, HOLISTIC PRACTICES AND ALL WATER SPORTS AND ACTIVITIES.

DEVELOPER OF IDEAS, A DESIGNER, AND AN IMPLEMENTER OF SOLUTIONS. HE HAS ALWAYS LEVERAGED TECHNOLOGY AND ORGANIZATION TO IDENTIFY THE BEST WAYS TO ACHIEVE PROFESSIONAL, BUSINESS, AND PERSONAL GOALS, WITH A KEEN FOCUS ON TECHNOLOGICAL INNOVATION AND THE EFFICIENT USE

OF AVAILABLE RESOURCES. HIS WORK IS GUIDED BY ACHIEVING THE OPTIMAL BALANCE BETWEEN OBJECTIVES, QUALITY, COST-EFFECTIVENESS, AND IMPLEMENTATION TIMELINES.

MANY YEARS DEDICATED TO TECHNICAL TRAINING HAVE FORGED HIS ABILITY IN COACHING TECHNICS AND APPLICATION OF THIS COMPETENCES ... DRIVES HIS KNOWLEDGE INTO CHILDREN EDUCATION.

ORIGINALLY FROM ITALIAN REGION ROMAGNA BY THE SEA, WHICH HE PROUDLY IDENTIFIES WITH FOR ITS CHARACTER, AMBITIONS, AND GOALS, HIS JOURNEY BEGAN WITH A BACKGROUND IN TOURISM AND LANGUAGES. HE MOVED TO MILAN IN THE 1980S TO IMMERSE HIMSELF IN THE BURGEONING FIELD OF INFORMATION TECHNOLOGY.

GRADUATING SUMMA CUM LAUDE IN COMPUTER SCIENCE FROM THE UNIVERSITY OF MILAN, HE ADOPTED A HANDS-ON APPROACH TO LEARNING. HIS THESIS FOCUSED ON INDUSTRIAL APPLICATIONS IN TELECOMMUNICATIONS. THEN HE SPECIALIZED IN COMPUTER NETWORKS AND SECURITY, STARTING MY CAREER AS BOTH A CONSULTANT AND PROFESSIONAL TRAINER.

HE HAD THE PRIVILEGE OF WORKING WITH LEADING GLOBAL COMPANIES OF THE TIME, INCLUDING IBM, SUN MICROSYSTEMS, SIEMENS, HEWLETT-PACKARD, DIGITAL, HONEYWELL BULL, INFORMIX, ORACLE, AND ITALTEL, AND, AFTER AN INITIAL FREELANCE EXPERIENCE, HE BECAME AN ENTREPRENEUR, FOUNDED A COMPANIES FOCUSED ON DESIGNING TECHNOLOGICAL NETWORKS AND ADVANCED IT SOLUTIONS. HIS CLIENTS INCLUDED PRESTIGIOUS ORGANIZATIONS LIKE SAN PELLEGRINO, NESTLÉ, IBM, FORZA ITALIA POLITICAL PARTY, AUTOSTRADE DEL BRENNERO, AND DIGITAL, AS WELL AS LOCAL AUTHORITIES SUCH AS THE MUNICIPALITY OF MILAN, AMSA (MILAN'S WASTE MANAGEMENT COMPANY), AND REGIONE LOMBARDIA.

FROM 1999 TO 2005, HE SERVED AS HEAD OF ICT FOR THE URBAN PLANNING DEPARTMENT OF THE MUNICIPALITY OF MILAN, OVERSEEING THE DIGITAL TRANSFORMATION OF APPROXIMATELY 600 EMPLOYEES. THIS ROLE REQUIRED CLOSE COLLABORATION WITH BOTH ORGANIZATIONAL AND POLITICAL TEAMS TO ALIGN VISIONS AND IMPLEMENT EFFECTIVE IT SOLUTIONS.

DURING THE COVID-19 PANDEMIC, HE DEEPENED HIS COLLABORATION IN THE FIELD OF FREQUENCY-BASED SOLUTIONS, FOCUSING ON MICROCURRENT AND FREQUENCY GENERATOR TECHNOLOGIES TO ENHANCE HUMAN, ANIMAL, AND AGRICULTURAL WELL-BEING.

OVER HIS DECADES-LONG CAREER, HE DEVELOPED AND SOLIDIFIED SIGNIFICANT EXPERTISE IN ORGANIZATION, TECHNOLOGY, AND INNOVATION. HIS UNWAVERING COMMITMENT TO FINDING SOLUTIONS IN EVERY CONTEXT HE FACES, COMBINED WITH A FOCUS ON THE WELL-BEING OF PEOPLE, ANIMALS, AND THE PLANET, DRIVES HIS PROACTIVE APPROACH TO NEW CHALLENGES. HIS COLLABORATIVE SPIRIT, TEAMWORK, AND CONSTANT DESIRE TO LEARN AND GROW REMAIN THE FOUNDATION OF HIS PROFESSIONAL AND PERSONAL ENDEAVORS.

HE IS .... STILL LEARNING ;-)

About the co-author Raoul Pucci

GRADUATED RAOUL PUCCI, 62, MOST OF HIS LIFE, TRAVELLING ALL OVER THE WORLD.

VERY YOUNG, HE STARTED WORKING AT CONTROL DATA CORPORATION DEVELOPING THE TECHNOTEC APPLICATION. THE FIRST SOFTWARE ABLE TO CONNECT PEOPLE AND TECHNOLOGIES LIKE THE TODAY- WEB. IN PARTICULAR HE DEVELOPED THE ITALIAN PATENT SYSTEM WHICH WAS CONNECTING THE SCIENTISTS OFFERING THEIR SOLUTIONS AND THE COMPANIES WHICH NEEDED THEIR INVENTIONS.

AFTER WORKING IN SEVERAL COMPUTER COMPANIES AT COMMERCIAL DEPARTMENT IN ITALY, HE WON MANY PRIMES AS THE BEST SALESMAN. THEN THE DECISION TO STOP SELLING AND TO TRAVEL ON DIFFERENT COUNTRIES.

FROM 28 YEARS UP TO NOW, HE VISITED AFRICA, ASIA, SANTO DOMINGO, THAILAND HELPING PEOPLE

IN 1989 HE DID, WITH HIS FAMILY, ALL THE JOURNEY OF THE GLOBE, MILAN, PARIS, NEW YORK, SAN FRANCISCO, LOS ANGELES, HONOLULU, MAUI, OACKLAND, SIDNEY, SOUTH OF CINA, SINGAPORE, BOMBAY, ROME, MILAN, THE STOP OVERS MOST IMPORTANT. (MORE THAN 2 MONTHS).

AFTER THIS TIME HE DECIDED TO WORK HARD IN ITALY IN ORDER TO HAVE TIME TO KNOW THE NATURE AND THE DIFFERENT CULTURES.

SPEAKING 4 LANGUAGES, HIS CHARISMA ,SYMPATHY, EMPATHY LET HIM COMMUNICATE SO EASY WITH PEOPLE. WITH ALL DIFFERENT GROUPS OF NATIVE PEOPLE.

NOW READY TO START AGAIN TO OTHER SPANISH COUNTRIES OR LAOS OR CAMBODIA? WE WILL SEE.

About the co-author Laura Mazza

AMONG ITALY'S 100 MOST POWERFUL WOMEN ACCORDING TO FORBES, SHE IS A PROFESSOR OF ECONOMICS, PRESIDENT OF FEDERFORMAZIONE AND SECRETARY GENERAL OF THE MEDITERRANEAN PARLIAMENT. SHE DIRECTS THE "INTERNATIONAL UNIVERSITY DEPARTMENT OF RESEARCH ON EDUCATION, INNOVATION, DIPLOMACY" OF CUIRIF AND IS THE GENERAL DIRECTOR OF THE UNITED NATIONS LEADERS FOR PEACE PROJECT. SHE HOLDS TOP POSITIONS IN INTERNATIONAL ASSOCIATIONS, SHE'S AN EXPERT AT MINISTERIAL TABLES AND SPECIALIZES IN COOPERATION AND DEVELOPMENT. SHE DEALS WITH THE CONDITION OF WOMEN IN ITALY AND ABROAD, PROMOTING TRAINING AND JOB PLACEMENT, PROTECTION OF HUMAN RIGHTS AND SUSTAINABILITY. SHE HAS OBTAINED SEVERAL MASTER'S DEGREES, INCLUDING EUROPEAN PLANNING, BUSINESS AND HUMAN RIGHTS, IMMIGRATION AND INTEGRATION, WITH THE PATRONAGE OF THE UNITED NATIONS AND CNEL. SHE IS ACTIVE IN INTERNATIONAL RELATIONS THROUGH THE WORLD INTERCULTURAL ORGANISATION, THE INTERNATIONAL DIPLOMATIC INSTITUTE, MOVIMENTO UNITI PER UNIRE AND OTHER ORGANIZATIONS. AN EXPERT IN TRAINING, ACTIVE POLICIES AND SKILLS CERTIFICATION, LAURA IS THE GENERAL DIRECTOR OF THE CHAMBRE DE COMMERCE ET INDUSTRIE ITALIE – MADAGASCAR, VICE PRESIDENT OF GUARDIE INTERNAZIONALI AMBIENTALI AND VICE OF NEW BUSINESS ORGANIZATION. SHE'S A MEMBER OF PLANET LIFE ECONOMY FOUNDATION AS A CONTACT FOR FEMALE LEADERSHIP

AGAINST GENDER VIOLENCE AND VICE PRESIDENT OF EMERGENZA SORRISI ONLUS AND IS AN HONORARY MEMBER OF VOCE DELL'ESSERE. THANKS TO HER SKILLS IN STRATEGIC CONSULTING, DEVELOPMENT, COMMUNICATION, DIGITALIZATION AND INTERNATIONALIZATION, SHE WAS AWARDED AMONG THE FIRST THREE WOMEN IN EUROPE FOR INNOVATION, CHANGE AND CREATIVITY. SHE RECEIVED THE EUROMED PRIZE FOR HUMANITY AND THE CARTHAGE PRIZE FOR INTERNATIONAL COMMITMENT. SHE PARTICIPATES IN THE ASVIS WORKING TABLES FOR THE OBJECTIVES OF THE UN 2030 AGENDA FOR SUSTAINABLE DEVELOPMENT, COORDINATES COOPERATION AND DEVELOPMENT PROJECTS, AND COLLABORATES WITH NATIONAL AND INTERNATIONAL INSTITUTIONS FOR ACTIVE LABOR POLICIES. VICE PRESIDENT TEAMSTV, SHE HOSTS COLUMNS ON THE ECONOMY AND INTERNATIONAL DIALOGUE AND IS THE AUTHOR OF ARTICLES IN INTERNATIONAL MAGAZINES. AUTHOR OF SEVERAL BOOKS, INCLUDING COVIDNOMICS IN WHICH SHE ANALYZES TRAINING AND SUSTAINABLE DEVELOPMENT. IN 2025 SHE PUBLISHED "THE PRIVILEGE OF BEING A WOMAN", AN ANALYSIS OF AUTHENTIC AND INCLUSIVE FEMALE LEADERSHIP TO BUILD A BETTER WORLD.

If you liked the ideas and proposals, give us confirmation, with the "like" and share on Facebook by subscribing to the group "Genitori COACH Orientati" to stay updated.